Ran

too

Mountain Names

12·XII·87.

Summit of Chimborazo, Ecuador. From Edward Whymper, Travels amongst the Great Andes of the Equator *(London: 1883).*

Mountain Names

Robert Hixson Julyan

The Mountaineers
Seattle

The Mountaineers: Organized 1906
"...to encourage a spirit of good fellowship
among all lovers of outdoor life."

Published by The Mountaineers
715 Pike Street, Seattle, Washington 98101

Published simultaneously in Canada by Douglas & McIntyre, Ltd.
1615 Venables Street, Vancouver, British Columbia V5L 2H1

Cover design by Elizabeth Watson
Text design by Barbara Haner
Illustrations from the Mountaineering Collection of the Special Collections,
Norlin Library, University of Colorado, Boulder.

Manufactured in the United States of America

Library of Congress Cataloging in Publication Data
Julyan, Robert Hixson.
    Mountain Names.

    Bibliography: p.
    Includes index.
    1. Mountains. 2. Gazetteers. I. Title.
GB501.2.J85 1984   910'.02'1430321   84-11581
ISBN 0-89886-091-1
ISBN 0-89886-054-7 (pbk.)

With love and hope, I dedicate this book to my wife, Mary.

Acknowledgments

During this project the names that came to mean most to me were those of the people who helped me along the way. Though I cannot list all the persons whose cooperation and assistance were so important, I would like to acknowledge with gratitude the contributions of the following: Celia Millward of Boston University and her conscientious students, Zhu Bin and Lin Ziyu, for their research and correspondence regarding Chinese names. Tom Schmidt of the Institute of Names Research in Oslo, Norway, for research into the origins of Norwegian mountain names. Carl Smith of the New Mexico Mountain Club, for the generous use of his mountaineering library. Place-names scholar T.M. Pearce, for use of his material. Greg and Mary Donohoe, translators and friends. Stuart White of the University of New Mexico geography department, for insight into Quechua mountain names. Nora Quinlan and Sonia Jacobs of Special Collections of Norlin Library at the University of Colorado, for their friendly cooperation, Klaus Weber, University of New Mexico ski coach and lover of mountains, for help with Swiss mountain names. Mohammed Ataee of the University of New Mexico, for help with Iranian names. The United States Board on Geographic Names, for information about their guidelines. John Pollock, Donna DeShazo, Ann Cleeland, Stephen Whitney, and Matt Harris, for their professionalism, goodwill, and timely encouragement, which this author, at least, does not take for granted. And above all, my family, for their patience, love, and understanding.

Introduction

The French mountaineer Gaston Rebuffat, writing years later about his first route in the Mont Blanc massif, the Pic de Roc, said: "Everything tempted me to it: its name, short and abrupt, its appearance, a granite spire, its situation on the Mer de Glace face of the Grepon...."[114]* This statement reminds us that we usually first come to know mountains as we become acquainted with people— through their names.

This book is an introduction to the names of the world's mountains. It is based on the belief that a mountain's name is not merely an insignificant or irrelevant appendage but rather an integral part of a mountain's identity. As Freud wrote of names generally: "For primitive men, as for savages today and even for our children, a name is not indifferent and conventional as it seems to us, but is something important and essential."[6] When we truly understand a mountain's name, we also understand much of that mountain's history and character.

In this book I have discussed the names of approximately three hundred of the world's mountains, but to truly understand mountain naming it is necessary to consider not only the names of individual peaks but also place-names in general and the ways humans have created them. As the American names scholar Erwin G. Gudde has written: "Names belong to the oldest elements of human speech. According to some authorities, they even antedate the verbs for eat, drink, sleep, or the nouns for hand, night, or child."[56] Thus, place-names, like other names, result from the fundamental and uniquely human need to label with words, and therefore the concepts of naming and identity are inextricably linked. As another American names scholar, Kelsie Harder, has observed, a place without a name in one sense isn't really a place.[60]

But while the world's place-names total in the millions, not all aspects of a landscape receive names. For primitive peoples particularly, places given names had to be (1) distinct and (2) useful. To contemporary peoples, mountains at first glance easily would meet both criteria, but this was not always so among early peoples. As George R. Stewart has explained in his *Names on the Globe*: "The failure to recognize entity even functions to make the name-pattern of a primitive people different from that of a more developed one. The difference is

---

* *Superscript numerals refer to numbered entries in the Reference List located at the end of the book.*

1

not in the small features. The most untutored of men can recognize a spring or a cave. But lacking maps, ignorant of physiographic studies, his capacity for travel limited to the length of his own legs, the primitive man cannot usually conceive of a mountain, though he may recognize a towering peak from a distance, especially if it is snow-covered and arouses feelings of religious awe. But anything like a mountain range is beyond him."[133] As a result, many of the world's great mountain systems were not named until relatively recently; the Appalachian mountain chain in eastern North America, for instance, was not known by a single name until the late nineteenth century.

Early peoples also had different naming needs than more developed peoples. Throughout most of human history mountains were mysterious, dangerous places, to be avoided where possible. More urgent than the need to name mountains was the need to name features such as rivers, fords, springs, meeting places, and places of abundant food. To be sure, contemporary preliterate peoples do have names for the mountains in their territories, but when we survey place-names historically, we find that the oldest names are not on mountains but on rivers and streams. This is one reason why so many mountains have taken the names of rivers, but not the reverse.

The Evolution of Mountain Names

There is no direct evidence about the nature of the earliest mountain names. Even the most primitive of contemporary cultures have fully developed languages, with mature complements of place-names, so we can only speculate about what truly primitive names must have been like. Still, it has been suggested that the first names would have been very simple, perhaps only identifying a feature as belonging to a certain class, such as mountains. An origin such as this—and it is only conjectural—could provide a clue as to which existing mountain names are the oldest. Certainly, no mountain name could be simpler than one meaning merely "mountain," and when we survey the mountain names still in use that mean, at least in part, "mountain," we find that they are indeed very old, so old that their original meanings no longer are readily apparent: Ararat, Balkans, Apennines, and possibly Atlas. Based upon linguistic evidence, a strong case can be made for the oldest mountain name still in use being *Alp*, a name that conceivably could antedate the arrival of Indo-European peoples in western Europe.

Names meaning "mountain" soon would have combined with qualifying terms to form simple descriptive names: white mountain, round mountain, sharp peak, and so forth. Other simple ways of distinguishing one mountain from another also would have been incorporated into mountain names: mountain-where-there-are-strawberries, mountains-where-our-enemies-live, and mountain-where-a-lion-killed-a-man.

The fact that names such as these are still in use throughout the world, even in highly developed nations, illustrates something important about place-names, including mountain names: although names are among the most ephemeral of human creations, existing only in human minds and capable of being changed or eliminated at whim, they nonetheless are among the most perdurable of all cultural artifacts. William Francis Ganong put it well: "Place names form a permanent register or index of the course and events of a country's history; they are fossils exposed in the cross-section of that history, marking its successive periods; and so lasting are they that records in stone or brass are not to be compared with them for endurance."[58] Of dozens of North American Indian groups obliterated by the advent of the Europeans, little remains to remind us of their existence except their names—Appalachian, Adirondack, Chehalem, Klickitat. Celtic-speaking peoples long ago were displaced in the Alps by people speaking Germanic and Romance languages, but Celtic names still survive there in words like *berg, horn, Pennine,* and *Alp* itself. And Mount Sinai at the southern end of the Sinai Peninsula still bears today approximately the same name by which it was known to the Israelites when Moses led them there during the exodus from Egypt.

An Approach to Mountain Names

By now it should be clear that mountain names, when examined closely, can yield much more information than would be at first apparent. Probably the best way to approach mountain names, to squeeze information from them, is to ask questions about them. For instance, the first question most persons ask about any name is, "What does it mean?" Certainly, knowing the meaning of a name is fundamental to an understanding of it.

But there are many other questions we can ask about a name to garner more information. For example, we can ask how old the name is. Age puts the name into an historical context, which often can be critical to understanding the relationship between the name and the mountain. The name of Norway's Jotunheimen Mountains means "home of the giants," and knowing this alone would tempt us to assume the mountains were named by Norse folk in pre-Christian times, when giants were an important part of Norse mythology. When we discover, however, that the name was a nineteenth-century creation, we must seek other explanations for the mountains having the name Jotunheimen.

Another question we can ask of a mountain name is who gave it. Very often this will be apparent from the name itself, but not always. The highest summit in Britain outside Scotland has two names, Yr Wydffa and Snowdon, whose forms tell us that one was given by the Welsh and the other by the Anglo-Saxons. But who could guess that the name of El Capitan in Yosemite National Park in California was given not by a Spaniard but by an American? Or that Pumori, a peak in Nepal, was named not by a Nepalese but by an Englishman? Moreover, knowing who gave the name reveals not only the ethnicity of the namer but also his or her social class or occupation, and this provides further information about the mountain's history.

We also learn much about a mountain's history when we learn what other names it has had. Rare is the mountain that has borne only one name during its history, and knowing all a mountain's names can yield clues as to who has lived or traveled near the mountain and how they perceived it. Mount Everest bears not only the name of an English surveyor but also native names—

Chomolungma and Sagarmatha—that express the mountain's religious significance for local peoples.

We also can ask how a mountain's names relate to other names in the region. In Britain, the juxtaposition of Celtic names in the mountains and Anglo-Saxon names in the valleys corroborates other evidence suggesting that Celtic settlements persisted in the mountains long after the Anglo-Saxon invaders had occupied the more hospitable lowlands.

Finally, we can speculate about *why* a namer chose a particular name for a mountain. Geographical features, like children, receive their individual names for many different reasons: to simply describe the place or otherwise identify it; to recall something that happened there; to confer honor; to evoke good fortune; and so forth. This array of intentions formed the basis for a classification of place-names by the American place-names scholar, George R. Stewart. His classification is especially useful in comparing how people of different cultures create names, and because of this it is worth considering mountain names in the context of Stewart's major categories: descriptive, associative, incident, commemorative, commendatory or religious, transfer, and folk etymology.

Descriptive Names

The fundamental function of any place-name is to identify its place, to distinguish it from other places. The easiest, most effective way to do this is simply to describe it, taking at least one distinguishing characteristic of the place and incorporating it into a name. So simple and natural is this process that descriptive names are the most common of all natural features names. Moreover, such names are bestowed universally; cultures may differ in the degree to which they bestow other types of names, but all human cultures bestow descriptive names in abundance.

Mountains, in particular, are well-suited for descriptive names. After all, mountains usually are more distinct than many natural features, such as bays and plains, and mountains' distinguishing characteristics easily lend themselves to succinct summation in a name. Indeed, many mountain characteristics, such as size and color, if anything fit too easily into descriptive names, and thus many descriptive names, because of their widespread application, lose much of their value as identifiers. The name "white mountain," for example, has been applied so frequently that it often is meaningless, except to a very localized audience.

Moreover, the qualities encapsulated in descriptive names often are relative. Contrast, for instance, Beinn Mhor (Gaelic, "big mountain"), at 1,874ft/571m the highest point on the Outer Hebrides island of Lewis, with Broad Peak, 26,400ft/8,047m, the third highest summit of the Karakoram. Both mountains were named because their size impressed the namers, yet the Hebridean summit would be a mere bump on the Karakoram peak.

Differences in perspective or viewpoint affect descriptive mountain names in other ways as well. Mountains that appear one color at one season might be a different color at another season. The Green Mountains of Vermont actually are not green for most of the year; in the fall they become orange, brown, and

4

red with the changing foliage, and in the winter they become gray. From the name Snowdon, highest summit in Wales, we can deduce that its Anglo-Saxon namers first saw the peak at a time when snow was on the mountain and presumably not on lesser summits. Similarly, a distinctive profile or outline giving a mountain its name may be apparent only from a certain perspective. In central New Mexico there is a hill that early settlers named Elephant Butte; modern observers, passing by the hill on routes not used by the settlers, have had difficulty seeing the resemblance.

Despite these limitations, however, descriptive mountain names have served humans well for as long as humans have named mountains. When we look at the most ancient mountain names, as well as names used by later preliterate peoples such as Indian tribes, we find these names to be overwhelmingly descriptive. Sometimes the description is elaborate and fanciful. A lake at the base of Crestone Needle in the southern Colorado Rockies was known to the local Indians by a name that meant "lake you come down to when you come down the wrong way," and the Abenaki Indian name for Mount Mansfield, highest summit in the Green Mountains of Vermont, was "mountain with a head like a moose."

But more often the names are starkly simple. The name Himalaya, derived from the ancient Sanskrit, means merely "abode of the snow." The ancient mountain names of Britain, when their meanings can be known at all, typically are simple descriptive names: Ben More, "big mountain"; Druim Fada, "long ridge"; Malvern, "bare hill"; Ochill Hills, "high ones"; and Trossachs, "transverse hills." The Arabic name of the Lebanon Mountains, the Jebel Liban, means simply "mountains white as milk." When Henry M. Stanley named the Ruwenzori Mountains of Central Africa, he merely borrowed a native name meaning "rainy mountains." The name of Mount Vesuvius comes from a pre-Latin word meaning "emitter of smoke and sparks." The ancient Chinese name of Song Shan was Song Gao, "lofty height." Galdhopiggen, highest summit in Norway, has a name meaning "pointed peak near the farms Galde." The list is long, and the older a name, the greater the likelihood that it will be a descriptive name. Indeed, the evolution of place-names parallels that of personal names. The names we bear today usually originated in an attempt to describe a specific individual, whether by occupation, as in Smith or Baker, or by coloring, as in Brown or White, or by place of residence, as in Gallegos (Spanish, "native of Galicia"), or by any one of numerous other ways of describing a person.

Given this, how have people named mountains by describing them? Clearly, the characteristics most commonly appearing in descriptive mountain names are color and shape. Although a mountain's color often is not very useful in distinguishing it from nearby mountains, that has not prevented color names from being very widespread. This reflects most such names having evolved through local usage, without conscious thought given to how the name might be interpreted elsewhere. For example, though almost *all* mountains appear blue from a distance, because of scattering and filtering of light, mountains and ranges named *blue* are very common: the Blue Ridge Mountains of North Carolina, the Blue Mountains of Australia, Blue Mountain Peak in Jamaica, the Cairngorms of Scotland, Azuljanka of Peru, and scores of less well-known examples. Similarly, *black* appears in many mountain names. Examples include the Black Range of New Mexico, the Black Hills of South Dakota, Black Tooth in Wyoming, the Cordillera Negra of Peru, Makalu (Tibetan, "great black one") in the Himalaya, Meall Dubh (Gaelic, "black mountain") in Ireland, and dozens of others. The color green, curiously, appears only infrequently in mountain names, even though as many mountains appear green as appear blue or black; perhaps this color is too indistinctive. The Green Mountains of Vermont and the Aiguille Verte (French, "green needle") in the Mont Blanc massif are among the few examples.

But without question the most common color appearing in mountain names is white. So common and important is this color in mountain names that the world's "white mountains" deserve special consideration.

In mountain areas throughout the world, wherever peaks are high enough to capture snow, regardless of the language or culture of the namers, the chances are great that at least one of the major mountains—and perhaps the entire range—will bear a name meaning "white mountain" or "snowy mountain." Examples are legion. In the Alps are Mont Blanc, Monte Rosa (a corruption of words that in a local dialect mean "white mountain," not "red mountain" as it appears), the Weisshorn, and the Weissmies, and it is possible that the name Alp itself originally meant something akin to "white mountain." In the Caucasus, the name of the range and its highest summit, Elbruz, have that meaning. In the British Isles are Snowdon in Wales, Slieve Snaght and Benbaun in Ireland, and Meall Geal (and very likely Ben Nevis) in Scotland. Elsewhere in Europe are Sneehatten in Norway, Sneekoppe in Czechoslovakia, Crêt de la Neiges in France, Snafell in Iceland, and the Sierra Nevada in Spain. In the Middle East are the Lebanon ("white as milk") Mountains, and in South Africa is Sneeuw Bergen. The major range on the island of New Guinea is the Snow Mountains, while Mauna Kea, highest summit in the Hawaiian Islands, means "white mountain" in Polynesian. "White mountain" names are relatively scarce in Central Asia, but they are not absent; Dhaulagiri and Muztagh are the best known examples, while the name Himalaya (Sanskrit, "abode of the snow") is a reference to the range's whiteness. But the greatest frequency of such names is in the western hemisphere, beginning with the hemisphere's highest summit, Aconcagua, whose name most often is translated as "white mountain." In South America, many of the continent's most important ranges and mountains have "white mountain" names: the Cordillera Blanca, Chimborazo, and Illimani, as well as numerous lesser known peaks—Chilpariti, Yuraqraju, and Loyaqjirka.

"White mountain" names are no less frequent in North America, appearing on at least four major ranges: the White Mountains of New Hampshire, the White Mountains of eastern Arizona, the White Mountains of eastern California, and facing them across the Owens Valley, the Sierra Nevada of California. The Spanish especially found it easy to name mountains for their whiteness, and no fewer than fifteen orographic features in California alone have *blanca* or *blanco* in their names. The name Sierra Blanca appears in both New Mexico and Arizona, and one of the great peaks of the southern Colorado Rockies is Blanca Peak. English explorers and settlers also found a mountain's whiteness a convenient handle for a name: Snowcap Mountain in Alaska, Snow Hill in

Great crevasse at the foot of Mont Blanc, France. From William H.D. Adams, Mountains and Mountain Climbing *(London: 1883).*

North Carolina, Snowmass Peak and Snow Peak in Colorado, and the Snowcrest Range in Montana. Many Indian mountain names translate to mean "white mountain," such as Mount Waumbek in New Hampshire, the Unaka Mountains in Tennessee, and Musinia Peak in Utah.

Not surprisingly, the region most lacking "white mountain" names is Antarctica. There, the color that appears most often in mountain names is black.

Several important general characteristics should be noted about "white mountain" names world-wide. First, such names tend to be old. This corresponds to the fact already mentioned that early peoples tended to give simple descriptive names; few names are more simply descriptive than "white mountain."

And because elevation largely determines which peaks capture snow first and hold it longest, "white mountain" names tend to appear disproportionately on peaks that are the highest in their regions: Mont Blanc, Elbruz, Aconcagua, Dhaulagiri, Blanca Peak, Sierra Blanca, Mauna Kea, Chimborazo, Snowdon, and Monte Rosa.

And finally, with "white mountain" names as with mountain names generally, we should never assume they mean what they appear to mean. The name of Florida's Thlauhatke Hills means "white mountain" in the Muskogean Indian language. Even given the extremely widespread distribution of such names, this one still is unexpected in a state not known either for mountains or snow. The whiteness in the name, however, comes not from snow but from the hills' rocks; examination of other "white mountain" names reveals other examples.

While colors other than white, blue, and black appear less frequently in mountain names, these names usually describe more specifically the mountains they identify. The numerous mountains named "red," for example, usually are conspicuously red. However, the presence of a color in a name does not always mean the name is descriptive. Green Mountain might be named for a man named Green. And while one of the Navajo Indian names for Mount Taylor in New Mexico is Turquoise Mountain, this is a ceremonial name that doesn't necessarily imply any resemblance between the mountain and the color turquoise.

Still, color is a sufficiently distinctive characteristic that its use in mountain names is very common, and often with unusual variations and metaphors: Buckskin Mountain in Oregon; Dripping Blood Mountain in California; Maparaju (Quechua, "stained mountain") in Peru; Altai Mountains (possibly Turkish, "speckled mountains") in Central Asia; Mount Greylock in Massachusetts; the Maroon Bells in Colorado; Purple Mountain in Colorado and Arkansas; and Polychrome Pass in Alaska. Several mountains in the American West reminded early settlers of calico, and now three western mountain groups have that name: Calico Hills and Calico Peaks in California and Calico Mountains in Nevada.

Mountain names describing a mountain's shape, whether directly or through metaphor, are perhaps even more common than color names. Indeed, some names describing mountain shapes have become so widely used that they have expanded to become terms of mountain morphology. This has occurred with the term *aiguille*, once restricted to France but now applied world-wide to any needlelike mountain formation. Similarly, *sugarloaf* still is widely used as a formal name but also has become accepted as a generic term for any mountain shaped like a "loaf" of sugar. The extremely common name Baldy also is becoming a generic term, as in Santa Fe Baldy in New Mexico.

Many shape names are relatively straightforward, and names such as Round Mountain, Long Mountain, and Pyramid Mountain are common examples. Such names, like common color names, often have great antiquity, if not great appeal.

Much more interesting are the myriad metaphor names based upon real or imagined resemblances between a mountain's shape and something else. A sample of these names includes Dent du Crocodile (French, "crocodile's tooth"), Mooses Tooth, Camels Hump, Jirishanca (Quechua, "hummingbird's beak"), Emei Shan (Chinese, "beautiful eyebrows"), Ixtaccihuatl, (Nahuatl, "white woman"), Sleeping Beauty Peak, Imp Mountain, Jungfrau (German, "maiden"),

8

Arrigetch Peaks (Indian dialect, "fingers extended"), Machapuchare (Nepalese, "fish's tail"), Grossglockner (German, "big bell"), Organ Mountains, Sandia Mountains (Spanish, "watermelon"), Shiprock, White Sail, Table Mountain, Eiger (German, "ogre"), Gooseneck Pinnacle, Cake Peak, and Ice Cream Cone Mountain. Many mountains take their names from their resemblance to headgear: Sombrero Mountain, Mitre Peak, Warbonnet Peak, Hat Crown Mountain, Night Cap, and Tam O'Shanter Peak. The variety of metaphor names based upon shape is virtually endless. The highest summit entirely within Switzerland, the Dom, takes its name from the German word for "cathedral." At the other extreme of reverence is a range of mountains in Arizona named by early cowboys for the mountains' supposed resemblance to an outhouse; they called the range the S.H. Mountains. Taboos are few; wherever a resemblance has been noted, a name has been created. The strong resemblance between certain mountains and a woman's breasts has resulted in "breast names" being found throughout the world in numerous languages.

Mountains occasionally are described by their geological composition. The best known example is the Dolomites, whose distinctive spongelike limestone inspired the name. Other examples are the Spanish Cerro Pedernal ("flint mountain"), the Erzebirge (German, "iron mountains"), Glass and Bottlerock Mountains (named for obsidian), the Whetstone Mountains, and Granite Peak. Such names presume at least a rudimentary knowledge of geology and consequently are rare in areas where most of the peaks were named by peoples indifferent to mineral composition, such as Europe, the Himalaya, and the Andes. Often a name such as Stone Mountain in Georgia reflects not the mountain's composition but its appearance; all mountains, after all, are composed of stone.

Still another way of describing a mountain is by its size, yet mountain names based on this are relatively rare. Beinn Mhor in the Hebrides and Broad Peak in the Karakoram have already been mentioned. And size clearly inspired the name of Mount Massive in the Colorado Rockies and Corno Grande (Italian, "big mountain") in central Italy, but other examples are hard to find, and the best explanation is that bigness is so integral a part of any mountain that only rarely does it preempt other characteristics to form the basis for a name.

Although most descriptive mountain names derive from visual characteristics, a few exceptions exist. Many volcanoes were named because of the heat they generate. And at least three mountains were named because of their sounds. In Brazil there is a mountain named Serra do Roncador (Portuguese, "the snorer"). Also in South America is El Tronador (Spanish, "the thunderer"). And Hurrungane in Norway is believed to take its name from an Old Norse Dialect word *hurra* meaning "to make a strong noise," a name presumed to have been inspired by the mountain's frequent avalanches. (Music Mountain in Nevada was named because horizontal strata on the mountain resemble a musical staff, and the Growler Mountains in Arizona were named not because they "growl" but for an early settler.)

Occasionally, mountains are described according to their geographical location relative to other features. The name Lhotse, for instance, means "south mountain"—south of Everest. The Front Range in Colorado, the Coast Range of Oregon, and the Meije (from French, "middle") are other examples. But while names of location are more precise than many descriptive names, they rob their mountains of individual identity; it's like naming people "big brother," "little sister," or "only child."

Also, mountains sometimes are named for the impression they make upon the namer. Mount Bellicose in the Chugach Mountains of Alaska was named by some mountaineers after their difficult first ascent, while Benign Peak nearby clearly made a different impression on its namers. Mount Remarkable in Australia was named by an explorer because that was how the mountain appeared to him, and the Remarkable Mountains of New Zealand presumably were named similarly. Bashful Mountain in Alaska was named by some mountaineers who felt the mountain was hiding coyly behind clouds. More typically, however, if the impression was strong enough to inspire a name, the impression was negative: Mount Disappointment in Australia, Mounts Fury in Washington and California, Mounts Deception in Washington and New Hampshire, Forbidden Peak in Washington, and Mount Horrid in Vermont.

Such names are closely related to what Stewart calls "hortatory descriptives," a rare but interesting type of name that describes by asserting, "at this place you should behave thus." Such intent is clear in the name of Goback Mountain in northern New Hampshire. Stewart gives the example of the Kiss Me Quick Hills in South Dakota, named, as he says, "because the road across them was full of the kind of irregularity which might give excuse for a girl to throw herself into her lover's arms and thus was known to American countryfolk as a kiss-me-quick."

And then there are volcanoes. Most of them have descriptive names, but just as volcanoes are not like other mountains, neither are their names, particularly those belonging to volcanoes that have been active in recent geological times. Many volcano names are very old, and typically these make reference to volcanoes' fiery nature. The name Fujiyama has defied definitive interpretation, but it is believed to go back to a pre-Japanese Ainu word having to do with heat. Similarly, Demavend, highest mountain in Iran, takes its name from a very old Persian word also meaning "heat." The name Vesuvius goes back to a pre-Roman Oscan word meaning "emitter of smoke and sparks." The Klickitat Indian name for Mount St. Helens in Washington was Tah-one-lat-clah, "fire mountain." And Popocatapetl, one of Mexico's three great volcanos, still carries the Nahuatl name the Aztecs gave it, "smoking mountain."

These names seem bland compared to some other names volcanoes have inspired. The Spanish name of Pico del Teide on the Canary Islands means "peak of hell," a meaning shared by the Quechua names of two of Ecuador's volcanoes, Sangay, "hell," and Tungurahua, "little hell." South America includes many volcanoes with intriguing names: Pichincha (Quechua, "boiling mountain") and El Reventador (Spanish, "the exploder") in Ecuador. But probably the grimmest volcano name is that on a volcano in the Aleutian Islands of Alaska, Pogramni; its name comes from the same Russian root as *pogrom*, an organized massacre of helpless people, and has been translated as "black destroying death," though "desolation peak" is perhaps more accurate.

Associative Names

During the early days of white settlement of central Oregon, many pioneers passed along a road that ran north of a prominent mountain. Beside this road for many years was a wagon tire, said to have come from a wagon burned by Indians. The wagon tire came to be well known in the region, so much so that people began to identify the mountain with the wagon tire. Eventually the current name Wagontire Mountain evolved, persisting long after the wagon tire disappeared.

This example is typical of associative names, a very large class of mountain names that identifies mountains by their association with something else. Associative names are very closely related to descriptive names, because to identify a place by its association with something else is, in a sense, to describe it. Yet some subtle but important differences do exist between associative and descriptive names.

For example, as the name Wagontire Mountain illustrates, a mountain with an associative name can bear the name long after the association has ceased. Bear Mountain is a very common mountain name, especially in eastern North America, yet how many "bear mountains" still harbor bears?

Not surprisingly, animals are the basis for most associative mountain names. Very often the animals are the large game species—Elk Range in Colorado, Big Horn Mountains in Wyoming, Cariboo Mountains in British Columbia, and Bear Mountain and Deer Mountain everywhere—but not always. The Cordillera Huayhuash in Peru takes its name from an obscure species of rodent, while Nevado Viscacha also is named for a rodent.

But mammals have no monopoly on inspiring mountain names. Birds are represented in Magpie Peak in Oregon, while Eryri, the mountainous region in northern Wales, has a Welsh name meaning "place of eagles." Reptiles appear in the names of Chuckwalla Mountain in California and Culebra (Spanish, "rattlesnake") Peak in Colorado. (The Drakensberg—Dutch, "dragon mountain"— of South Africa doubtless take their name from something other than an actual physical association with dragons!) And a surprising number of mountains are named for insects: Ladybug Peak in Arizona; two mountains in New Mexico named Mosca (Spanish, "fly"); Pinecate Peak in California (Spanish for a type of beetle); and Scorpion Mountain in Oregon. One can only shudder to imagine the experiences that led to the name of the Mosquito Range in Colorado!

Often the association is with vegetation. The Matterhorn, for all its awesome singularity, bears a humble name that in German means simply "peak of the meadow," a shepherd's name. A major Iranian peak, Kuh Laleh-zar, was named for a species of wildflower. In the Palasade Group in California is Polemonium Peak, named for a genus of mountain flower, while Montana has Tobacco Root Mountain. Nevada Wamanripa in Peru was named for a plant species. Mountains named for trees are especially common, at least in North America, and just as every region seems to have one or more "bear mountain," so each has at least one "pine mountain" or "spruce mountain."

Natural features other than mountains commonly are named for wildlife and vegetation, but only mountains are named for clouds. Cloud Peak, highest summit in Wyoming's Big Horn Mountains, and Banner Peak in California both were named for the clouds that form around their summits. So was Mount Hekla in Iceland, whose Old Norse name usually is explained as meaning a "cowled or hooded frock," a reference to the cloak of clouds and smoke the volcano wears. And despite a folk etymology that relates the name of Mount Pilatus in Switzerland to Pontius Pilate, the name actually comes from a Latin word referring to the clouds around the peak.

These examples are only the most common inspirations for associative names; virtually anything associated with a mountain can inspire a name. A mountain in Alaska was the site of a marathon footrace, so the mountain became Marathon Mountain. Mount Mansfield, highest summit in the Green Mountains of Vermont, was named for the nearby town of Mansfield. Many mountains in the western United States, such as Mother Lode Mountain in Oregon and Treasure Mountain in Nevada, were named for their association with mines or mining. Outlaws hid in many western mountains, spawning names such as Outlaw Mountain in Arizona and the Sierra Ladrones (Spanish, "thieves' mountains") in New Mexico. During his campaign in Arizona against the Apaches, General Nelson Miles stationed his men atop mountains where they used mirrors to flash signals; one of the mountains became Heliograph Peak. TV Mountain in Montana was named for the television transmission towers on its summit. In the Cordillera Blanca of Peru, a battle left a pile of bones at the base of a peak, and that is what the Quechua name Tullujuto means—"pile of bones." At least two mountains in the British Isles were named for their association with fairies, the *sidh* of Celtic mythology: Knockshee (Gaelic, "fairy hill") in Northern Ireland and Schiehallion (Gaelic, "fairy hill of the Caledonians") in Scotland. At the other extreme of romance is a mountain that took its name from a local industry—Cannery Mountain.

Very often mountains are named for their association with people, individuals or groups who lived near the mountains and whose names came to be identified with them. When the Romans began their conquest of what is now Spain, they encountered a people living in the rugged northwest of the Iberian Peninsula whom they referred to as the Cantabrii. The Cantabrii long ago lost their separate identity as a people, their language and culture absorbed into the larger Iberian culture. But their name remains, now applied to the mountains where they lived—the Cantabrians. And it is quite possible that the name Pyrenees also preserves the tribal name of a people long since vanished. Throughout the world, mountain names preserve the names of people who once lived there, or still do. In the Sahara of southern Algeria are the Ahaggar Mountains, which were named because they are in the territory of the Al-hoggar branch of the Tuaregs.

As these examples point out, mountain names given for peoples or tribes typically were not given by the peoples themselves but by other peoples. And because of tribal animosities, such names, when examined closely, often are derogatory. The Adirondack Mountains of New York State took the name that tribes living outside the mountains had for the mountain-dwelling people, "bark eaters," a pejorative term. Mount Klickitat of coastal Oregon preserves the name local peoples had for a tribe that raided in the region; Klickitat means "robbers." Navajo Mountain, Comanche Mountain, and Apache Mountain in New Mexico all were named for these well-known tribes, yet none of these names is the name these tribes have for themselves; rather the names come from the languages of other peoples.

Mountains named for their association with tribal groups are particularly common in North America, where very often the names are the only reminders of the tribes that once lived in these regions. Examples of these names include the Uinta Mountains and the Timpanogos Mountains of Utah, the Absaroka Mountains of Wyoming, Mount Athabasca in Alberta, the Monashee Mountains of British Columbia, the Chugach Mountains of Alaska, Mount Shasta in California, and Mount Assiniboine on the British Columbia-Alberta border. It has been suggested that even the name of the great Rocky Mountain chain is not really a descriptive name but rather is a reference to the Assiniboine Indians, whom other tribes often called "the stonies" from their practice of cooking with heated stones. (The name Assiniboine means "stone cookers.")

Mountains occasionally are named for their association with a specific person or family. Such names are not necessarily intended to honor the person but merely recognize that the person lived near the mountain and became identified with it. Cochise Peak in Arizona was named by white settlers because it was associated with the Apache chief Cochise, whose warriors battled soldiers in a canyon near the peak. Throughout the American Southwest are mountains named because they are associated with early Spanish land grants made to specific individuals; the Ortiz Mountains in New Mexico are an example.

Outside North America, mountains named for their association with specific individuals or families are more rare, but they do occur. Galdhøpiggen, highest summit in Norway, was named at least in part for its association with farms owned by the family Galde, and in Scotland many mountains bear personal names, very likely those of people who long ago once lived near them.

Incident Names

When early miners in the Trinity National Forest region of California overindulged in alcohol, they referred to the jittery aftermath as the "jim jams." In the 1890s three miners hiked up a previously unnamed ridge, made camp, and began drinking heavily. In the course of their carousing one of them fell into their campfire, his pockets filled with rifle shells. This triggered such an attack of the jim jams among the miners that they named the ridge for the incident, and in 1935 the name Jim Jam Ridge was put on the Trinity National Forest map.

The name that resulted from this incident is typical of a large, extremely diverse, and very interesting class of place names known as incident names. Incident names identify a place and distinguish that place from all others by referring to something that happened there, something that became so closely identified in the public's mind with the place that a name resulted. Almost by definition, the incidents behind such names are colorful and dramatic, and as the name Jim Jam Ridge illustrates, the incident doesn't have to be historically significant, just memorable.

Hasty descent of the Aiguille du Midi, France. From the Alpine Journal, *Vol. 5, 1870-1872.*

Probably the greatest incident ever to inspire a mountain's name was the ascent of Moses to the top of the Sinai massif, there to receive from God the tablets on which were engraved the Ten Commandments. Though the name of the massif itself was untouched by the incident, one of the group's individual summits came to be known as Jebel Musa (Arabic, "Mount Moses"). According to legend, the name of Adams Peak in Sri Lanka had a similarly extraordinary origin; Adam, the first man, is believed to have left his footprint on the summit after ending there a thousand-years penance for his fall from grace.

Most naming incidents, however, are much less momentous. Indeed, very often the only record that survives of an incident is the name itself—and that can create problems. For example, a mountain named Massacre Peak clearly was named for a specific incident, even though other details might be lacking, but what of Bear Mountain? Was it named because of an abundance of bears there, or because of an incident involving a specific bear? Stewart argues convincingly that most such names began with specific incidents involving specific animals and that people later assumed the name came from association with an animal species only after the incident was forgotten. A similar ambiguity exists with mountains named for people when the naming circumstances have been lost. Was Prospector Peak named because prospectors sought minerals there, or because of an incident involving a specific prospector?

When we survey the incidents that have inspired mountain names, we cannot help but wonder at their diversity. In fact, there seems to be no common factor among them, least of all significance. Bug Butte in Oregon was named because bark beetles had killed many trees on it. Crazy Peak in New Mexico was named because a woman became demented and jumped from a cliff there. At Mount Destruction in Australia an expedition's horses died of thirst. Fusillade Mountain in Montana was named because a party of hunters fired many times at some goats without hitting them. Regulation Peak in California was named by a man placing copies of Forest Service regulations on trees there. Mount Chocorua in New Hampshire is where an Indian chief of that name is believed to have leaped to his death. Captain James Cook gave Mount Fairweather in Alaska its name because of good weather on the day of its discovery. Quandary Peak in Colorado was named because some miners were perplexed by some ore they found there. No incident is too trivial. The Ophthalmia Range in New Zealand was named because the namer had an eye infection.

Still, a few general observations can be made about incident mountain names. One is that such names tend to lose their meanings with time. Incidents are forgotten, and languages change. A name that made sense when it was created often will become unintelligible to later inhabitants of the region. The name of Plynlimon in Wales comes from the Celtic and means "five lights," almost certainly inspired by an occasion when five fires burned on the summit, but the details have been lost and even most Welshmen now would have difficulty guessing the name's meaning. When we survey the oldest mountain names, we notice that very few of them are recognizably derived from incidents. Conversely, most incident mountain names occur in regions where the mountains were named relatively recently—North America, Australia, New Zealand, and Antarctica. (Incident names are not altogether lacking elsewhere. In the

Diablerets group of the Alps there is a rock wall immediately below the summit named the Pas du Lustre, "pass of the chandelier." It was named from an incident in 1857 when the guide leading the botanist Jean Muret down the mountain forced Muret to pass a rope under his armpits to descend. Later the scientist recounted his experience, saying, "Everything went well, even if at a rough spot these rascals suspended me like a chandelier!")

Also, because memorable incidents are more likely to happen to people who frequent mountains, mountaineers have given mountains proportionately more incident names than other types. Unfortunately, the incidents that inspired the mountaineers often were bad ones. Bivouac Peak in Wyoming was named because climbers making the first ascent were forced to make an unplanned bivouac on the mountain. Mount Defiant in Alaska had defied the climbers' efforts, and mountaineers named Peril Peak in Alaska for the dangers of its ascent. Disaster Peak in California was named when a climber was injured by a boulder. But probably the worst time of it was had by the climbers who in 1925 named Disappointment Peak in the Tetons. Though they made a successful first ascent, they were barred from reconnoitering the Grand Teton by a huge mountain gap. Then they were unable to descend its northwest face and had to retreat another way. And finally, one of the party was injured in a glissade. Disappointment indeed!

But not all mountaineer incident names are as ill-omened. Easy Day Peak in Wyoming was named for the mountaineers' day of rest before making the ascent. The Revelation Mountains in Alaska fulfilled the expectations of their namers. And Pabst Peak in Wyoming was named when the climbers making its first ascent celebrated by drinking beer!

Commemorative Names

In the mid-1800s, when British scientists and explorers with the zeal of missionaries and the adventure lust of conquistadors were delving into the world's unmapped regions, T.H. Huxley had penetrated the interior of the vast, mountainous island of New Guinea. There he found, unexpected in so tropical a land, a commanding, snow-capped mountain range. It lacked a name, at least an English one, so to Huxley fell the responsibility—and the privilege—of supplying one. In that jungle wilderness, Huxley remembered the skipper on whose ship he had first sailed the South Seas. The skipper, a tragic figure, had committed suicide in Australia, but Huxley, years later at the moment of discovery, decided to commemorate his old shipmate and named the mountains the Owen Stanley Range.

Such commemorative or honorific names have been bestowed by the thousands throughout the world, primarily by Englishmen or their descendents. These names differ fundamentally from the other kinds of names previously discussed in that the givers of these names were motivated not so much by the simple desire to identify a place as by the more complex impulse to confer honor, or at least ensure remembrance. Whereas the other types of names—descriptive, associative, and incident—usually evolve through local usage, commemorative names typically are deliberately created by a single individual. And whereas the other types of names represent a close connection between the place and the name—describing the place, mentioning an association, or recalling something that happened there—commemorative names often are independent of any such links. Owen Stanley had virtually no connection with the mountains that bear his name; he never even saw them, or only from a distance. Yet Huxley's main intention has been achieved: to use the permanence of names to preserve the memory of his comrade.

Such a name as the Owen Stanley Range illustrates the best and the worst of commemorative naming. Huxley's sentiment was laudable and sincere, far better than the motives of those sycophantic namers who have used their naming prerogative to honor patrons, or worse, potential patrons. A long tradition exists of explorers naming mountains for persons or groups responsible for their expeditions. Probably the best known example is the British navigator Captain George Vancouver. As he coasted along northwestern North America, he saw nothing unusual or objectionable in naming the features he saw for friends and prominent figures in the British naval establishment, and thus Mounts Rainier, Hood, and St. Helens acquired their names.

But while Huxley's intentions at least were honorable, he nonetheless put onto a major mountain range the name of a minor figure, a name that reveals nothing of the range's character. Mismatches such as these often are an unfortunate characteristic of commemorative mountain names, and when we survey the often bitter controversies that have arisen about mountain names, inevitably a commemorative name is involved: Everest, McKinley, Rainier, and many more.

Early peoples experienced no such difficulties. As we have seen, mountain names given by preliterate peoples tend to evolve either from local mythology or from a need to identify the mountain, and the idea of using names to confer personal honor was unthinkable. This author can think of no example of a natural feature in North America named by Indians to honor a specific individual. Even Mount Tyee in Oregon, whose name is a Chinook jargon word meaning "chief," was named to indicate prominence, not to honor a chief. To be sure, numerous North American mountains bear the names of Indian chiefs, but without exception these names were given by non-Indians. Examples similarly are lacking in South America, Africa, and Asia. And while many very old European mountain names include personal names, these most likely evolved from a close association between the person and the mountain. The Brecon Beacons of Wales, for instance, preserve the name of an ancient Welsh prince, Brychan, but it is unlikely the mountains were deliberately named to honor him; more likely, the mountains were within his realm or an incident occurred there involving him.

With the development of civilization and writing, peoples' views of posterity—and how to achieve it—changed. Alexander the Great certainly was confident of the durability of place-names when he put his name on many of the cities he founded during his conquests. And his estimation was correct; more than two thousand years later, Alexandria in Egypt still bears his name. But the notion of using mountains as packhorses to immortality came later. As

Stewart has written: "Through history and even before it, human beings have looked upon great peaks, perhaps with feelings of esthetic pleasure, but certainly with wonder, and even with religious awe. To put a person's name upon such a towering mass is to bestow outstanding honor and seeming immortality upon him. It is almost to make him a god. The idea, however, was not grasped in early times. Even Alexander the Great named cities for himself, not mountains."[133]

Eventually, of course, the idea was grasped, and by many peoples, but particularly by a people who have had a disproportionate role in the naming of the world's mountains—the English and their descendents. Driven by a singular compulsion to explore the blank spaces on the world's map, English explorers in the eighteenth and nineteenth centuries found there innumerable peaks and ranges that lacked names, or at least English ones. And by then the idea of using names to confer honor was well established.

Mount Everest, the Fitzroy Mountains of Patagonia, the Flinders and Darling Ranges of Australia, Mount Rainier of Washington State, Mounts Cook and Tasman in New Zealand, the Aberdare Range in East Africa—wherever the English found unnamed mountains, as often as not they seized the opportunity to honor someone. Even some seemingly native names were created this way: Pumori near Everest was named by Sir George Mallory for his daughter, Clare; *pumori* in the native language means "daughter." To be sure, other European peoples also have given many commemorative names to mountains; the Russian Pamirs are littered with names honoring heroes of the Russian Revolution, and the Italian mountaineer, the Duke of the Abruzzi, was hopelessly addicted to commemorative names. But the English names scholar C.M. Matthews has shown convincingly in her *Place-names of the English-speaking World* that English-speaking countries—Australia, New Zealand, Canada, and the United States—have a much higher frequency of commemorative names than regions settled by other peoples, such as the Spanish. Indeed, the propensity to bestow commemorative names is the single most distinguishing naming characteristic of English-speaking peoples. (Ironically, Britain itself has very few commemorative mountain names, most mountains there having received their names long before commemorative naming came into vogue.)

Commemorative names now are among the most numerous of all mountain names. Nor are such names bestowed only to preserve the memories of the powerful and famous. They honor settlers (Lassen Peak, California), ranchers (Barton Peak, California), artists (Bierstadt Peak, Colorado, and Mount Moran, Wyoming), schoolteachers (Mount Maggie, California), novelists (Mount Wister, Wyoming, and London Peak, Oregon), humorists (Mount Leacock, Alaska), poets (Robert Frost Mountain, Vermont, and Mount Robert Service, Alaska), composers (Mount Verdi, California), and even courtesans (Mount Lola, California). They honor wives (Mount Ulmer, Antarctica), daughters (Pumori, Nepal), aunts (Mount Hunter, Alaska), great-grandfathers (Mount Sanford, Alaska), and girl friends (Mount Judith, Montana). They honor not only multitudinous political figures but also their wives (Mount Lady Washington, Colorado) and their children (Mount Ishbel, Canadian Rockies).

But the groups that are best represented in commemorative mountain names are scientists, particularly geologists, surveyors, and explorers. They, after all,

18

discovered and described many of the mountains, and it was only natural that when they had the opportunity to bestow honor through naming, they would choose from among their colleagues and predecessors. Josiah Dwight Whitney, head of the geological survey of California, forbade his subordinates from naming features for him, but when a peak in the Sierra Nevada was discovered to be the state's highest, the surveyors ignored his directive and named it Mount Whitney. Similarly, the highest summits in four other western states are each named for a surveyor—Gannett Peak in Wyoming, Humphreys Peak in Arizona, Kings Peak in Utah, and Wheeler Peak in New Mexico. Dozens of lesser mountains bear similar names. Indeed, the preponderance of scientists' names is one characteristic that distinguishes mountain names from those of other features. As Stewart has written: "Mountains, so long neglected by Indians, pioneers, and practical men, became the special field of scientific naming. Not only did scientists name mountains, but also mountains were named for scientists. The Humboldt is almost the only river bearing a scientist's name, but there are many mountains, east and west. The magnificent chain of the Sierra Nevada might be called the Scientists Range as properly as a lesser row of eastern peaks is the Presidential."[134] Actually, Stewart's Scientists Range has been realized, though on a smaller scale; in Kings Canyon National Park in California are eight peaks each named for a scientist associated with evolution, and together the peaks are called the Evolution Group.

While the names of scientists, surveyors, and explorers are particularly numerous on mountains in western North America, their names are also common on mountains elsewhere. The eminent nineteenth-century American geographer Arnold Guyot is honored not only by a mountain in California but also by one in Tennessee, and Mount Jackson near the Presidential Range of New Hampshire honors not President Andrew Jackson but New Hampshire State Geologist Charles T. Jackson. In New Zealand Mounts Tasman and Cook and the Haast Range honor explorers and scientists, as do the Flinders Range of Australia and Carstencz Pyramid in New Guinea. When the Duke of the Abruzzi named the summits of the Ruwenzori Range, he chose as eponyms important figures in the exploration and development of East Africa. Antarctica, all of whose natural features were named after commemorative names became popular, has virtually all its mountains named for people, many important in the continent's exploration. But even the Alps, where one would expect earlier names to have preempted most opportunities for commemorative naming, nonetheless has a few examples: the Durfourspitz on Monte Rosa honors a pioneer mapmaker, and the Hugihorn in the Schreckhorn group honors a pioneering geologist and winter mountaineer.

Curiously, mountain names honoring scientists, surveyors, and explorers are largely lacking from one region where these groups have been conspicuously active—Central Asia. To be sure, the dominant peak there bears the name of a surveyor, Sir George Everest, and another surveyor, Henry Godwin-Austen, has been proposed, albeit unsuccessfully, as the eponym for the region's second highest mountain, K2. But considering how many peaks, particularly in the Karakoram, were unnamed before British exploration, and remembering that British exploration of Central Asia came at a time when British explorers elsewhere were applying commemorative names with a vengeance, the relative lack of commemorative names in Central Asia is surprising. Several highly conjectural reasons could be advanced to explain this, but one would like to think the British explorers, confronted with the overwhelming size and majesty of the mountains, shrank from putting on them the names of mere mortals. When Sir Martin Conway, exploring the Baltoro region of the Karakoram, encountered a mountain larger than any other in his experience, he named it not for a monarch or any other human, however significant, but instead called it simply Broad Peak.

While the expansion of the British empire was the heyday of commemorative mountain naming, the practice has slowed since, only because fewer mountains remain to be named. Nor have commemorative mountain names been limited to honoring just individuals. Indeed, virtually anything someone deems worthy of commemoration is a potential source for a commemorative name. The Duke of the Abruzzi named two peaks for ships—Mount Bona in Alaska and Mount Lucania in the Yukon. The Centennial Range in western Canada was named to commemorate Canada's centennial celebration. Mount Sanhedrin in California recalls the council body of the ancient Hebrews. Mount Mazama in Oregon was named by and for the Mazamas mountaineering club, which took its name from the Spanish for "mountain goat," while Explorers Peak in Alaska honors the Explorers Club. Expanding to still larger groups, Mount Democrat in Colorado honors a political party, while English Mountain in Oregon was named during World War II to honor "the English people." From the grandiose to the trivial, anything attracting enthusiasm or loyalty is a potential subject for a commemorative mountain name. Shortly after World War II some climbers in Wyoming made a first ascent of an unnamed peak. They were using a new type of rope that wartime rationing had made previously unavailable, and so enthusiastic were they about its properties that they named the mountain for it, calling it Nylon Peak! Is it only a matter of time before a summit somewhere is named Perlon Peak? Or Dent du Gore-tex?

Needless to say, the widespread and extremely varied use of commemorative names has led to what many people feel are abuses. Surely, these people argue, mountains deserve to be more than mere insignia bearers for the sometimes trivial, often ephemeral, and occasionally debased fancies of humans whose naming prerogatives frequently result from little more than accident. Surely mountains deserve names more in keeping with their history and character, names in which the mountain's identity is more important than the namer's. It is difficult not to concur with these arguments in the face of mountain names such as Antarctica's Executive Committee Range, named by its discoverers for the Antarctic Service Executive Committee, the group that had authorized their expedition; individual peaks in the range were named for individual committee members. And surely few lovers of mountains would wish upon them names such as those the Soviets have bestowed upon peaks in the Pamirs: Communist Academy Peak, Pravda Peak, German Communist Party Peak, and Peak of the Proletarian Press.

To prevent inappropriate commemorative names, governmental geographic agencies have adopted certain guidelines for naming mountains for people. For example, the New Zealand Geographic Board stipulates that "only persons who have climbed or traversed on mountain features have the right to submit names for them,"[87] but as the Duke of the Abruzzi's namings illustrate, mountaineers are as capable of inappropriate namings as anyone else. In the United States, the Board on Geographic Names rejects proposals naming natural features for living persons, thus trying to ensure that the eponyms have at least some historical significance, but occasionally this stricture is waived, or at least avoided by the namers. This author has personal knowledge of one such instance, one that reveals much about the weaknesses of commemorative naming. In the small village of Groveton in New Hampshire's White Mountains, the fish and game club decided to honor a popular local conservation officer by placing his name on a minor and previously unnamed mountain. The officer, a modest man who was only a passive participant in the effort, was still alive at the time of the initiative, but the Groveton sportsmen, working through their local politicians, succeeded in having the name adopted nonetheless, and so the obscure peak was christened Muise Mountain. Soon after, Officer Muise wearied of law enforcement—and became a car salesman.

Mountains Named for Mountaineers

Given the close association between mountains and mountaineers, we would expect numerous mountains to bear the names of those who climb them. Not so. In fact, mountain names honoring politicians are much more common. The most obvious reason for this is that mountaineering as a recognized, organized activity came relatively late, after most mountains already had names. Even though Edward Whymper will be closely associated with the Matterhorn forever because of his dramatic first ascent, his name could not dislodge the centuries-old name the mountain already possessed.

But even in regions such as the Andes, western North America, and Central Asia, where many mountains were unnamed until persons interested in mountain conquests arrived, mountains named for mountaineers are relatively rare. The mountaineering Duke of the Abruzzi named the major summits of Africa's Ruwenzori Range, but he named them for African explorers, not fellow mountaineers. Indeed, when we consider the almost legendary figures in mountaineering's history, we cannot help but be perplexed by the virtual absence of their names from the peaks, particularly when lesser figures, many with no direct connections with the mountains, are routinely honored.

To be sure, examples of mountains named for mountaineers do exist, particularly if the term *mountaineer* is defined to include persons such as surveyors, geographers, and frontier guides who climbed mountains in the course of other activities. Given this definition, mountains such as Mount Guyot and Clingmans Dome in the Great Smoky Mountains, Mount Mitchell in the Black Mountains, and Mount Crawford in the White Mountains would be included.

But restricting *mountaineer* to mean someone whose primary purpose in the mountains is not gaining knowledge but gaining the summit, the list contracts considerably. In Patagonia, Torre Egger honors the Austrian climber Toni

Egger, who died descending nearby Cerro Torre. In Switzerland, the Ulrichshorn above Saas Fee honors Melchior Ulrich, an early member of the Zurich school of climbing who made pioneer explorations of the glaciers around Zermatt. Three crags in the Dolomites are named Winkler, Stabler, and Delago for the mountaineers who were first to climb them. In the Pyrenees, Pic Schrader bears the name of the first climber to complete the ascent. And in the Cuillin Hills on the Isle of Skye, Sgurr Alasdair preserves the name of the local writer, lawyer, and climber who in 1873 made the first ascent of the peak, Sheriff Alexander Nicolson. (Sgurr Alasdair means "Mount Alexander" in Gaelic.)

Most other "climber peaks" are in western North America, especially in California and Wyoming. They include Ellingwood Peak, Bollinger Peak, Buchtel Peak, Mount Fryxell, Mount Owen, Philsmith Peak, Mount Theodore Koven, and Walt Bailey Peak, all in Wyoming; Mount Clark, Colby Mountain, Foerster Peak, Mount Gould, Mount Mallory, Peter Peak, Mount Starr, and Mount Tyndall, all in California; Ellingwood Peak, Wilson Peak, and Mount Wilson in Colorado; Bill Williams Mountain in Arizona; Mount Fanny in Oregon (named for the first woman to reach the summit); and Stutfield Mountain in Alberta.

Needless to say, numerous routes and individual features on mountains are named for mountaineers closely associated with them, such as Petzoldts Pinnacle Ridge in Wyoming's Gannett region, but as for the mountains themselves, the names of mountaineers are conspicuously absent.

Commendatory or Religious Names

Mountains always have been holy places. Since earliest times, among all peoples, the mountain world has been a world apart, a realm midway between the known earth and the divine firmament, partaking of both. To primitive peoples in any time, the mountain world was to be approached with fear and trembling; in the mountain world humans were especially vulnerable to all the evil happenstance possible in a universe governed by nightmarish confusion of easily offended, powerfully vindictive, utterly bewildering spirits. Even in the twentieth century, mountaineers know mountains to be dangerous places, where accidents are more likely to happen than elsewhere; to primitive peoples, to whom there are no accidents, to whom avalanches and falling stones are the work of malevolent forces, mountains would have been terrifying beyond our imagining.

Thus, most primitive peoples avoid mountains whenever possible, but they name them nonetheless, and very often their names reflect their attitudes toward mountains: Kinabalu, highest summit in Borneo, "mountain of the dead"; Khan Tengri in the Tien Shan, "prince of the spirits"; and Kilimanjaro, highest summit in Africa, "mountain of the snow devils."

As primitive animism developed into more sophisticated religions, mountains did not become less fearsome or mysterious, but their place in the supernatural order did change. Still infested by myriad malicious spirits, mountains also

The Chimney, on the southwest ridge of the Matterhorn, Switzerland. From Edward Whymper, Scrambles amongst the Alps 1860-1869 (Philadelphia: 1873).

became the home of more important deities. All of nature had been the habitat of spirits, but mountains were the abode of the gods.

Indeed, the universality of the tendency to find God in the mountains suggests that the profound impact mountains have on the human psyche is a deeper emotion than we have imagined, one that transcends culture or locality. Everywhere, mountains have been where gods and humans meet.

As a result, the list of mountain names with origins in religion is long. In Ireland there is Croagh Patrick, where the saint prayed. In Iran there is Takh-e-Suleiman—"throne of Solomon." In Sri Lanka, Adams Peak, bearing the footprint of Adam, the first man. In Mexico, Ixtaccihuatl, "sleeping woman," and Citlaltepetl, "mountain of the star," both from Aztec mythology. In the American Southwest are the Sangre de Cristo Mountains, "the blood of Christ"; in northeastern North America, the Laurentian Mountains, for St. Lawrence; in New Zealand, Aorangi, Maori name for Mount Cook, from Maori mythology; and in west-central Europe, the Graian Alps, from the Graiae of Roman mythology.

But without question, the most fertile soil for religious mountain names is Asia. The Himalaya come quickly to mind. Of the Himalayan peaks with native names, most carry some religious meaning: Annapurna, "the bountiful goddess"; Chomolungma (Everest), "goddess, mother of the world"; Gosainthan, "home of the saint"; Cho Oyu, "goddess of the turquoise"; Chomo Lhari, "mountain of the goddess"; and many, many more. Particularly plentiful are mountains whose names indicate they are sacred to worshippers of Siva: Nanda Devi, "the goddess Nanda," consort of Siva; Trisul, "trident" of Siva; Gaurisankar, consort of Siva; Ganesh, a child of Siva; and even Shivling, "penis of Siva."

This density of religious names in the Himalaya is not surprising, when one considers how much concern is given in the region to honoring and propitiating the deities. As Stewart has written: "Naming a place for a god, with the idea that the god will then be favoring, constitutes one of the commonest manifestations of commendatory naming. The more dominating the religiosity of a culture, the commoner this type of naming. India is an outstanding example, a numerous pantheon making it possible for names of good omen to be placed even upon the smaller natural features."[133] In mountains where prayer wheels are driven by winds, where trailside cairns are heaped with offerings, where monasteries and shrines are carved from the living rock, it was inevitable that the mountains themselves would become shrines.

Throughout Asia, not just in the Himalaya, mountains are religious objects, whether or not this is reflected in the mountains' names. In Japan the mountain name Ontake can be translated as "the venerable one," and pilgrims by the hundreds of thousands have climbed to its summit. China has its Wu Yue, its five sacred mountains, one for each of the four cardinal directions and one for the center, each with a name indicating which yue it is and each richly embellished with shrines and temples. The name of one of China's great ranges, Tien Shan, means "celestial mountains." In Mongolia, dominating the capital of Ulan Bator, is Bogdo-ol, "the mountain of God."

On mountains throughout the world are names indicating that still, as in the past, mountains are holy places.

Transfer Names

The highest mountain in West Africa, Mount Cameroon, is best known by a name that, traced to its Portuguese origins, means "prawns." On such an enormous mountain this name is unexpected, particularly as no prawns are associated with the mountain, nor does the mountain's shape in any way resemble a prawn. Where did the name come from? From a nearby river, which in turn was named for a bay—which did have prawns.

This process, in which one feature shares its name with one or more nearby features in much the same way a schoolchild spreads a cold, is known as *transfer naming*. The transfer usually evolves unintentionally. For example, a stream is known for its trout and with time comes to be known as Trout Stream. The stream's headwaters are beneath a group of unnamed peaks which come to be known as Trout Stream Peaks. Eventually the *stream* is dropped, and the peaks are left with the odd name Trout Peaks. The next step would be for other features to pick up the name—Trout Canyon, Trout Ridge, and possibly even a town. By this process, the Truchas (Spanish, "trout") Peaks and the village of Truchas in New Mexico received their names.

The geographic features most likely to transfer names to mountains are waterbodies, particularly rivers. Some examples include the Finsteraarhorn in Switzerland, Glittertinden in Norway, Kitaraju in Peru, and the Hindu Kush in Central Asia, as well as numerous North American examples: the Wind River Range, the Medicine Bow Range, the Big Horn Mountains in Wyoming, the Catskill Mountains in New York State, and the Wallowa Mountains in Oregon.

Waterbodies, however, typically have not taken their names from mountains. Scotland's famous Loch Lomond owes its name to nearby Ben Lomond, but other examples are difficult to find.

Mountains Named for Other Mountains

We can hardly imagine today how pioneer homesteaders in North America must have felt arriving for the first time at the land that was to be their home. For many the journey through the wilderness had been long and difficult, perhaps dangerous, but now their journey was over, their destination achieved. It must have been a deeply moving moment, and for some a deeply religious one. From moments such as these surely must have come the many North American mountains with the Biblical name Pisgah, the name of the mountain from which Moses beheld the Promised Land. Mountains named Pisgah exist in at least four U.S. states, with three in Vermont alone. Other biblical names—Carmel, Hermon, and Nebo, for example—are also widespread.

Mountains are often named because of some real or imagined resemblance to other mountains. The mountain whose appearance has made its name the most widely borrowed is the Matterhorn. In the United States, Matterhorns are found in California, Colorado, Oregon, Nevada, and even Vermont. Throughout the world fang-shaped mountains are known as "the Matterhorn of ———."

When Captain John Mears saw the mountain dominating what is now Washington's Olympic Peninsula, he was reminded by its majesty of the mountain home of the Greek gods, and so he named the peak Mount Olympus. Less lofty sentiments caused a mountain near Los Angeles, California, to be named Mount Vesuvius. In 1893, a weekly fireworks display on the summit concluded with an imitation of the Italian volcano erupting, and so another Mount Vesuvius was born.

Folk Etymology and Mountain Names

The ancient Romans were remarkably uninterested in mountains in general, much less their names, but had anyone asked a citizen of the late Roman Empire the origin of the name of the Apennine chain running like a spine down the Italian peninsula, the Roman very likely would have had an answer. The name, the Roman would have explained, was derived from the time of Hannibal. During the Punic Wars, the Carthaginian general crossed these mountains when he invaded Roman territory, and because of this the mountains came to be known as the Poenine, or Punic, mountains, later corrupted to Apennine. It's an appealing etymology, but probably incorrect. The name Apennine is likely derived not from the Carthaginians but from the Celts, who had inhabited the region before the ascendency of Rome. The Celtic language included the root *pen*, "summit," from which came the name of the Italian mountains and also that of the Pennine Alps in Switzerland, also once inhabited by Celtic-speaking peoples. The Romans would not have known this, of course—the Celts and their language having long since vanished—so when the Punic explanation appeared, it sounded plausible and was widely accepted. Only much later would persons knowledgeable in linguistics and the region's ancient ethnology unravel the name's true origins.

This process of a people evolving a plausible explanation for a name in ignorance of the name's actual origins is known as *folk etymology*. For example, in Maine there is a minor mountain with the odd name Sowbungy, sometimes spelled Sourbungy. Explanations for this name vary, but they usually involve a pig or something sour. Early records indicate that *Sowbungy* evolved from an earlier form, *Soubangen*, which in turn was derived from an Algonquian Indian word, *sowangen*, "eagle," a perfectly understandable associative name for a mountain. Early white settlers surely were aware of this meaning when they adopted the name, but the meaning and sounds of the Indian word gradually were lost, and later white inhabitants eventually came to spell and interpret the name according to more familiar patterns. Hence the name Sowbungy.

The Hindu Kush provides what may be the most noteworthy example of folk etymology at work upon a mountain name. The etymology that has been popular since Mongol times in this great range extending west from the Karakoram is that *kush* means "killer," so that the name can be variously translated as "Hindu killer" or "Hindu death." The explanation for these meanings is that Hindus, driven as slaves over the high mountain passes by Central Asian invaders, perished from cold and altitude in such numbers that the mountains acquired an evil reputation—and an ominous name. But the name Hindu Kush has no direct connection either with the Hindus or their enslavement. Rather, Hindu is just one of many manifestations of the Sanskrit word *sindhuh*, "river," (a word from which the names India and Indus are derived), and Kush most likely is related to *kuh*, a Persian word meaning "mountain." Thus, the name Hindu Kush really means simply "river mountains," most likely explained by the Indus having its headwaters there.

The trouble with folk etymology is that explanations created this way are

26

assumed true until suspected false; if no basis for suspicion is detected, the explanation is accepted. Often, however, folk etymology betrays itself. Medieval villagers near Mount Pilatus in Switzerland had no difficulty believing a local legend that the mountain's name came from Pontius Pilate having drowned himself in a lake there, but modern researchers, skeptical of the legend, were able to determine that the name came instead from a Latin word referring to the mountain's cloudcap. And while researching mountain names in the White Mountains of New Hampshire, this author once asked a local resident about the name of an odd squiggle of a mountain called Cape Horn. "It was called that," the informant said, "because early settlers noticed that the mountain from the air resembles Cape Horn in South America." Folk etymology immediately was suspected—how would early settlers have seen the mountain from the air?

Regulation of Mountain Names

Because mountains have names, like people, and not numbers, like library books, we have access to all the history and folklore inherent in names—but we also sometimes encounter their problems. A name such as Bear Mountain can occur often in an area, leading to confusion. Often an individual mountain will have several competing names, again resulting in confusion: which is the proper name of North America's highest summit, McKinley or Denali? Frequently mountain names exhibit inconsistencies in spelling: the name of Maine's highest summit has been spelled both Katahdin and Ktaadn, among other ways. Occasionally names will be deemed inappropriate or in bad taste: Should North America's highest summit really bear the name of an Ohio politician who never saw the mountain and probably never cared to, and do names such as Nigger Nose and Nellies Nipples belong on standardized maps?

To avoid these and other problems—if indeed they are problems—official governmental bodies have been created to issue guidelines, resolve inconsistencies, and adjudicate conflicts. The effect of these efforts generally has been benign, functioning not to bureaucratize naming but rather to untangle some of the snarls that inevitably result from such an unregulated, wildly individual activity. One reason for this is that these official bodies recognized early the primacy of local usage. As the great Swiss-American geographer Arnold Guyot wrote more than a century ago: "It is evident that popular usage will decide in the last resort and that the name universally adopted will, in time, become that which geography ought to accept."[50] Similarly, Colonel Sir Sydney Burrard of the Indian Trigonometrical Survey, who studied many Himalayan and Karakoram mountains, stated: "The nomenclature of a mountainous region should not be forced, it should grow spontaneously, and we should never invent a name until its absence has become inconvenient."[11] These wise sentiments were echoed on an international level by a 1967 United Nations conference of geographers who said in their report: "The whole basis of its [the conference's] immediate program was to encourage governments to standardize place names in their own countries. Once the highest national authority has given its ruling...the proposed commission will try to obtain worldwide acceptance of names approved in local usage."[142]

In the United States, the body responsible for mountain names is the United States Board on Geographic Names (USBGN), created in 1890 "to establish and maintain uniform geographic name usage throughout the federal government." Because the United States still has unnamed mountains, it is worth summarizing here some relevant USBGN guidelines:

1. The USBGN "prefers imaginative names that are relatively unique or distinctive provided they are not incompatible with the forms of other names existing in the areas in which they will be used. Names descriptive of topographic form or suggested by local history, folklore, or incident, or by associated natural life or other phenomena are preferred. This includes Indian and other ethnic names appropriate to the area in which the features are located."

2. "A proposed name should not duplicate another name in the state or nearby in an adjoining state."

3. New names should be suitable as proper names. "They normally should be as short as possible and easily pronounced. Preferably, the pronunciation should be apparent from the spelling."

4. Qualifying and relational terms (big, second, north, and so forth) should be avoided. "Wherever possible, new names should be distinctive."

5. Personal names "will not be adopted unless it is determined to be in the public interest to honor the person or persons for historical reasons. To justify adoption by the board the person or family being honored should have been directly associated with the feature being named or have made a significant contribution to the area of the feature or the state in which it is located.... Proposals honoring exceptional national or international persons also will be considered." Because many commemorative names have only temporary significance, the USBGN will "not adopt names that commemorate...living persons." Also, "a person must have been deceased at least one year before a commemorative proposal will be considered."

6. The USBGN "will not adopt a name proposal that implies discrimination or is derogatory to any particular person, race, or religion. This also applies to names considered obscene or blasphemous in a present-day culture or context."

These guidelines, if heeded by persons naming mountains, will not obstruct any good mountain names and will avoid many bad ones.

A Final Word

I began this project because I like mountains and I like names, and writing this book has allowed me to learn more about both. But from the outset I was aware that I could present no more than a selection of the world's mountains and that many important mountains, many with interesting and appealing names, could not be included. This is regrettable, if unavoidable, and to those readers disappointed that certain mountains are not present I extend my sympathy, for I too have seen omitted many peaks I deemed important. Often this resulted not

Hut on the Matterhorn, above Zermatt, Switzerland. From the Alpine Journal, *Vol. 9, 1878-1880.*

from a judgment as to the peak's significance but rather because the information about its name was inadequate or nonexistent. The Alps, where mountaineering was born, proved ironically to be the region for which adequate name information was most difficult to obtain. The Pyrenees and the Caucasus also deserved better than I was able to give them.

Very often I encountered conflicts among my sources; where a consensus appeared or where evidence allowed, I attempted to resolve the conflict. But many conflicts defied resolution, and in these instances I have attempted to include all relevant explanations without arbitrating among them.

The study of mountain names is a continuing search. I invite readers who can supply information about names not in this book, or additional information about names I have included, to contact me.

These, then, are the names of the world's mountains. In writing this book I have attempted to remain mindful of mountain names scholar Francis P. Farquhar's admonition that a book about names should not present mere skeletons but should attempt to convey the living character and personality of the peaks. It is my hope that persons who love mountains will find in their names many of the same qualities of the mountains themselves—beauty, excitement, individuality, discovery, always the unexpected, and infinite variety and delight.

ABSAROKA RANGE
Highest elevation, 13,140ft/4,005m, Francs Peak.
See Introduction.

Wyoming, USA

ACONCAGUA   22,835ft/6,960m
First ascent, 1897, M. Zurbriggen.

Argentina

Throughout the world, when the preliterate native peoples of a region have applied names to the natural features surrounding them, the names usually have been descriptive. It isn't that the local people are unimaginative, they're just practical. In a primitive world where being able to identify local landmarks quickly and accurately often means survival, descriptive names are very popular.

Certainly none of the Indian peoples living in what is now Argentina northeast of Santiago in Chile would have had any doubt which mountain was referred to when the name Kon-kawa, "snowy mountain," was mentioned. The summit, the highest in the western hemisphere, can be seen from the Pacific coast of Chile 100mi/160km away. Aconcagua has been called "the greatest and best-known landmark on the continent"[69], and because of its elevation, its summit is white when others are not.

The *Toponimia Quechua*, a work in Spanish about Quechua place-names, says the name Aconcagua comes from Quechua words that can be roughly translated as "vantage point from which to contemplate God." While most Quechua mountain names are simpler, usually naming the mountain by describing it or mentioning an association, such a meaning would not be completely out of character for a Quechua mountain name. But as the *Toponimia* suggests, this etymology is complex and perhaps is best regarded as tentative.

Although Aconcagua most likely was named for its whiteness, when mountaineers first attempted to climb the mountain they discovered more on its upper slopes than just snow. It has been called by climbers "an intolerably monotonous slag-pile"[76]—an unkind reference to the volcanic rocks comprising the mountain. (Aconcagua is not a volcano, however; its volcanic strata, laid down earlier, have been uplifted by nonvolcanic forces to form the mountain.) The mountain also has been called "the dump-heap of South America." James Ramsay Ullman suggested it might well be called "the Mountaineer's Nightmare."[140] Its upper slopes are savaged by severe storms; the altitude is formidable; the cold is intense; and the mountain is immense.

Actually, the entire region around Aconcagua suffers from a bad reputation. When the South American patriot and liberator San Martin in 1816 wanted to push his troops against those of the Royalists in Chile, he wrote: "It is not the opposition which the Royalists can offer to my soldiers that disturbs my sleep but the passage of these immense mountains."[88] In January 1817—summer in the southern hemisphere—San Martin's troops undertook a crossing of the mountains through Uspallata Pass, called by the Spanish Camino de los Andes, located in the shadow of Aconcagua. The trek took eighteen days. It was a daring move, but it was successful, and the Royalists were defeated.

Yet for all the scarifying epithets applied to it, Aconcagua has been climbed often since the first ascent in 1897. In 1934 an Italian party took two dogs to the summit, and in 1952 two priests carried a statue of Our Lady of Carmel up the mountain and placed it on top.

Most mountain names in Argentina are of Spanish origin, the native names having been lost since the Conquest. Aconcagua and Andes are two indigenous names that have survived.

MOUNT ADAMS   5,798 ft / 1,767m   New Hampshire, USA
First ascent unknown.

Mount Adams in the White Mountains of northern New Hampshire is the second highest peak in New England. Actually, the mountain is a composite of three summits, all named for an American patriot named Adams, two of whom were related. In 1820 a naming party from nearby Lancaster, New Hampshire, christened the highest summit for John Adams, second president of the United States. Then in 1857 the Reverend Thomas Starr King named the northernmost of the three peaks for another president, also named Adams and also named John. This peak honors John Quincy Adams, sixth president and son of John Adams. And finally, in 1876, some Appalachian Mountain Club members jokingly referred to the most westerly peak in the complex as Sam Adams—and the name stuck. Today this summit honors the American pamphleteer and advocate of independence, Samuel Adams.

MOUNT ADAMS   12,307ft / 3,751m   Washington, USA
First ascent, 1854, B.F. Shaw, E.J. Allen, A.G. Aiken, and A.J. Burke.

A dormant volcano located 35mi/56km due east of Mount St. Helens, Mount Adams is one of only a few peaks in the Pacific Northwest named for United States presidents, but if a proposal put forward last century had been adopted, many of the region's important peaks would have had such names. Between 1830 and 1843 efforts were made to change the name of the Cascade Range to the Presidents Range, with individual peaks renamed to honor individual presidents. A man named Hall J. Kelley championed the proposal, under which St. Helens would have become Washington; Baker, Taylor; Rainier, Harrison; and Olympus, outside the Cascades, Van Buren. Naming a range's peaks for presidents had a precedent. Just a few years earlier, in 1820, the peaks of the highest range in northeastern North America were formally named to honor United State presidents, and the range itself was dubbed the Presidential Range (see entry).

Kelley's proposal came to naught, most likely because of the prior naming of the eastern Presidential Range and because most of the Cascade Peaks, unlike those in New Hampshire, already had well-established names. But while the proposal was alive, the second highest summit in the range, previously known only by its Indian name, Pah-to, acquired the name Mount Adams. For a time there was confusion as to exactly which mountain honored which president, but by 1855 the name Adams had settled permanently upon Pah-to.

This relatively late naming of such an important peak is unusual and would not have occurred had not Lewis and Clark missed an important naming opportunity during their expedition in 1806. They did notice the mountain, for Captain William Clark mentioned it in his journal entry of 2 April 1806, when he was at the mouth of the Willamette River: "From the entrance of this river, I can plainly see Mt. Jefferson which is high and covered with snow S.E. Mt. Hood East, Mt. St. Heliens [and] a high humped mountain to the East of Mt. St. Heliens."[43] The "high humped mountain" certainly was Adams, but while it was Lewis and Clark who had named Mount Jefferson for the president then in office who had authorized their expedition, they neglected to name the other mountain, leaving it to be named eventually for another president.

The Indians of the Northwest gave personalities to the region's great mountains, and in an often-told legend (see Mount Hood) Mount Adams is Pah-to (sometimes Klickitat), son of the Great Spirit. He competed with his brother, Wy'east (Mount Hood), for the hand of a beautiful maiden, Loo-wit (Mount St. Helens). After a titanic battle that created the present topography of the Northwest, Pah-to won Loo-wit's hand—but not her heart. William Gladstone Steel, in *The Mountains of Oregon* (1890), says the name Pah-to signifies "high" and was applied by the Indians to snow-capped mountains generally.[43]

ADAMS PEAK   *7,360ft/2,243m*   *Sri Lanka*
First ascent ... Adam (?)

If Christian and Moslem legends regarding this mountain in southwestern Sri Lanka are believed, then its first ascent was the first ascent of any mountain anywhere, for it was made by the first man—Adam. To the faithful, the evidence exists to this day on the mountain's summit; there, in an oblong rock platform, is an indentation 64in by 30in/162.56cm by 76.8cm shaped like an outsize human foot. According to Moslem traditions, the footprint was made by Adam when he ended one thousand years of penance here.

The Moslems were not the first to notice the indentation or to venerate it. When the Buddhists came to Sri Lanka in the fourth century B.C., they found the indentation on the mountain and heralded it as belonging to Buddha. Hindus also were aware of the footprint; they claimed it for their god Siva. Later, in the Christian era, some Gnostic Christian sects proclaimed the footprint had been made by Adam, a belief adopted by Moslems when the island came under their dominion; they gave the mountain the name Adams Peak. Still later, Portuguese explorers consecrated the mountain to St. Eusebius.

33

No matter who is believed to have made the footprint, for more than two thousand years pilgrims by the hundreds of thousands have climbed the 3,306 steps to the summit, there to worship what they regard as material validation of their religious traditions. Only a few of the world's mountains—Fujiyama in Japan, Croagh Patrick in Ireland, Mount Sinai in Egypt, and Mount Olympus in Greece—are as sacred or have been climbed as often.

ADIRONDACK MOUNTAINS
New York, USA
Highest elevation, 5,347ft / 1,630m, Mount Marcy.

To many contemporary Americans, the Adirondack Mountains of north-eastern New York represent welcome relief from urban life, offering beauty, respite, and recreation amidst abundant, unspoiled nature. But to the Indians of colonial times, the vast wilderness was a harsh, undesirable place, difficult to traverse, unsuitable for most Indian crops, niggardly of game. Thus the branch of Algonquian Indians that lived in the mountains was regarded with contempt by the tribes living in the more accommodating lowlands. They called the mountain dwellers a name that sounded like *adirondacks* or *hatirontaks* and that meant "leaf eaters" or "eaters of trees." It was intended as an insult, something like calling a person a poor relation, and it implied that the Indians in the mountains had nothing better to eat in times of scarcity than the leaves or bark of trees.

Actually, it's not unusual for mountains to take on the pejorative names of Indian tribes associated with them. Mount Klickitat, in Oregon, bears the name of a tribe which dwelt far away, near The Dalles on the Columbia River in Washington, and conducted raids around the mountains now known for them. The name Klickitat means "robber" or "marauder" and doubtless was applied by a more local tribe that was the object of the Klickitat's raiding. Similarly, the many natural features in the American Southwest named for the Comanche Indians preserve not the name the Comanches called themselves—Nermernuh, "the people"—but rather the name by which they were known to other peoples of the region, from a Ute Indian word meaning "enemy."

The name Adirondack was first applied formally to the New York mountains in 1838 by Ebenezer Emmons, chief geologist of the New York Topographic Survey. It's possible Emmons was aware of the original meaning of the name Adirondack, but more likely the name's association with the mountainous wilderness had already eclipsed its earlier association with the people who lived there.

Emmons also named the highest summit in the Adirondacks, Mount Marcy, whose location in the east-central part of the region he had determined by triangulation. Emmons named the peak for William Learned Marcy, who was governor of New York at the time of the naming and who had instituted the geological survey of the Adirondacks. The Iroquois Indians of the region knew the mountain as Tahawus, "cloud splitter."

The first recorded ascent of Mount Marcy came in 1872 when the lawyer and topographical engineer Verplanck Colvin climbed the peak and discovered there Lake Tear-in-the-clouds, the source of the Hudson River. Colvin, who

Elephants before Adams Peak, Sri Lanka. From Frederic Zurcher and Elie Margollé Les ascensions
célèbres *(Paris, 1867).*

spent his summers exploring the Adirondacks, later initiated the survey of the
region that eventually resulted in the great forest preserve there today; a peak in
the mountains he loved bears his name.

AGATHLA NEEDLE   7,100ft/2,164m   Arizona, USA
First ascent, 1949, L. Pedrick, H. Conn, and R. Gardner.

   At the southern end of Monument Valley in northeastern Arizona is a black
volcanic needle towering 1,500ft/457m above the surrounding landscape. The
frontier guide and Indian fighter Kit Carson named it El Capitan, "the chief,"
because it dominated the entrance to the valley, but its present name is a Navajo
word meaning "much wool." According to the Navajo Bead Chant, the Indians
once killed a herd of antelope at the base of the rock. They set about cleaning
the hides there, and so many skins were scraped against the rough, volcanic
stone that it became known as "the place of wool and hair." That Agathla
Needle was the place in the chant is corroborated by the Spanish name for the
peak, Lana Negra, "black wool."

As a climbing site, Agathla Needle begs comparison with Shiprock, another volcanic formation located relatively nearby in northwestern New Mexico. Shiprock's height is greater, but its sides are no more precipitous.

AGUNG   10,308ft/3,142m   Bali
First ascent unknown.

Rising 10,000ft/3,048m from sea level and dominating the tiny island of Bali is the volcano Agung. It has erupted often in recent history, sowing widespread destruction, so it is not surprising that the people of Bali regard it with awe and reverence. Their name for it, Agung, means "the navel of the world." Farmers, cultivating their rice paddies, hang palm leaves on tree branches as votive offerings.

AHAGGAR MOUNTAINS   Algeria
Highest elevation, 9,574ft/2,918m, Mount Tahat.

Alain Barbezat, writing in *Mountain World*, has succinctly summarized the Ahaggar Mountains of southern Algeria: "There are no chains of an Alpine type in the Hoggar region. But there are many small massifs and many isolated mountains. It is a chaotic world, with a confused relief, with ravined summits, bare plateaus, rocky domes, strange volcanic peaks, deep gorges, and wide wadis of pale sand."[9] In this bizarre, inhospitable land live the Kel-Ahaggar Toureg, one of seven main Toureg groups claiming the Sahara as their dominion, and from them the mountains derive their name, just as Saudi Arabia takes its name from the reigning Saud family. According to Barbezat, the term Hoggar is an Arab distortion of Ahaggar, as used by the Toureg.

Though the entire Ahaggar is mountainous, the highest region usually is designated by the name Atakor, a Tamacheq Toureg term, or Koudia, an Arab name, both meaning "summit."

MONT AIGUILLE   6,880 ft/2,097m   France
First ascent, 1492, A. de Ville and party.

Mont Aiguille in the Dauphiné Alps of southern France is one of many "needle mountains" found throughout the world. However, Mont Aiguille's looming limestone bulk, rising abruptly 1,000ft/305m above the surrounding countryside, more closely resembles a fortress than a slender sewing implement. A fortress, certainly, would have been in the mind of Captain Antoine de Ville on 26 June 1492 when he and his men, on orders from King Charles VIII of France, attacked the peak. It was a formidable task; as early as 1211 English writers had referred to the mountain as Mons Inascensibilis, "unclimbable mountain," but then this climbing party was accustomed to difficult and dangerous ascents. De Ville and his men were *schelliers* in the army of King Charles, and in wartime it was their role to use ladders and mechanical devices known as "subtle engines" to surmount the walls of beseiged cities. With similar seige tactics they assaulted Mont Aiguille, using ladders and other aids to ascend vertical chasms and conquer their objective. They built a hut and occupied the summit for three days before withdrawing, sending reports to their king. It was the first major rock climb—and the first bivouac hut—for which adequate records are available, and it was an impressive feat, even by later standards; the climb was not repeated until 1834 when some local men, armed with masons' tools to cut hand and foot holds, made the ascent.

ALASKA RANGE
Alaska, USA

Highest elevation, 20,320ft/6,193m, Mount McKinley.

It's typical of the tortuous ironies of naming that the largest U.S. state—and one of North America's greatest mountain ranges—came to bear a name originally applied to an obscure island that geographers eventually concluded didn't exist. In 1762 a Siberian merchant named Bechevin wintered in Isanotski Strait between Unimak Island and the Alaskan Peninsula. He incorrectly perceived the western end of the peninsula to be an island, and he is reported to have called it Alaksu, or Alakshak, from a local Aleut Indian name meaning, ironically, "great country," or "mainland." Later, in 1768, two seamen with the Imperial Russian Navy made the same mistake, again referring to a large island, probably a peninsula, as Alaxa.

With time and usage the name Alaska, in various forms, expanded, especially as its application was not limited to an identifiable feature, such as the non-existent island. Soon the name referred to the entire southwestern part of what is now known as the Alaskan Peninsula. Then, in the manner of such names as Andes and Appalachia (see entries), it expanded still further so that by 1778 Captain James Cook was able to write: "I have already observed that the American continent is here called by the Russians, as well as the islanders, Alaschka, which name, though it properly belongs only to the country adjoining to Oonemak (Unimak) Island, is used by them when speaking of the American continent in general."[100]

The name Alaska was first applied to the mountain range in 1870 in a volume entitled *Alaska and its Resources* by the surveyor and explorer William H. Dall. In it he wrote: "The Coast or St. Elias Range contains the highest peaks and most of the volcanoes. It extends along the whole northwest coast from California to the peninsula of Alaska. . . . [It] merges with the ranges which join it from the north and east, forming the Alaskan Range."[42] The chief United States geologist in Alaska, Alfred H. Brooks, wrote in 1911: "This name [Alaska Range] was first applied by W.H. Dall to that part of the range which lies between the Susitna and Kuskokwim basins."[42] The name, however, true to its expansionist past, has continued to spread and now encompasses a larger area, stretching in a 650mi/1,046km arc from Lake Iliamna in the southwest to the White River in the Yukon in Canada.

The early mountaineering history of the Alaska Range is the history of

Mount McKinley, 20,320ft/6,193m, nearly 3,000ft/914m higher than the second highest peak, Mount Foraker, 17,400ft/5,304m, and nearly 1mi/1.6km higher than the third highest, Mount Hunter, 14,570ft/4,441m. But in the Alaska Range, timberline is at 3,000ft/914m, and when mountaineers' attentions turned from McKinley to the other peaks in the range, they found that many were formidable indeed. Peaks such as Foraker, Hunter, Mooses Tooth, Deborah, Huntington, and the Kichatna Spires are regarded as among the most difficult and challenging in North America. And as the mountaineer James Monroe Thorington has written: "The vast extent, great elevation, uncertain weather, and proximity to the Arctic Circle make of the Alaska mountains a territory of special technical problems to the mountaineer. Here, alone in North America, conditions demand equipment, time, and persistence not required in ordinary Alpine ascents."[69]

ALLEGHENY MOUNTAINS
East-central USA

Highest elevation, 4,860ft/1,481m, Spruce Knob, West Virginia.

Its ridges running like long ribbons through Pennsylvania, Maryland, Virginia, and West Virginia, the Allegheny Mountain chain is part of the great Appalachian system. The name Allegheny has been said to be derived from an Indian word meaning "endless mountains," but while this is an appealing etymology, and certainly a possible one, it lacks corroboration. It is more likely that *Allegheny* is from the Delaware Indian language, according to the American names scholar Kelsie Harder, but "its origin and meaning are unknown." Harder mentions as possible derivations *welhikhanna* or *oolik-hanne*, "fine river" or "beautiful river," and points out that its stem *-aha(n)*, "lapping, or alternate motion," may also refer to the river.[60] Certainly, ample precedent exists for mountains acquiring the names of nearby rivers. Moreover, while Indians tended to name individual mountains within a range, they often had no name for the range itself, particularly when the range was as extensive and as ill-defined as the Allegheny Mountains.

Indeed, so elongated and complex is the mountain system of the eastern United States that as late as the mid-nineteenth century even the region's white settlers hadn't agreed upon a single name for the huge range, and one of the names being considered was Allegheny. Professor Arnold Guyot in 1861 settled the matter in favor of Appalachian (see entry), and the name Allegheny now seems unlikely to spread farther.

ALPAMAYO 19,600ft/5,974m
Peru

First ascent, 1957, G. Hauser, F. Knauss, B. Huhn, and H. Wiedmann.

Though the name of this peak in Peru's Cordillera Blanca sounds Spanish and has *alp* as its first syllable, the name has no connection with either the language of Spain or the mountains of Switzerland. Rather, it comes from Quechua, the language of the Incas, and the name originally was applied not to the mountain at all but to a river. According to the Peruvian mountaineer and Quechua speaker, César Morales Arnao, the name comes from two Quechua words: *allpa*, "earth," and *mayu*, "river," together meaning "muddy river."[2] The term is appropriate for the Rio Alpamayo, which begins at the glacial lake of Jancarurish and frequently is muddy.

THE ALPS

Highest elevation, 15,771ft/4,807m, Mont Blanc.

The English poet Shelly wrote, "I never knew what mountains were until I saw the Alps."[137] The English climber-philosopher Leslie Stephens called them "the playground of Europe." The American mountaineering writer James Ramsay Ullman said that the Alps "were the first place where it ever occurred to men to climb mountains—where not merely a sport was born, but an idea."[140] To the Swiss and Austrian herdsmen who for centuries have lived and worked there, however, the Alps are primarily good places for grazing livestock, for the local meaning of *alp* is simply "high mountain pasture."

But the term *alp* was used in the mountains even before Germanic peoples early in their history moved there from the northern European lowlands. When the Germans arrived they encountered Celtic-speaking peoples, and the Germans, lacking mountain words, tended to adopt local words and names already in use. Little now remains of the Celts in west-central Europe except a few stone ruins—and a few mountain names. The German word for "mountain," *berg*, has a Celtic origin, as does the name of one of the Alps' most important ranges, the Pennines (see entry). And while the matter is far from settled, most authorities agree that the word *alp* also was a legacy of the early Celts, meaning to them what it still means among their Welsh and Gaelic descendents, "height" or "mountain."

The likelihood is great, however, that the term predates even the Celts, and here one enters an alder thicket of deduction and speculation. The close correspondence in sound and meaning between the Celtic *alp*, "mountain," and the Latin *albus*, "white," strains coincidence, particularly when some Italic dialects said *alpus* instead of *albus*. This led the Roman lexicographer Festus to write: "It is possible to believe that the Alps took their name from the whiteness of their snows."[133] With *alp* possibly linked to the meaning "white," some writers have speculated that the term might be related to such names as Albania, the land which when seen from the west often appears as a long, snowy range, and Albion, an early name for Britain possibly derived from the white chalk cliffs that persons crossing the English Channel would see as they approached the island.

If *alp* and *albus* are related, then they might share a common origin in the ancestral Indo-European language from which sprang virtually all modern European languages and many in India and the Middle East as well. Or, as the names scholar George R. Stewart has suggested, *alp* might even have come from a long vanished pre-Indo-European language, spoken, perhaps, in the Alps.[133] If "mountain" was the word's original meaning, this possibility is real indeed, for linguists have deduced from the Indo-European vocabulary and other evidence that before their dispersal the Indo-Europeans dwelt in the region north of the Black Sea in what is now southern Russia—a region not noted for its mountains. Either origin—Indo-European or pre-Indo-European—would make *alp* a strong candidate for the world's oldest mountain name still current.

Alp also remains one of the most vigorous mountain names in existence, continuing to acquire new meanings despite millennia of use. As early as 1551 the term *alp* was used as a specific place-name by the English writer William Turner, who wrote in his *Herbal* of "the alpes that depart Italy and Germany. . . ."[91] The word also has retained—or regained—its original meaning as a synonym for "mountain," and in 1589 Hakluyt's *Voyages* mentioned "certaine alpes or mountaines directly southward. . . ."[91]

Since then, the word has continued its tendency to become a generic as well as a specific term, and it now appears on mountain masses throughout the world: the Lingen Alps of Norway, the Trinity Alps of California, and the Southern Alps of New Zealand. Indeed, in the Green Mountains of Vermont is a group of modest, forest-covered hills known locally as the Alps because their 2,000ft/607m summits are the highest around! The long, complex evolution of the term *alp* appears far from over.

ALTAI MOUNTAINS   *Central Asia*
Highest elevation, 14,783ft/4,506m, Gora Belukha.

The Soviet Union, China, and Mongolia all contain portions of this great range stretching for 1,200mi/1,931km in Central Asia, but it was the Mongols who gave the range its name. Their words for the mountains were *altain ula,* "mountains of gold," and as early as the seventh century A.D. people in the region believed that the mountains were rich with precious metals. That may have been true, but through the centuries extremely difficult access has left the Altai Mountains richer in name than in fact.

The highest peak in the range is Gora Belukha in the Soviet Union. The higher of this mountain's twin summits was first climbed in 1914 by the well-known explorers of the Altai, the brothers B.V. and M.V. Tronov. The smaller western summit (14,567ft/4,440m) was not climbed until 1937, when it was ascended by Y.A. Alekseyev.

AMA DABLAM   *22,494 ft/6,856m*   *Nepal*
First ascent, 1961, M. Gill, B. Bishop, M. Ward, and W. Romanes.

The traditional route to Everest passes by the famous Thyangboche Monastery, and thus Ama Dablam, 6mi/10km to the north and visible from the monastery, has become one of the best known mountains in Nepal. Of it John Cleare has written: "The magnificent chisel of Ama Dablam is the classic peak of Khumbu. Almost isolated, it is another impossible-looking 'Matterhorn peak.'"[27]

To the people living near the mountain, however, the most striking thing about Ama Dablam was the resemblance between the glacier suspended on the peak's steep sides and a religious amulet, and from this resemblance has come, at least in part, the mountain's name. Thus, in a region where most local mountain names have religious significance, Ama Dablam is no exception. The American mountaineer Tom Frost, who in 1979 made the second ascent of Ama Dablam, via the south ridge, has explained the name's meaning: "*Ama* means 'mother.' *Dablam* is the picture of a god worn by lamas around the neck and shoulder down about the right front side of their bodies inside a box. To the old Sherpas and Tibetans in the area, Ama Dablam is a god, and they carry the painting of this god on their persons—and in like manner Ama Dablam displays its hanging glacier for all to see."[51]

ANDES   *Western South America*
Highest elevation, 22,835ft/6,960m, Aconcagua.

The Andes exemplify how a name with a rather localized meaning can acquire global significance when it acquires another meaning. The Andean mountain system is one of the greatest on earth; its peaks exceed in altitude all but those of Central Asia (Aconcagua is the highest non-Asian mountain) and the range is the world's longest, extending 4,000mi/6,436km from Venezuela to Cape Horn. Indeed, it would extend even into Antarctica had not one segment subsided into the sea below the tip of South America, for the heights of the Palmer Peninsula in Antarctica are due to Andean mountain building. Thus the Andes richly deserve their full Spanish title, Cordillera de los Andes; *cordillera* sometimes means "backbone," and the Andes are truly the rocky spine of the South American continent.

The name Andes originated among the Inca Indians of Peru. It was first applied, with several possible meanings, to the mountains east of Cuzco only. Most sources agree that the name comes from the Quechua word *anti*, but interpretations of its meaning have varied. The historian Garcilaso de la Vega, who was half-Inca and who wrote less than a century after the Conquest, stated with some authority that the name referred to an Indian tribe living east of Cuzco. This name might easily have come by association to denote the local mountains and to later have spread with the course of Spanish communications to include the entire range. (The Appalachian Mountains of eastern North America owe their name to a process almost identical to this.) Other scholars, however, have suggested the name means simply "east mountains," or "copper," because that mineral was found in the mountains east of Cuzco.

Whatever its humble origins, the name now has achieved world-wide recognition and surely must be included in any list of the earth's "great names."

ANNAPURNA   26,504ft/8,078m   *Nepal*
First ascent, 1950, M. Herzog and L. Lachenal.

The Annapurna massif, a gleaming white wall dwarfing the green foothills between the range and Pokhara, has a name as beautiful as the mountains themselves. It combines two Sanskrit words: *anna*, "sustenance," and *purna*, "goddess." Thus the name has been translated as "goddess rich in sustenance" and "goddess of harvest," but perhaps a better translation is "bountiful goddess."

(The sound—and some of the meaning—of the name Annapurna is echoed in the name of a less well-known Himalayan peak, Dunapurna. According to the explanation of the Sanskrit by Nima Norbu Sherpa of Namche, *duna* refers to a plate made from the leaves of the *salla* tree.[17] Thus Dunapurna means "leaf plate of the goddess.")

Considerable confusion has existed as to which names identify which peaks in the Annapurna massif, particularly Roc Noir and Gangapurna. According to the chronicler of the Himalaya, Louis C. Baume, the sequence of peaks, running west to east in the Annapurna Himal, is Annapurna I, Roc Noir, Glacier Dome, Gangapurna, and Annapurna III, with a ridge running south from Annapurna III to Machapuchare.[11]

Annapurna has been "rich in sustenance" for mountaineers, yielding many important firsts in Himalayan mountaineering. It was the first 8,000m peak to be climbed—an achievement that owed much to chance, as the strong French party that climbed it in 1950 had set its sights originally on Dhaulagiri and turned to Annapurna only after being disappointed in its reconnaissance of the other mountain. In 1970 the first successful climb of a big Himalayan wall was made when a British attack led by Chris Bonington on the 9,000ft/2,743m south face put Dougal Haston and Don Whillans on the top. Then in 1974 Annapurna became the first 8,000m peak to be climbed by a women's expedition when M. Mori, N. Nakaseko, M. Uchida, and Sherpa Jambu reached the summit.

APENNINE MOUNTAINS   *Italy*
Highest elevation, 9,560ft/2,914m, Corno Grande.

One explanation for the name of these mountains forming the backbone of Italy is that it comes from the time of the Punic Wars, when Rome and Carthage struggled for dominance in the Mediterranean basin. According to this theory, The Romans called the mountains the *poenine*, or *punic*, mountains because Hannibal, the Carthaginian general, crossed them when he invaded Italy. A more likely explanation, however, is that the name has evolved from the ancient Celtic root word *pen*, meaning "summit," and thus is related to other European mountain names such as the Pennine Alps in Switzerland and the Pennine Chain in England. Before the Christian era, Celtic-speaking peoples were widely distributed throughout western Europe, and though the Celts later were displaced by other peoples, many Celtic place-names survive in their former territories (see Pennine Alps).

API 23,399ft/7,132m   Nepal
First ascent, 1960, K. Hirayashi and G. Norbu.

NAMPA 22,162ft/6,755m   Nepal
First ascent, 1972, F. Kimara and S. Takahashi.

The Api-Nampa group is the most westerly of Nepalese mountains. The names of the two peaks come from two Tibetan words: *ap'i*, applied to the higher summit, means "grandmother," while *gnampa-p'a* means "holy or heavenly father." It has been suggested that these names are derived from the mountains having a rather benign appearance viewed from certain perspectives, but it is more likely that the names have their origin in Nepalese mythology or folklore.

APPALACHIAN MOUNTAINS   Eastern USA
Highest elevation, 6,684ft/2,037m, Mount Mitchell.

It's a curious fact that place-names are at the same time the most permanent and the most pliable of human cultural artifacts, and few names illustrate this better than that of the ancient mountain range stretching from Maine to Georgia in the eastern United States. The name first appeared in written history in 1528 when the records of the Spanish explorer Navarez mentioned a poor Indian village named Apalchen. The Indians were of Muskohegan linguistic stock, and etymologies that have been suggested include *hitchiti*, "on the other side," and the Choctaw *apelachi*, "helper." The Spanish explorer De Soto (1500?–1542) also mentioned the "Apalachee" Indians in his chronicles.

Before long the name came to refer not only to the Indian tribe but also to the area where they lived, and it got onto maps as a vague name designating the unexplored, mountainous interior. The name was far from being applied to the entire mountain chain, however. In fact, it was not until the nineteenth century that the huge system had a single name; early settlers, like the Indians, had a limited, localized perspective and thus had difficulty recognizing the mountains as a single geographical unit. Indeed, early settlers came to know parts of the Appalachians under many different names. Slowly, as awareness grew of the unity of the range, most of the more local names were dropped until at last only two names remained as rivals—Appalachian and Allegheny. The matter finally was settled in 1861 by the geographer Arnold Henry Guyot as he prepared to publish an important geological study of the mountains. As the American names scholar George R. Stewart tells it: "He apparently hesitated between the names. His map, prepared in advance, used Allegheny, but his final title was *On the Appalachian Mountain System.* The authority of his study apparently established scientific usage, which filtered down through school geographies and eventually became popular usage also."[134]

Thus the name of an obscure Indian tribe in northern Florida came to be affixed to one of North America's greatest geographical features. Indeed, the name conceivably could have expanded even further. The American author Washington Irving (1783–1859), writing when the new republic stretched only along the Atlantic coast, once proposed adopting the name Appalachia as a name for the entire nation. The United States of Appalachia is as euphonious and at least as meaningful as the present name, derived by historical accident from the first name of an Italian geographer, but generations of schoolchildren and their spelling teachers still should be grateful Irving's proposal came to naught.

MOUNT ARARAT 16,916ft / 5,156m Turkey
First ascent, 1829, F. Parrot.

When Noah stepped from his ark onto the top of Mount Ararat on the seventeenth day of the seventh month, he became one of the first persons credited, in legend at least (see Adams Peak), with having attained the summit of a major mountain. (The first ascent of Ararat in more recent times was made by the German Dr. Frederic Parrot.) That Ararat was regarded as the terminus of Noah's epic voyage is testimony to the mountain's widespread prominence even in Biblical times. Indeed, Ararat is one of the greatest volcanoes on earth,

Mount Ararat, Turkey. From Frederic Zurcher and Elie Margollé, Les ascensions célèbres *(Paris: 1867).*

rising 14,000/4,267m above the plain of the Aras River, forming the Turkish-Russian border 20mi/32km to the northeast, and visible for 100 mi/161km in all directions. Anthropologists have traced the legend of the flood back to Sumer, one of the earth's oldest civilizations. The legend reappears in various forms among many of the Middle Eastern peoples, most of whom were, like the Sumerians, dwellers of plains and river valleys. To them the commanding cone of Ararat would have seemed a natural place for the ark finally to find haven.

Given the mountain's long history, it's not surprising that Ararat has had many names, surely more than have been recorded. Turks call it Agri Dag, "crooked mountain," while its Persian name is Kuh-i-Nuh, "Noah's mountain." The origins of the name Ararat are more obscure. Legend links the name with the story of the Armenian king, Ara the Handsome, who spurned the love of the Babylonian princess Shamiram and was defeated by her troops at Ararat's base. Some scholars have suggested a connection with the ancient people of Urartu (ninth to sixth centuries B.C.). But the most likely explanation is that the name comes from the Old Persian word *ara*, meaning "mountain." (Thus the name Mount Ararat is a redundancy, or better, an example of a generic term, *ara*, taking on a more localized meaning and becoming a specific term.) The root *ara* also is found in the name of the land encompassing Mount Ararat, Armenia, which originally was Har-minni, "mountains of Minni."

Like most Biblical mountain names, such as Pisgah, the name Ararat has been echoed wherever people familiar with the Bible have settled. For example, four California mountains bear the name Ararat, and the name is found frequently elsewhere. A mountain in Washington State was named Ararat by a man who believed he had discovered traces of Noah's ark there.

ARRIGETCH PEAKS *Alaska, USA*
6,000ft/1,828m to 7,200ft/2,195m

The Arrigetch Peaks are a group of dramatic rock spires in the Brooks Range that increasingly have beckoned climbers since first being reported in 1931 by Robert Marshall. The peaks bear an Eskimo name said to mean "fingers extended," a name sure to be interpreted in many ways by mountaineers climbing there.

For mountaineers, the Arrigetch Peaks have presented a rare opportunity, not only to make first ascents of the mountains but also to name them. In most areas mountaineers arrive to find the mountains' names already in place, applied by earlier visitors—native peoples, surveyors, prospectors, settlers, and so forth—many with only an incidental interest in the mountains themselves. Not so in the Arrigetch Peaks. Because these were explored relatively late, and then by persons interested in climbing them, the Arrigetch Peaks bear the kind of names contemporary mountaineers give to mountains, and like recent names of climbing routes, many of these are fanciful indeed: Mount Nevermore, Xanadu, the Albatross, Parabola Peak, Elephants Tooth, the Melting Tower, and Ariel.

BEN ARTHUR   2,892ft/881m   Scotland
First ascent unknown.

In the Arrochar group of hills of the Grampian Mountains is the craggy summit of Ben Arthur, more commonly known as the Cobbler. As a writer named Stoddart explained in 1800: "This terrific rock forms the bare summit of a huge mountain, and its nodding top so far overhangs the base as to assume the appearance of a cobbler sitting at work, from whence the country folk call it—*an greasaiche crom*, 'the crooked cobbler.'"[111] (It also has been suggested that the name is a corruption of the Gaelic *an gobaileach*, "the twin peaks," an explanation made less likely by Ben Arthur having three main summits, not two.) As often happens with such fanciful folk-names as the Cobbler, the temptation to stretch the metaphor further has proved irresistible. The Cobbler has three tops: South Peak is known also as the Cobbler's Daughter or the Cobbler's Last; Central Peak is the Cobbler; and North Peak is the Cobbler's Wife. Edward Pyatt has pointed to the name Cobbler also appearing in the Alps: "It is said that similar rocky summit tors in the Eastern Alps are often called *schuster*, or Cobbler—the Dreischusterspitze in the Sextenthal is a notable example."[111]

MOUNT ASGARD   6,600ft/2,012m   Baffin Island, Canada
First ascent, 1953, H. Weber, J. Marmet-Rothlisberger, and F. Schwarzenbach.

It's not known exactly where the Norse mariners sailing west from Greenland in the tenth century made landfalls on North America, but had they touched the northeastern coast of what is now Baffin Island, they would have found a landscape strongly reminiscent of their native Norway—deep fjords, glacier-filled valleys, and stark, forbidding mountains often cloaked in mist. Appropriate it is, then, that many of the mountains of Baffin Island, particularly those of the Cumberland Peninsula, bear names taken directly from Norse mythology. There, in a long valley connecting the South Pangnirtung and North Pangnirtung fjords are peaks such as Mount Loki, Mount Odin, Mount Thor, and Mount Friga—all derived from the Norse pantheon. Mount Asgard is not the highest summit in the group—that distinction goes to Tête Blanche (7,074ft/2,156m)—but Asgard's curious shape, resembling a flat-topped tree stump, and its difficult vertical walls have led John Cleare to call it the finest in the area.[27] Appropriately, Asgard in Norse mythology is the home of the gods.

It's ironic that in Norway itself, few mountains bear similar names from Norse mythology, most bearing names with humbler, more commonplace meanings. When references to Norse mythology do appear, as in the Jotunheimen Mountains in southwestern Norway, such names, like the Norse names on Baffin Island, are of relatively recent origin.

MOUNT ASPIRING   9,959ft/3,036m   New Zealand
First ascent, 1909, C. Graham, A. Graham, and B. Head.

Mount Aspiring, highest peak in the Haast Range in New Zealand's Southern Alps, could not avoid its nickname, "the Matterhorn of the South"; the resemblance to the peak in the Swiss Alps is too strong. Mount Aspiring rises

46

like a great white fang from the glaciers below, and despite its difficult access—it's located 100mi/161km south of Mount Cook—it is one of New Zealand's most popular mountains, and certainly one of the most dramatic. The name Aspiring doubtless was suggested by the mountain's appearance, its slopes "aspiring" upward with strength and exaltation. The Haast Range, in addition to Mount Aspiring, includes other peaks with intriguing names: Stargazer, Moonraker, Skyscraper, Rolling Pin, and Spike—all named for the topsails of a square-rigged ship.

MOUNT ASSINIBOINE   11,870ft/3,618m   Alberta–
First ascent, 1901, Sir J. Outram with   British Columbia, Canada
C. Bohren and C. Hasler.

Like Jirishanca in Peru and Mount Aspiring in New Zealand, Mount Assiniboine's real or fancied resemblance to the peak rising above Zermatt in Switzerland has caused it to be dubbed "the Matterhorn of the Canadian Rockies." The mountain is indeed a spectacular pyramid, and the British mountaineer Sir James Outram described it as rising "like a monster tooth when seen from the north."[12] Located 30mi/48km south of Banff on the Continental Divide, the peak is the highest summit between Banff and the international boundary to the south.

Despite its prominence, Mount Assiniboine was named relatively recently. In 1885 G.M. Dawson of the Canadian Geological Survey saw the mountain from afar and named it for the Assiniboine Indians, a tribe of Siouan linguistic stock. Their name came from the Ojibway *usini*, "stone," and *upwana*, "he cooks by roasting," meaning "stone-cookers," from the Assiniboine's practice of cooking by dropping hot stones into water. English settlers, aware of the origin of the tribal name of the Assiniboine Indians, often called them the "Stonies," and some persons have suggested their name was responsible for that of the range in which Mount Assiniboine is located—the Rocky Mountains (see entry).

MOUNT ATHABASCA   11,452ft/3,491m   Alberta–
First ascent, 1898, J. Norman Collie and H. Woolley.   British Columbia, Canada
See Introduction.

ATLAS MOUNTAINS   Northwest Africa
Highest elevation, 13,655ft/4,162m, Jebel Toubkal.

In classical mythology, the Titan Atlas was depicted as standing at the end of the earth, near the Hesperides, with his feet in the ocean and his great shoulders supporting the firmament. To ancient Greek sailors familiar only with the Mediterranean, the Strait of Gibraltar, with the unknown ocean beyond, certainly fit descriptions of the realm of Atlas, and it took little imagination for them to associate the mountains on the strait's southern flank with the Titan's shoulders. This is an appealing and plausible explanation for the name, especially as the Atlantic Ocean beyond the strait also owes its name to the myth, but it's also possible that the name comes not from Greek mythology but from a Berber word *adrar*, "mountain," which evolved into its present form through folk etymology.

For centuries, the Atlas Mountains lived up to their reputation as barriers guarding the unknown; beyond them were vast, forbidding expanses of water or sand, mostly unexplored but permeated by rumors of wealth in strange, distant lands. Even the people of the Atlas Mountains were strange. Warlike and aloof, the Berbers had found in the high valleys of the Atlas a refuge where they could preserve their distinct culture despite successive conquests of the lowlands by invaders such as the Carthaginians, the Romans, and the Arabs. Even today the High Atlas is crossed by only two passes, and the climate further discourages travel; the mountains are hot and parched in summer and cold and snowbound in winter. It was not until the latter half of the nineteenth century that extensive exploration was undertaken, and the high peaks of the Atlas, topped by Jebel Toubkal, still invite mountaineers and adventurers.

MOUNT BAKER   10,778ft / 3,285m   *Washington, USA*
First ascent, 1868, E.T. Coleman, T. Stratton, J. Tenant, and D. Ogilvy.

Mount Baker, located only 15mi/24km from the Canadian border, is the northernmost big volcano of the Cascade Range. It certainly would have appeared as a conspicuous landmark to Joseph Baker, who on 30 April 1792 became the first Englishman to view the mountain. Baker was third lieutenant to the British navigator George Vancouver, and Vancouver named the mountain for him. Baker was not the first explorer to notice the mountain, however; two years earlier the Spanish explorer Manuel Quimper saw the peak and named it La Montana del Carmelo, which has been translated fancifully as "great white watcher." This is not far from the Nooksak Indian name for the mountain, Koma Kulshan, meaning "white, steep mountain." These descriptive names are appropriate because Mount Baker, with 31sq mi/80sq km of glaciers, has an ice system second in the Cascades only to that of Mount Rainier.

Despite its mantle of snow, Mount Baker occasionally reminds us of its volcanic origins. The mountain exhibited volcanic activity in 1975 and was still steaming in 1978. The Lummi Indian name for the mountain is reported to mean "shot at point," apparently a reference to an early eruption that shattered the mountain's once conical summit.

MOUNT BAKER   15,889ft/4,843m   *Uganda*
First ascent, 1906, the Duke of the Abruzzi, J. Petigax, C. Ollier, and J. Brocherel.

Like the other major peaks of the Ruwenzori Range, this mountain was named by the Duke of the Abruzzi for an explorer who helped fill in the blank spaces on the early maps of Africa, just as the Duke himself had done with the peaks of the Ruwenzori. Sir Samuel White Baker (1821–1893) shares with John Hanning Speke, for whom Mount Speke was named, the distinction of having discovered the sources of the Nile. Sir Baker named Lake Albert, the 100mi/161km lake between Zaire and Uganda, and he helped put down the slave trade in east and central Africa. His name on the third highest summit in the Ruwenzori Range—after Mounts Stanley and Speke—is fitting recognition of his achievements.

BALKAN MOUNTAINS   *Bulgaria*
Highest elevation, 7,795ft/2,376m, Botev Peak.

The Balkan Peninsula of southeastern Europe has had a long and tangled history of political intrigue and petty warfare among tiny and often short-lived states. This turmoil has been encouraged by the region's complex topography, where the isolation imposed by the mountains has reinforced ethnic and political fragmentation; even the name Balkan, of uncertain origin, is evidence of this. One explanation for the name is that it is connected with the Slavonic word *balka*, meaning "gorge" or "ravine," which was imported, ironically, by Turkish-speaking Bulgarians from the southern Caucasus, who in turn borrowed it from Slavic-speaking peoples. (Modern Bulgarians know the mountains as Stara Planina, "old mountains.") Another explanation for the name is that it is linked with the Old Turkish word *balak*, "high, tall," but also carrying the meaning "mountain." This name would have been applied to the Balkans when the Turks conquered the peninsula between 1350 and 1450. The name for the mountains that is easiest to explain is that used by the ancient Greeks. They called the range Haemus, from their word for "blood," a reference to the ruddy color of the Balkan's rocks.

MONT BLANC   15,771ft/4,807m   *France*
First ascent, 1786, M. Paccard and J. Balmat.

The name Mont Blanc means simply "white mountain," a common descriptive name shared by Dhaulagiri in the Himalaya, the Weisshorn in the Alps, Chimborazo in the Andes, Elbruz in the Caucasus, and many, many other of the world's high mountains. While descriptive mountain names usually are very old and reflect some unique aspect of the mountain's appearance, some descriptive names are so commonplace that they mask identity rather than reveal it. Of the dozens of mountains named Sugarloaf, most bear some resemblance to a

The south side of Mont Blanc, France. From the Alpine Journal, *Vol. 8, 1876-1878.*

symmetrical cone of sugar, but of the mountains named "white," many actually appear no more white than their neighbors.

Mont Blanc, however, is unmistakable. The highest summit in central Europe, capping that continent's greatest mountain massif, Mont Blanc is a huge white snow-dome that once seen could hardly be confused with other white mountains in the region. The mountain dominates the Alpine landscape along the French–Italian border southeast of Geneva and overlooks some of Europe's most important trade routes. A boundary stone on the road to Geneva was inscribed in the time of Vespasian (A.D. 9–79) indicating that Roman legions passing on the road would have seen the great white mountain, but history does not record how they referred to it. The name Mont Blanc first appears in a letter written by Francois de Sales in 1603.

Until the 1750s, Mont Blanc also was commonly known as the Montaigne Maudite (French, "accursed mountain") because of superstitious fear surrounding it. The successful ascent of the mountain in 1786 by Dr. Michel-Gabriel Paccard and Jacques Balmat brought even the highest mountains into the human realm and thus gave birth to mountain exploration as we know it. Indeed, just as Africa was the womb of human evolution, Mont Blanc was the site of mountaineering's early development into a systematized, respectable, and even popular activity. Until a wealthy Swiss natural scientist named Horace Benedict de Saussure in 1760 offered a prize of two guineas to the first person to stand on Mont Blanc's summit, no serious interest had existed in Europe in climbing Mont Blanc or any other high mountain. Saussure's challenge and personal enthusiasm for the ascent stimulated several assaults on the mountain prior to the successful one in 1786, and in 1787 Saussure himself organized a party of twenty to make an ascent that captured the world's imagination.

People have been climbing Mont Blanc in increasing numbers ever since. For decades after Saussure's ascent, the Mont Blanc massif was almost the sole focus of European mountaineering as the mountain was climbed again and again, and new routes and techniques were developed. It was on the mountain's glaciers, such as the huge Mer de Glace (French, "sea of ice"), that early snow and ice techniques evolved, and the famous aiguilles are regarded as the birthplace of modern rock climbing.

CORDILLERA BLANCA   *Peru*
Highest elevation, 22,205ft/6,768m, Huascaran.

Running north of Lima in Peru for approximately 120mi/193km is a range that William Bueler has called "the greatest tropical mountains on earth."[20] Because of the range's nearness to the equator the snow conditions are quite different from those of mountains in the higher latitudes. Above the snowline even the steepest slopes are draped with ice, while the summits often consist of incredible overhanging cornices. This accounts for the range's name, which translates from the Spanish as "white range" and distinguishes it from the lower Cordillera Negra, "black range," to the west. Actually, the term *cordillera* comes from *cordilla* meaning "rope," or "cord," but *cordillera* has been used so often in

Spanish as a metaphor for mountain range that this meaning has all but eclipsed the original meaning. The Cordillera Blanca includes approximately forty peaks exceeding 19,685ft/6,000m, including several well-known to mountaineers: Huascaran, Huandoy, Huantsan, Chacraraju, and Alpamayo.

In his guide to the Cordillera Blanca, John F. Ricker recounts a poignant Indian legend about the range's creation: The highest peak, Huascaran, was once a woman with several children. Her husband, Canchon, was seduced by a woman, Sutoc, who was a better cook. Inflamed by jealousy, Huascaran castrated her husband, then fled, followed by her children. The strongest and biggest stayed close to her, while the smallest was farthest away; on her back Huascaran carried her favorite child. When they halted their flight, they were transformed into the peaks of the Cordillera Blanca. Canchon, too, was turned to stone, becoming the most beautiful mountain of the Cordillera Negra.[116]

BLANCA PEAK   14,317ft/4,364m   Colorado, USA
First ascent unknown.

At first glance it might seem ironic that the highest peak in the range named Sangre de Cristo, Spanish for "blood of Christ," has a name, also Spanish, that means "white." Yet Blanca Peak, standing at the northern end of the Sangre de Cristos, taller than its neighbors, and much more formidable, so dominates the region that it seems to exist independent of the range. Indeed, some Coloradoans were so disappointed when surveys showed Blanca Peak not to be the highest mountain in the nation—or even in Colorado—that they mounted a futile campaign to make up the missing elevation by cairns and poles.

Blanca Peak is among the more difficult of Colorado's "Fourteeners," and some routes on it have been compared to those on the Matterhorn. Nevertheless, when members of the Wheeler Survey in 1874 made the first official ascent of Blanca Peak, they found on its summit a curious Indian-made structure most likely intended either for trapping eagles or as a lookout.

The name Blanca is the Spanish form of the ubiquitous descriptive mountain name "white." As *blanco* or *blanca* the name appears on approximately twenty orographic features in California alone. One of New Mexico's major peaks is Sierra Blanca, 12,003ft/3,659m. And while some people have claimed that Blanca Peak of Colorado was named for a prominent outcropping of white rock near the mountain's summit, the mountain more likely received its name as did all the other big *blanca* mountains in the American Southwest, from persistent snow.

BLUE RIDGE MOUNTAINS   North Carolina–Virginia, USA
Highest elevation, 6,684ft/2,037m, Mount Mitchell.

As the writer Ferdinand C. Lane has put it, the numerous mountains and ranges around the world named Blue "remind us only that all ranges, observed at a distance and particularly through summer haze, appear blue." Mountains bearing this rather nondescript descriptive name are found in almost every U.S. state and every nation having mountains. Among the better known are the Blue Mountains of Oregon, the Blue Mountains of Australia, and the Blue Mountains of Jamaica—that nation's highest range.

If the name Blue is appropriate anywhere, however, it is on the Blue Ridge Mountains of North Carolina and Virginia. Though these mountains are larger than the more rugged mountains of New England—Mount Mitchell is the highest point in eastern North America—they are forest-covered to their tops, and the characteristic most visitors remember about them is their soft, blue appearance—an effect possibly reinforced, as in the nearby Great Smoky Mountains, by the fires and hearths of isolated settlements.

MOUNT BONA   16,550ft/5,044m   Alaska, USA
First ascent, 1930. A. Carpé and T. Moore.
See MOUNT LUCANIA.

BRECON BEACONS   Wales
Highest elevation, 2,907ft/886m, Pen y Fan.
See Introduction.

BROAD PEAK   26,400ft/8,047m   Pakistan–China
First ascent, 1957, M. Schmuck, H. Buhl, F. Winterstaller, and K. Diemberger.

On 12 August 1892 William Martin Conway, leader of the British Karakoram expedition, and A.D. McCormick climbed from the Baltoro Glacier to an 18,750ft/5,715m pass that afforded a view of the surrounding region. There, Conway later wrote, was "a fine breadth of mountain splendor displaying itself—a huge Breithorn, as it were, filling the space between K2 and the hidden Gasherbrum."[11] The mountain was massive, even by Himalayan standards, its three summits joined by a long crest dominating almost the entire left flank of the Godwin–Austin Glacier, and Conway was so impressed by its enormous bulk that he named the mountain Broad Peak.

Broad Peak, remote from human habitation, apparently had no local name, so Conway's name has been accepted. Indeed, P'alchan Ri, the name by which some Balti people in the area reportedly refer to the peak, is merely Broad Peak translated into Balti. (English transliterations only approximate Balti sounds.)

Names derived from a mountain's "bigness" are relatively common, although they usually refer to the length of a mountain's summit ridge rather than to its breadth; Long Mountain is a very common mountain name. Such names are more common among preliterate peoples, for whom descriptive names have practical value. The trouble with such names, of course, is that bigness of mountains is relative; a mountain that might seem enormous to a people with a limited perspective might not be regarded as big at all by other peoples. Moreover, the name loses usefulness when it appears often throughout a region.

For example, the name Ben More (see entry) is found throughout Scotland, and while each mountain with this name usually is the largest in its immediate vicinity, their elevations vary greatly, from 3,843ft/1,171m Ben More in the Cairngorms to 1,874ft/571m Beinn Mhor on the island of Lewis.

The name of the peak in the Karakoram suffers from none of these problems. Not only is it the only Broad Peak in the region, but the peak it identifies would be considered big anywhere. Indeed, Broad Peak is the world's biggest "big mountain."

BROOKS RANGE   Alaska, USA
Highest elevation, 9,060ft/2,761m, Mount Isto.

In 1916 Alfred Hulse Brooks, chief geologist of the United States Geological Survey (USGS) in Alaska, wrote in a report: "A new name, Arctic Mountain system, is proposed for the east and west trending mountain system of northern Alaska formerly regarded as part of the Rocky Mountain system."[100] Brooks's conclusion that these mountains in northern Alaska are separate from the Rocky Mountains has been generally accepted by geologists and geographers, but the name he proposed has not; the mountains bear his name instead.

Actually, Brooks was not the first person to see the range as distinct and give a name to it. In 1826 Sir John Franklin of the Royal Navy gave the range the name Rocky Mountains. Then in 1880 Ivan Petroff, who surveyed Alaska as part of the tenth United States census, gave the name Hooper Mountains, after Captain C.L. Hooper of the United States Revenue Cutter Service, to an unidentified range in northern Alaska—possibly the Brooks Range. And in 1885 Lieutenant P.H. Ray of the United States Army proposed still another name: "From the break of the country, I have no doubt Meade River has its source in that range, so I named them the Meade River Mountains."[100]

The name that has survived, however, is that proposed in 1925 by the USGS to honor Brooks, who had died the year before after having been chief geologist for twenty-one years. Even without his name on one of the state's best known mountain ranges, Brooks's memory would be preserved in Alaska. His name also is found on a mountain and a glacier in Denali National Park, on a mountain in the York Mountains, and on a lake and a falls in Katmai National Monument.

The western section of the Brooks Range is divided by the Noatak River into two sub-ranges, the Baird and the DeLong, both named in 1886 by Lieutenant G.M. Stoney of the United States Navy. The Baird Mountains bear the name of Spencer Fullerton Baird (1823–1887), a pioneer American naturalist noted for his studies of North American birds. The DeLong Mountains were named for Lieutenant Commander Washington DeLong, commander of the steamer *Jeannette*; DeLong died in 1881.

BUGABOOS
British Columbia, Canada

Highest elevation, 11,150ft/3,399m, Howser Spire.

Anyone seeing the Bugaboo Peaks of British Columbia's Purcell Range would instantly assume that their name was inspired by the frightful verticality of the jutting rock spires. Such an assumption would be wrong. As mountaineer and author Fred Beckey explains, the Bugaboos actually took their name from nearby Bugaboo Creek and Bugaboo Pass, named by disgruntled miners. The peaks were unnamed when surveyors Tom Longstaff and Arthur O. Wheeler, accompanied by the young Austrian guide Konrad Cain, penetrated the region in 1910, and only later was the name Bugaboo transferred to them. (Beckey also points out that, strictly speaking , the Bugaboos are *nunataks*, rock outcrops projecting from the surface of a glacier, typically single but in the Bugaboos grouped in an awesome cluster.)

On the Upper Lamar River of Wyoming is a group of peaks whose name, the Hoodoos, is reminiscent of the Bugaboos. The three men who first explored the region found its wildly eroded landforms so strange and spectral that they named it "Hoodoo" or "Goblin" land.

BEN BULBEN *1,730ft/527m*
Ireland

First ascent unknown.

A traveler taking the main road north from Sligo will soon pass beneath the looming, chisel-shaped mass of Ben Bulben, overlooking Donegal Bay like the prow of a huge ship. Like other Irish mountains, Ben Bulben is ancient, its limestone strata having been laid down in seas remote in geologic time. The mountain's name is also ancient; in Gaelic it's Beann Gulban, "Gulba's mountain," and its origins have been lost in the mists of Irish history.

Ben Bulben has been made famous throughout the English-speaking world through the poetry of William Butler Yeats, who returned often to the mountain in his search for meaning in his life and that of Ireland. The concluding poem in his volume entitled *Last Poems* is "Under Ben Bulben."[156] Its final stanza reads:

> *Under bare Ben Bulben's head*
> *In Drumcliff churchyard Yeats is laid.*
> *An ancestor was rector there*
> *Long years ago, a church stands near,*
> *By the road an ancient cross.*
> *No marble, no conventional phrase;*
> *On limestone quarried near the spot*
> *By his command these words are cut:*
> > *Cast a cold eye*
> > *On life, on death.*
> > *Horseman, pass by!*

CADER IDRIS   2,927ft / 1,892m   Wales
First ascent unknown.

Cader Idris is a prominent mountain near the Welsh coast in Merionethshire. Its long summit ridge connects the towns of Barmouth and Dolgellau, and its north face is steep and rugged, giving rise to the local saying, "The walls of Dolgellau are three miles high."[111] It was on Cader Idris that Owen Glynne Jones made one of his first rock climbs in Britain, a landmark in the history of British climbing.

The mountain's name, like that of many Welsh mountains, is derived from Welsh mythology. It means "seat of Idris" (from Old Welsh *cadeir*). Idris was of the race of giants, and Cader Idris was his chair.

CAIRN GORM   4,084ft / 1,245m   Scotland
First ascent unknown.
See CAIRNGORM MOUNTAINS.

CAIRNGORM MOUNTAINS   Scotland
Highest elevation, 4,296ft / 1,309m, Ben Macdhui.

The Cairngorms of north-central Scotland are the highest mountain group in the British Isles, covering approximately 300 sq mi / 777sq km and including four of Britain's five highest summits: Ben Macdhui, 4,296ft / 1,309m; Braeriach, 4,248ft / 1,295m; Cairn Toul, 4,241ft / 1,293m; and Cairn Gorm, 4,084ft / 1,245m. It is from this last mountain that the entire group gets its name; Cairn Gorm is Gaelic and means "blue cairn," *cairn* referring to a heap of rocks, but the origins of this name have been lost. Also likely to be lost is the ancient name for the mountains, Monadh Ruadh (pronounced *monarua*), Gaelic for "red mountains." They were called this to distinguish them from the Monadh Liath (pronounced *monalea*), "gray mountains," located on the other side of Strathspey. As the name Cairngorm becomes generally accepted for this mountainous region, little chance exists that the name Monadh Ruadh will survive in popular usage.

The Cairngorms have been described as stony rather than craggy. Though their slopes occasionally have fine granite cliffs, their remoteness has limited climbing until relatively recently. One of the best known mountains in the Cairngorms is the granite mass of Lochnagar, which takes its name from a small loch at its base. The poet Byron, who spent his boyhood in Aberdeen, later wrote of the "steep frowning glories of dark Lochnager," and some of Britain's most severe climbing conditions are found there. For hikers in the Cairngorms, however, distance rather than difficult terrain is the main obstacle.

CAMELS HUMP   4,083ft/1,244m   Vermont, USA
First ascent unknown.

The second highest elevation in the Green Mountains is Camels Hump, a peak that unlike most in the range rises above timberline and presents a rugged, striking profile. The French explorer Samuel de Champlain could not help but notice it when in 1609 his canoes explored the lake later named for him; he called the mountain Le Lion Couchant, a term from heraldry meaning "the lion lying down, its head erect." It's not known when or why the English settlers of Vermont preferred to see the mountain as a camel's hump rather than a reclining lion, but something of the spirit of the earlier name survived in the name that at least some residents of Calais and other Vermont villages had for the mountain. They called it Catamountain, *catamount* being a Northern New England term for "mountain lion." It has been suggested that the Abenaki Indians knew the mountain as a "resting place" or "a place to sit down." Their name for it was Ta-wak-be-dee-eeso-wadso, which meant "prudently, we make a campfire in a circle near water and rest at this mountain."

MOUNT CAMEROON   13,350ft/4,069m   Cameroon
First ascent, 1861, G. Mann and R.F. Burton.

Mount Cameroon, an enormous active volcano encompassing 700 sq mi/ 1,813 sq km, is by far the largest and tallest mountain in West Africa. The local people call the Great Cameroon, highest of the mountain's two summits, Mongo-ma-loba, "mountain of thunder," while the entire upper part of the massif usually is called Mongo-mo-ndemi, "mountain of greatness." But the name by which Mount Cameroon is most widely known originally did not belong to the mountain at all but to a river, which in turn was named for some lowly prawns.

In 1571 the Portuguese explorer Fernando Poo discovered in the right-angle bend of the West African coast a great bay with a river running into it. The bay, Poo noticed, was plentiful with prawns, so he named the river Rio dos Cameraos, Portuguese for "river of prawns." Poo's name failed to stick to the river, now known by the native name Wouri, but the Portuguese word for "prawn" came to be applied to the entire coast near the bay and eventually to the region's highest mountain.

CANTABRIAN MOUNTAINS   Spain
Highest elevation, 8,678ft/2,645m, Torre de Cerredo.

There is a mountainous region in northeastern Spain that in ancient times was inhabited by a people known to the Romans as the Cantabrii. They were conquered by Augustus in the Cantabrian War of 29–19 B.C. and soon were assimilated into the Roman Empire. Their ancient name, however, persists in the name of the mountains of their homeland.

57

The Cantabrians are an east-west range some geographers have suggested is a western extension of the Pyrenees. The Cantabrians form an effective boundary between the coast of the Bay of Biscay to the north and the sun-baked interior plateau to the south. The range's western terminus is the uplands of Galicia, another region named for an early tribe conquered by the Romans. Though the Cantabrians are relatively low, they do offer some limited but excellent climbing in the Picos de Europa, "peaks of Europe," pointed limestone formations some persons have found reminiscent of such well-known Austrian groups as the Karwendel.

Mountain ranges such as the Balkans, the Caucasus, and the Cantabrians historically have been important in preserving cultural diversity, isolating and then sheltering numerous tiny and varied populations. In the Cantabrians the cultures of the Basques and the Astrurians persist.

MOUNT CARMEL   1,791ft/546m   Israel
First ascent unknown.

Mount Carmel is a wooded mountain range running approximately 13mi/21km southeast from the Israeli port city of Haifa to the Plain of Jezreel. Like Mounts Hermon and Sinai, Mount Carmel is one of the sacred mountains of the Holy Land, and according to tradition events occurred there that have made it revered by persons of many faiths. On Carmel the prophet Elijah met King Ahab and was challenged to confront the "multitudinous priests of Baal and Astaroth," who had temples on the mountain. The scene of this great trial has been located by tradition at the summit el-Mahrakah, Arabic for "the place of the burnt sacrifices," and nearby is the spring from which Elijah is believed to have drawn water for his sacrificial libation. El-Mahrakah is especially venerated by the Druses, a dissident Islamic sect. Because of Carmel's association with Elijah and also with his disciple Elisha, Christians in the fourth century began making pilgrimages to the mountain. Monasteries were built, and in 1156 a religious order was established that took its name from the mountain—the Order of the Carmelites. The mountain's significance is not all ancient history, either—on Carmel are the tombs of Bab ed Din and Abdul Baha, who in the nineteenth century founded the Baha'i faith.

To the ancient Hebrews who gave the mountain its name, the religious significance of Carmel transcended the events that occurred there, a significance reflected in the name itself. *Karmel* is a Hebrew word meaning "fruitful garden," and in the figurative language of the Old Testament, Mount Carmel appears as the symbol of beauty, fruitfulness, majesty, and a prosperous and happy life. This identification is deserved. The mountain's steep slopes on the northeast are mostly forested, but the more gentle south and west slopes fall away to the sea in a series of long, fertile valleys. As one observer wrote, "the sheen of fruitful olives fills many a hollow, and in the time of flowers Carmel is beautiful in a garment of many colors."[99] Thus the ancient Hebrews saw in the mountain the favor of God made manifest—and when the bounty of Carmel faltered, the vengeance of God was upon the land.

CARPATHIAN MOUNTAINS

Highest elevation, 8,737ft/2,663m, Garlachovka.

Czechoslovakia–Ukraine–Romania

The Romans knew these important eastern European mountains as the Carpates, and their name for the range has survived, in various forms, to the present. The origin of the name is unknown, but doubtless Carpates was only one of many names given to the mountains by the peoples whose ethnic and political diversity the mountains helped foster. Like the Alps to the west and the Balkans to the south, the Carpathians have been a major influence on the complex cultural development of their region.

Along much of its 900mi/1,448km length the Carpathian Range consists of wooded hills most noted for their wildlife, but in the Vysoke Tatra (the High Tatras) rise peaks reminiscent of those in the Alps. Many walls exceed 1,000ft/305m, and the north face of Maly Kezmarsky, 8,281ft/2,524m, is nearly 3,000ft/914m high. Although the range contains no glaciers, winter climbing has become increasingly popular as more challenging routes are sought. The name of the highest peak in the Carpathians, Garlachovka, sometimes is Anglicized as Gerlach.

CARRAUNTUAL   *3,414ft/1,041m*   *Ireland*

First ascent unknown.
See MacGILLYCUDDYS REEKS.

CARSTENCZ PYRAMID   *16,400ft/4,999m*   *Irian Jaya*

First ascent, 1962, H. Harrer, P. Temple, R. Kippax, and A. Huizinga.

Carstencz Pyramid, one of the major peaks of the Snow Range (see entry) in western New Guinea, was named for the Dutch explorer Jan Carstencz, who made the first sighting of the peak in 1623 from on board his ship. Carstencz Pyramid has been described as the most technically demanding of the major peaks in the Snow Range, and it resisted all attempts on its summit until the 1962 expedition led by Philip Temple of the New Zealand Alpine Club.

CASCADE RANGE   *Northwestern North America*

Highest elevation, 14,410ft/4,392m, Mount Rainier.

Because of their great size and complexity, some major mountain ranges have not been known by a single name until relatively recently, and very often the name finally adopted is one that originally was given to a single, localized feature within the range. The Appalachians of the eastern United States and the Andes of South America are examples. So is the Cascade Range of the Pacific Northwest.

Most of the Indians of the region lacked a name for the range; they would have had difficulty seeing the range as a distinct geographic unit, and a single name, had one existed, would have had little practical value for them. The Klamath Indians are reported to have called the mountains Yamakiasham Yaina, "mountains of the northern people," but the origins of this name and the boundaries of the mountains it labeled are both vague. The first recorded attempt at a name came from the Spanish explorer Manuel Quimper, who saw the mountains in 1790 and labeled them as Sierras Nevadas de San Antonio, "snowy mountains of San Antonio." Two years later the British explorer George Vancouver saw the mountains and gave names to many of their more prominent peaks, but he referred to the range itself merely as the "snow range" and "ridge of snowy mountains," names similar to that given by Quimper. Thirteen years later, the explorers Lewis and Clark saw the range and mentioned specific peaks, but the closest they came to a name for the entire group was "western mountains." "The range of western mountains are covered with snow," wrote Lewis, and Clark wrote simply "western mountains covered with snow."[43]

The name Cascades first appeared in the writings of David Douglas, the botanist, for whom the Douglas fir is named. He referred several times to the "Cascade Mountains" or the "Cascade Range of Mountains." Yet Douglas didn't claim to have originated the name, and it almost certainly was in common usage at the time of his journal, kept from 1823 to 1827.

By 1843 the name Cascade was firmly established. The frontier explorer John C. Fremont wrote in his journal in November that year: "We were now approaching one of the marked features of the lower Columbia, where the river forms a great cascade, with a series of rapids, in breaking through the range of mountains to which the lofty peaks of Mount Hood and St. Helens belong, and which rise as great pillars of snow on either side of the passage. The main branch of the Sacramento river, and the Tlamath, issue in cascades from this range; and the Columbia, breaking through it in a succession of cascades, gives the idea of cascades to the whole range; and hence the name of the Cascade Range, which it bears, and distinguishes it from the Coast Range lower down."[43]

The American names scholar George R. Stewart has offered insight into the likely evolution of the name Cascade: "Like all travelers, the emigrants (of the 1840s) gave names only along a line. A stream usually took the name which the place of crossing brought to mind. If there was a rock there, that would be Rock Creek, even though there might be no other rock on the whole stream. Travelers even earlier than the covered wagon emigrants established a great name in that manner. Most of them followed the course of the Columbia River and came to what were called the Cascades, where the river flowed through a range of high mountains. They called these 'the mountains of the Cascades' and later the Cascade Mountains, and the name spread north and south along the great range (just as Apalchen did in the East) just as the names given to hundreds of little streams at their crossings spread to cover the whole."[134]

In 1839 an Oregon booster named Hall J. Kelley, also known as "the Boston schoolmaster," asked Congress to change the name of the Cascade Range to the Presidential Range and to rename individual peaks to honor United States presidents (see Mount Adams–Cascade Range and Presidential Range–New

Hampshire). Although the well-intentioned proposal eventually came to naught, it was adopted at least temporarily by some people and sowed considerable confusion as to which mountain honored which president.

CATHEDRAL PEAK   *10,940ft/3,335m*   *California, USA*
First ascent, 1869, J. Muir.

Cathedral Peak in Yosemite National Park, like dozens of other Cathedral Peaks worldwide, takes its name from its summit spire, reminiscent of the tower on a cathedral. In 1862 the Yosemite peak was named by Henry G. Hanks, James Hutchings, and Captain Corcoran, representatives of the San Carlos Mining and Exploration Company, while on a journey to mines near Independence. They designated the peak as the Cathedral Spires, but the Whitney Survey changed the name to Cathedral Peak. Rock formations opposite El Capitan in Yosemite Valley now bear the names Cathedral Spires and Cathedral Rocks. Cathedral also is the name of a range and a pass in Yosemite, both named for Cathedral Peak.

CATSKILL MOUNTAINS   *New York, USA*
Highest elevation, 4,204ft/1,281m, Slide Mountain.

Early Dutch settlers in southeastern New York State named this low mountain group, part of the Allegheny Plateau. Though folk etymology continues to suggest that the name referred to the killing of wildcats in the dense deciduous forests of these hills, the name actually is derived from that of a stream and only later was applied to the mountains. The Dutch word was Katskill; Kat probably was a personal name, while -*kill* was a suffix meaning "stream" or "river." (Dozens of streams in the northeastern United States bear this ending; Schuykill in Pennsylvania, Battenkill in Vermont, and Beaverkill in New York State are only a few examples.) Thus the name Catskill means nothing more than "Kat's stream."

CAUCASUS MOUNTAINS   USSR
Highest elevation, 18,481ft/5,633m, Mount Elbruz.

The Caucasus Range, stretching approximately 550mi/885km between the Black Sea and the Caspian, is accepted as one of the boundaries between Europe and Asia. The range's highest mountain, Elbruz, is 12mi/19km north of the Eurasian divide and thus is Europe's highest mountain, but just as the name Elbruz doesn't *seem* European, neither does the name Caucasus, though European it quite possibly is.

The name Caucasus is old. Indeed, the American names scholar George R. Stewart suggests it could include the very old name element *cuc*, "mountain," that appears often coupled with more recent name elements as in the French mountain name Cocumont. This is purely speculative, however. The Caucasus Mountains were mentioned by the Greek classical writers Aeschylus and Herodotus, and the Roman writer Pliny said the name came from a Scythian word meaning "snow-white," a very plausible etymology. A connection also is possible with the Gothic word *haus*, "height," and the Avestan *kahrkasa* and the Lithuanian *kaukas*, both meaning "bump." Still more likely is that Caucasus is a Persian word meaning "ice-glittering"; this has been the most common translation of the name.

While the Caucasus Mountains geographically are rather simple, having only one main crest, they harbor a linguistic topography that's among the world's most complex, with dozens of separate languages, each often having only a few thousand speakers, kept isolated by the Caucasus's ridges and valleys. This, and the variety of languages and cultures surrounding the mountains, make any explanation of the name tentative.

MONT CENIS   *11,792ft/3,594m*   *France–Italy*
First ascent unknown.

According to one account, the name of this mountain in the northern Cottian Alps on the Franco–Italian border originated during Hannibal's invasion of the Italian peninsula in 218 B.C. When the Carthaginian general and his army marched over the Col du Mont Cenis to attack the Romans, so the story goes, they burned the forest on the mountain. Because of this, the peak came to be known in Latin as Mons Cinereus, "mountain of ashes." Raising doubts about this explanation, however, is the fact that the Col du Mont Cenis is not widely accepted as being the pass Hannibal crossed; the issue will likely never be settled, but the preponderance of evidence seems to favor the Col du Traversette as the probable route. Mont Cenis is one of only a handful of Alpine peaks mentioned in Roman records, and like another peak mentioned, Monte Viso (see entry), Mont Cenis was noteworthy to the Romans because of its strategic location.

CHACRARAJU WEST   *20,055ft/6,113m*   *Peru*
First ascent, 1956, L. Terray and his six-man party.

Mountaineers and travelers seeing this peak in Peru's Cordillera Blanca have mentioned the flutings in the ice walls flanking the sharp summit ridge. The Quechua-speaking Indians of the region noticed this fluting too, and the most likely explanation for the Quechua name this peak bears stems from the resemblance of the ice furrows to the furrows of plowed earth. *Chacra* in Quechua means "cultivated field" and *raju* means "snow or ice peak." Thus the mountain's name can be translated as "snowpeak that seems cultivated." An alternative though less plausible explanation for the name is that its first part comes from the Quechua *chaki*, "foot"; the name could then be translated as "ice at the foot of the mountain." From the east the Chacraraju peaks are known in Quechua as Mataraju, "twin mountains."

CHANGABANG   22,520ft/6,864m   *India*

First ascent, 1974, C. Bonington, B. Sandhu, M. Boysen, D. Haston, D. Scott, and Tashi Chewang Sherpa.

Changabang is one of the peaks on the rim of the "Sanctuary," the ring of peaks surrounding Nanda Devi in the Garhwal, and apparently the relationship is reflected in the mountain's name. According to H. Adams Carter, who interviewed local people about the place-names of the Nanda Devi region, Changabang can be translated from the Garhwali to mean "shining mountain," and his informant, Dharam Singh of Lata, explains further, "It gives Nanda Devi light." (Actually, Carter points out, Changabang would be more accurately transliterated Changvanga.) "Shining" is hardly a novel adjective for a mountain, but it's particularly appropriate for Changabang, which William Murray has described as "a vast eyetooth fang...its rock milk-white granite."[27]

CHANGTSE   24,764ft/7,548m   *Tibet*

See LHOTSE.

CHIMBORAZO   20,561ft/6,267m   *Ecuador*

First ascent, 1880, E. Whymper, J. and A. Carrel.

Chimborazo is the highest peak in Ecuador, and since Spanish colonial times the huge volcano south of Quito has been a landmark in the Andes. Simon Bolivar called it "the watchtower of the universe."[76] A Franco–Spanish expedition to Ecuador in 1836–1844 proclaimed it the highest mountain in the world, a claim that was to stand for three-quarters of a century. Alexander von Humboldt in 1802 attempted to climb Chimborazo—and very nearly succeeded. When the first ascent finally came, it was by the famous mountaineer Edward Whymper and his two Swiss guides.

Despite all the attention paid to the mountain, it has retained the name, only slightly altered, by which the pre-Columbian Quechua Indians of the region knew it, Chimpu-raza, "mountain, or crater, of snow." Though some persons have suggested an association between the name and a Chimpo River in the area, the most widely accepted interpretation of the name makes it one of many "snow mountains" in the world. Like most such mountains, it earned its name by being much taller than its neighbors. Although Chimborazo rises only 10,000ft/3,048m above the intercordilleran valley to the east, the mountain's elevation at more than 20,000ft/6,000m—seen dramatically from the west—puts it more than 5,000ft/1,524m above the permanent snowline for the region, helping to make its great white bulk its most noteworthy characteristic. The icecap on Chimborazo has so deeply buried the volcano's crater that nothing now is visible except the bumps comprising the true and false summits on the mountain's broad summit plateau.

MOUNT CHOCORUA   3,475ft / 1,059m   New Hampshire, USA
First ascent unknown.

A long history of exploration and settlement have made the White Mountains of northern New Hampshire and western Maine especially rich in folklore, but few White Mountain peaks have been as celebrated in legend as Mount Chocorua, west of Conway. All the legends agree that the peak was named for the Sokosis Indian chief Chocorua, who lived in the early 1700s, and all agree that he met a tragic end on the mountain. The most prosaic of the stories says Chocorua died while hunting, apparently by falling from a high rock. But other tales speak of massacre and vengeance.

According to many of the tales, Chocorua's young son died after eating some poisoned food left for foxes by white settlers, who had previously enjoyed good neighborly relations with Chocorua. The chief blamed the settlers for his son's death and in revenge slew the wife and children of a settler named Cornelius Campbell. Campbell and other settlers, seeking vengeance in their turn, pursued Chocorua to the mountain's summit, where he was shot. As he lay dying on the rocks, so the story goes, he said to his slayers, "Chocorua goes to the Great Spirit—his curse stays with the white man." Soon after, cattle began dying in the region. This, however, was supposedly traced not to the chief's malediction but to unusually high concentrations of muriate of lime in the water; a dose of soapsuds solved the problem.

CHOGOLISA   25,110ft / 7,654m   Pakistan
First ascent, of Chogolisa Northeast, 1958, N. Fujihara and K. Hirai; first ascent of Chogolisa Southwest, 1975, Austrian expedition.

Chogolisa is one of the great Karakoram peaks rimming the Baltoro Glacier. It received international attention in 1909 when the Duke of the Abruzzi's well-equipped party reached 24,700ft / 7,529m on the mountain, an altitude record that stood for many years. It received attention again in 1957 when the famous Austrian mountaineer Hermann Buhl lost his life there after a career of several important Himalayan and Karakoram victories, including the bold Alpine-style ascent the same year of Broad Peak. According to H. Adams Carter, mountaineer and linguist, the name Chogolisa is derived from several Balti words together meaning "great hunting ground": *chogo*, "great"; *ling*, "hunting"; and *sa*, "ground."[22]

CHOMO LHARI   23,997ft / 7,314m   Bhutan–Tibet
First ascent, 1937, Lt. Col. F.S. Chapman and Sherpa Pasang Dawa Lama.

A conspicuous landmark along the ancient caravan route between India and Tibet and one of the mountains sacred to the Tibetans, this mountain for centuries has been known to the outside world by its Tibetan name, Chomo Lhari.

The mountaineer in repose. From the Alpine Journal, *Vol. 2, 1864-1866.*

This has been translated variously as "goddess of the holy mountain" and "lily white mother of snow," but Charles Bell, an authority and writer on Tibet, has given its meaning as "mountain of the goddess."[69]

Because of its proximity to the trade route, Chomo Lhari was among the first Himalayan giants to be known to Europeans. Two Jesuits, Stephen Cacella and John Cabral, traveling to Lhasa in 1627, returned to tell of having seen a great white mountain on the border between Tibet and the kingdom of Bhutan, and the mountain was included in Charles D'Anville's 1735 *Atlas of China*. But while physical access to Chomo Lhari is less difficult than for many Himalayan peaks, diplomatic access has been formidable indeed. Tibetans always have been reluctant to permit climbers to approach their sacred peaks, and the Chinese occupation of Tibet has only added further complications. Bhutan allows access only rarely. Once was in 1937 when F. Spencer Chapman and the Sherpa Pasang Dawa Lama made the first ascent. In their descent from the summit, bad weather forced them to spend four nights on the mountain before reaching safety.

CHO OYU   26,750ft/8,153m   Nepal–Tibet
First ascent, 1954, H. Tichy, S. Jochler, and Sherpa Pasang Dawa Lama.

The name of the world's seventh highest mountain, located in the Khumbu West region of the Nepal–Tibet frontier, can be translated from the Tibetan to mean "goddess of the turquoise." It's a beautiful and poetic name, but like so many others in the Himalaya, the specific circumstances that inspired it are unknown. Color names are not unusual among the world's mountains. One of four mountains sacred to the Navajo Indians of the American Southwest is *dzil dotlizi*, "turquoise mountain," and examples of color names from the Himalaya include Dhaulagiri, "white mountain," Saser Kangri, "yellow mountain," and Makalu, "the great black one." But "goddess of the turquoise" is a rather atypical color name, and like the Navajo name the color likely has religious significance.

Cho Oyu has been described as the easiest of the 8,000m peaks to climb, and the paucity of successful ascents since the first ascent in 1954 is due not so much to technical problems as to political circumstances barring access, as the easier northern and western approaches require entering Tibet.

CHUGACH MOUNTAINS   *Alaska, USA*
Highest elevation, 13,176ft/4,016m, Mount Marcus Baker.

The Chugach Mountains, one of the coast ranges of Alaska, are a 250m/402km western extension of the St. Elias Mountains. The name Chugach appears not only on the range but also on an island group, a national forest, a sound, and a marine passage. It originated with an Eskimo tribal name, first recorded by the Russians and written as both Chugatz and Tscougatskoi. In 1898 Captain W.R. Abercrombie of the United States Army spelled the name Chugatch and applied it to the mountain range.

CLINGMANS DOME   6,642ft/2,024m   *North Carolina, USA*
First ascent unknown.

Thomas Lanier Clingman came to the Great Smoky Mountains of North Carolina in the 1850s and quickly established a reputation locally as an adventurous explorer, an indefatigable promoter of the mountains, and a highly controversial character (see Mount Mitchell). His personality was summarized by Dr. F.A. Sondley in the *History of Buncombe County*: "He was an intrepid man of most arrogant and aggressive character, greatest self-confidence, unlimited assurance, prodigious conceit, stupendous aspiration, immense claims, more than common ability, no considerable attainments of culture, great boastfulness, and much curiosity. His scientific knowledge was not large, yet he rendered public service by arousing interest in western North Carolina, in local mineralogy and geography."[50]

In 1858, Clingman's zeal for exploration made him a member of a party of six whose objective was a peak known locally as Smoky Dome. Also in the party was Samuel B. Buckley, a well-known naturalist of the day who also had traveled extensively in the Smokies. Buckley made barometric measurements, somewhat inaccurate, of the peak's elevation, and later he proposed that this, the highest summit in the mountains, be named for himself. Buckley's intent was not altogether vain or unbefitting; he truly loved the region and made major contributions to its study. But the last word on the peak's name was to belong to the man who even more than Buckley or Clingman dominated scientific exploration of the region, Professor Arnold Henry Guyot (see Mount Guyot). Guyot insisted the dome be named for Clingman. Not only had Clingman warmly welcomed Guyot when he arrived in the area, but as Guyot wrote in a letter to the *Asheville News*, "I must remark that in the whole valley of the

Tuckasegee and Oconaluftee I heard of but one name applied to the highest point, and it is that of Mount Clingman."[50]

Though many of the names Guyot proposed in the Smokies did not endure, this one did. As for Clingman himself, he died homeless and impoverished in 1897, his energy dissipated, his schemes and visions bankrupted.

CLOUD PEAK   13,365ft/4,074m   Wyoming, USA
First ascent, 1897, N.H. Darnton and other surveyors.

Mountains and clouds exist in such close proximity that it is not surprising to find many mountains named for clouds. Banner Peak in California was named for the cloud banners streaming from its summit. In the Never Summer Range of the Colorado Rockies there are four peaks named for cloud types—Cirrus, Cumulus, Nimbus, and Stratus. Cloud Peak in Wyoming, highest in the Big Horn Range, was named simply because its summit, like all high summits, is a focus of cloud formation. This characteristic of the mountain was noticed by early traders and explorers; the name was appearing on maps by 1859.

COLLEGIATE PEAKS   Colorado, USA
Highest elevation, 14,420ft/4,395m, Mount Harvard.

When Professor Josiah Dwight Whitney in 1869 named what he thought was Colorado's highest peak for the school where he taught, Harvard University, he set a precedent that eventually determined the names of an entire mountain group—the Collegiate Peaks. Whitney was the distinguished geologist and surveyor for whom Mount Whitney in California was named (see entry). In 1869 he brought Harvard's first mining school graduates to Colorado, and with them he explored and surveyed much of the state, including the Sawatch Range in central Colorado where many of Colorado's "Fourteeners," peaks exceeding 14,000ft/4,267m, are found. Among these are the five Fourteeners making up the Collegiate Peaks.

Whitney was wrong in believing the peak he named Mount Harvard to be the state's highest—it's the third highest—but had the quixotic efforts of some other Harvard loyalists succeeded, Whitney eventually would have been proven correct. Many years after Whitney's naming, some Harvard students attempted to erect a 20ft/6m aluminum pole on the mountain's summit to make up the elevation needed to attain preeminence. They had neglected their homework, however, and planted the pole on the wrong summit. Later, some Cornell University partisans erected another pole, this time on the correct summit, as part of their equally quixotic efforts to have the peak renamed Mount Cornell.

Mount Harvard was not Whitney's only collegiate peak. In 1869, the same year he named Mount Harvard, Whitney gave Mount Yale (14,196ft/4,327m) its name. Though Whitney was then a professor at Harvard and founder of the mining school there, he nonetheless felt loyalty to his own alma mater, Yale University.

67

These two namings—Mounts Harvard and Yale—established a pattern in the region, so when the Princeton University Scientific Expedition of 1877 climbed an apparently unnamed big peak in the range, they named it for *their* university, dubbing it Mount Princeton (14,197ft/4,327m). (The surveyor George M. Wheeler earlier had named it Chalk Mountain, for the impressive chalk cliffs on the mountain's southern slopes, but the name had not stuck.)

In 1916 Roger Toll of the Colorado Mountain Club followed suit by giving still another peak a collegiate name, Mount Columbia (14,073ft/4,289m). The Colorado Mountain Club officially accepted this name in 1922.

Finally, shortly after 1925, the last of the Collegiate Fourteeners was named, this time for an English college but a college nonetheless. The Colorado Mountain Club, recognizing an inconspicuous summit as a true Fourteener, named it Mount Oxford (14,153ft/4,314m) for Oxford University.

MOUNT COLUMBIA   14,073ft/4,289m   Colorado, USA

First ascent unknown.
See COLLEGIATE PEAKS.

PEAK OF COMMUNISM   24,590ft/7,495m   USSR

First ascent, 1933, V.M. Abalokov.

In the Soviet Union it is not uncommon for the names of even major geographical features to be changed to reflect current political trends and ideals. Thus the city known as Tsaritsyn in the time of the tsars became Stalingrad during Stalin's regime only to become Volgograd after his death and fall from popular esteem. And by the same process the highest peak in the Soviet Union, located near the Afghanistan border, received its present name.

Prior to the 1930s, the complicated geography of the Western Pamirs was little known even in the USSR, which shares the range with China and Afghanistan. The Soviet scientific expeditions that penetrated the region in 1932 found most of the high peaks devoid of names. Indeed, before these expeditions a mountain in the Trans–Alai Range, Lenin Peak (formerly Mount Kaufmann, 23,382ft/7,127m) was believed to be the highest in the Soviet Union. This absence of names provided an excellent opportunity for Soviet namers to honor persons and ideals of the Russian Revolution, which had occurred less than twenty years before, as well as persons and institutions of the new regime, and so the peaks of the Pamirs received names that many of them still bear—Patriot Peak, Communist Academy Peak, Lenin Peak, Izvestia Peak, Pravda Peak, Karl Marx Peak, Engels Peak, and so forth. One that does not bear its original name, however, is Peak of Communism. It was named Stalin Peak during the Stalin era. (Fortunately for geographers, Stalin preferred not to be known in the USSR by his original Georgian name—Iosif Vissarionovich Dzhugashvili.) After Stalin's death, the USSR experienced a strong reaction against the police-state terrorism Stalin had instituted, and statues and memorials honoring him were expunged. The city of Stalingrad became Volgograd, and Stalin Peak became Peak of Communism.

To many ears, political use of place-names reduces naming to sloganeering, relegating major features such as mountains to being mere insignia bearers for political entities that sometimes are debased or trivial and that very often are short-lived. Certainly some names in the Soviet Pamirs encourage this view: German Communist Party Peak, Free Korea Peak, Peak of the Proletariat Press, and OGPU Peak—named for the Soviet secret police! And as Peak of Communism illustrates, such names frequently are as shifting as the currents of politics themselves. One peak in the Soviet Pamirs originally was named Moscow-Peking Peak; when relations between the USSR and China soured, the mountain became Marshall Zhukov Peak, 22,480ft/6,852m.

MOUNT COOK *12,349ft/3,764m*   *New Zealand*
First ascent, 1894, T. Fyfe, G. Graham, and J. Clarke.

Mount Cook, Mount Everest, Mount McKinley, and Mount Rainier all have one thing in common regarding their names: each continues to bear a locally popular native name despite the presence of a more widely accepted English name. The name Everest coexists with Sagarmatha, McKinley with Denali, Rainier with Tacoma, and on New Zealand's South Island the name Cook shares New Zealand's highest mountain with the Maori name Aorangi. Mount Cook's English name is easy enough to explain. English settlers in New Zealand gave the name in the nineteenth century to honor Captain James Cook (1728–1779), the English explorer and navigator whose voyages along the coast of the islands a century earlier brought them to the attention of the western world. It was Cook who first noted the great range that includes the peak now named for him, and it was he who gave the mountains their name, the Southern Alps.

But the English were not the first seafaring people to reach the remote South Pacific islands and give names to the features they found there. In one of the world's great migrations a Polynesian people left their ancient homeland of Tahiti to cross vast stretches of open ocean, eventually to make landfall at New Zealand. They found the islands uninhabited, the landscape a tabula rasa, all the mountains, rivers, lakes, bays devoid of names. Thus the names the Maoris gave are of special interest to names scholars, who rarely are able to study a culture's naming habits in a setting uninfluenced by previously existing names or patterns.

Though they were not interested in climbing mountains, the Maoris could not help but notice the great white peak dominating the southern island, and they named it Aorangi. *Ao* means "bright cloud," whether on the mountain or elsewhere, but it also carries the meaning of "land" or "world"; *rangi* means "sky." But to translate Aorangi to mean "bright cloud in the sky" ("world in the sky" might be better) would be altogether inadequate. Like the English settlers who followed them, the Maoris tended to use place-names as links with their homeland and to apply names from former habitations in new situations to preserve a sense of familiarity and continuity. Aorangi is an example. It's an ancient Maori name and is found not only in the ancestral Maori homeland of Tahiti but also in the Cook Islands, along the Maori's migration route. The Maoris applying the name Aorangi to the mountain in the Southern Alps was little different than the English settlers of Otago Harbor, also on South Island, naming a nearby mountain Ben Nevis.

CORNO GRANDE   9,560 ft/2,914m   Italy
First ascent, 1794, O. Delfico.

Corno Grande, dominating the Gran Sasso massif in central Italy, is the highest summit in the Apennines and the highest in Italy beyond the Alps. The mountain sometimes is called Monte Corno or Mount Corno, but these names contain redundancies; *corno* in Italian means "mountain." Thus the name Corno Grande means simply "big mountain." (The third highest summit in the massif, after Corno Grande's East Peak, is Corno Piccolo, "small mountain.") While Corno Grande's summit can be reached by some steep scrambling, rock climbers can find difficult routes on the mountain, and there are no non-technical routes up Corno Piccolo.

COTOPAXI   19,347ft/5,897m   Ecuador
First ascent, 1872, W. Reiss and A.M. Escobar.

Cotopaxi, the second highest peak in the Andes of central Ecuador and the highest active volcano in the world, bears a name derived from two Indian words: *ccota pasca*, meaning "shining pile." It's an ambiguous name, at least in translation, but it expresses something of the dual nature of the mountain.

Edward Whymper, who climbed Cotopaxi in 1880, described it as "an ideal volcano." Others have commented on the nearly perfect symmetry of its cone, comparing it to Fujiyama in Japan, and it has been called the most majestic peak in Ecuador, surpassing even Chimboarzo, 20,561ft/6,267m, its neighbor to the south. The Prussian traveler and scientist Alexander von Humboldt also was attracted to the mountain, and in 1802 he made an unsuccessful attempt to climb it; the ascent, he said, was impossible.

While volcanic forces have made Cotopaxi an exceptionally beautiful mountain, they also have made it an exceptionally dangerous one. Eruptions were recorded by Europeans as early as 1532, and subsequent eruptions of varying intensity have occurred ever since; from 1742 to 1942 fifty explosive eruptions took place, with frequent loss of life due to lahars (mudslides) and floods triggered by the rapid melting of snow and ice on the mountain. A devastating eruption in 1769 sent such a curtain of ashes over the area that people in Quito to the northwest had to use lanterns to travel even during the daytime. In 1803, the year after Humboldt attempted to climb Cotopaxi, he recorded an eruption of the mountain that even in the port of Guayaquil—160mi/257km away—

Cotopaxi, Ecuador, during its 1743 eruption. From the Alpine Journal, Vol. 10, 1880-1882.

sounded "day and night like continued discharges of a battery."[69] And Whymper reported that when he camped on Cotopaxi, the volcanic ash on the ground was so hot it scorched the ground sheet of his tent.[69]

COTTIAN ALPS   France–Italy
Highest elevation, 12,602ft/3,841m, Monte Viso.

Anthony Huxley suggested that this range along the French-Italian border might well be called "the cockpit of the Alps"; rarely have mountains been so in the way of events that shaped history. The major passes of the Cottians have witnessed battles and the passage of troops for as long as armed conflict has ebbed and flowed in southern Europe. Hannibal crossed the Cottians in 218 B.C., though exactly where has long been a source of controversey (see Mount Cenis). Then came Julius Caesar in 58 B.C., Charlemagne in 773, Charles VIII in 1494, French troops in World War I, and French and Italian armies in World War II, as well as uncounted other armies in wars less momentous under generals less famous. Yet despite the mountains' strategic importance, they have taken the name of a comparatively minor figure in the history of the region, King Marcus Julius Cottius, who perhaps prudently offered no resistance to Augustus's pacification of the Alpine regions. The territory, later annexed by Nero, was commonly known as the Alpes Cottiae.

One reason the Cottian passes have been so important in southern European history is that the surrounding mountains allow few alternative routes. Although the Cottians only occasionally rise above 11,000ft/3,353m and have only a few small glaciers, they nonetheless include several major peaks, such as Monte Viso, 12,602ft/3,841m, Viso di Vallante, 12,048ft/3,672m, and Aiguille de Scolette, 11,500ft/3,505m, and the terrain and weather were sufficiently harsh to inflict heavy losses on Hannibal's formidable army.

CRESTONE NEEDLE   14,191ft/4,325m   Colorado, USA

CRESTONE PEAK   14,294ft/4,357m   Colorado, USA
First ascent, 1916, A. Ellingwood and party, both summits.

"Peak-baggers" aspiring to climb all of Colorado's 14,000ft/4,267m peaks—"Fourteeners"—often reserve these two peaks for last because of their difficulty. Indeed, when explorers, surveyors, travelers, and prospectors had climbed all of Colorado's other Fourteeners, the first ascents of Crestone Needle and Crestone Peak in the Sangre de Cristo Range of southern Colorado waited until 1916 when Albert R. Ellingwood brought modern rock climbing techniques to bear on them. Crestone Needle was climbed first, then Crestone Peak soon thereafter.

The peaks' steep, distinctive appearances have been reflected in the names they have borne. Early names for Crestone Peak, Crestone Needle, and their neighbors included the French name Trois Tetons, "three breasts," and the English names Spanish Crags and the Needles. The present name most likely is an Americanization of the Spanish *creston*, which has been translated as "cockscomb" and "large crest"; either meaning would apply to the peaks. *Creston* also can refer to a mineral outcropping, raising the possibility that the mountains' names, like so many in Colorado, were derived from the mining era.

Apparently the Crestones also had a reputation among the Indians for difficulty. A small lake on the approach to Crestone Needle once had an Indian name that meant "lake you come down to when you come down the wrong way."

MOUNT CRILLON   12,726ft/3,879m   Alaska, USA
First ascent, 1934, B. Washburn and H.A. Carter.

Mount Crillon, one of seven peaks in the Fairweather Range exceeding 12,000ft/3,658m, is known as much for the glaciers surrounding it as for its summit. The area encircling Crillon comprises Glacier Bay National Monument—

Crillon is only 12mi/19km from the sea—and Crillon's North and South Glaciers were the object of pioneering research in glaciology. The first ascent of the mountain itself was accomplished only after several attempts, and the second ascent was not made until 1972, thirty-eight years after the first.

Just as Mount Crillon's glaciers have posed difficulties for mountaineers, so the mountain's name has posed problems for scholars. Indeed, the name Mount Crillon is an excellent example of how a single misinterpretation can, through time and repetition, become widely accepted. There's no doubt when the mountain was named or by whom; in 1797 the journals of J.F.G. de la Perouse were published in which the French explorer mentioned his sighting of the mountain in the 1780s and also the name Mount Crillon.[42] The surveyor William H. Dall in 1874 noted that Mount Crillon was named by Perouse after "the French minister of marine," and most references to Crillon's name since then have repeated Dall's assertion.[42] They are wrong. By going to la Perouse's original work and by researching French records, the expert on mountain names Francis P. Farquhar demonstrated that not only had la Perouse not specified for whom he had named the mountain but also that there never had been a French marine minister named Crillon. After further research, Farquhar concluded that the Crillon la Perouse had in mind "would hardly be other than the great General Louis des Balbes de Berton de Crillon (1543–1615), who distinguished himself at Lepanto and fought for Henri III and Henri IV."[42]

It's possible Farquhar, too, is mistaken, but until more information is available, his explanation is the best we have.

CROAGH PATRICK 2,510ft/765m   Ireland

First ascent unknown.

"In a country like Ireland, of broad undulating plains, the smallest hill may take upon itself an importance that it could never have in more mountainous terrain. So it is that the Irish lowland has many small hills which both command vast outlooks across the fields and bogs, and whose names are linked with the great events of Irish history."[90] Thus D.D.C.P. Mould in *The Mountains of Ireland* introduces Croagh Patrick, an isolated peak rising out of the desolate moorland of western Connacht, that history and religion have made Ireland's most sacred mountain and the island's most frequently climbed summit. Here St. Patrick, according to his own account, retreated to spend Lent praying and doing penance for the people of Ireland. And here the Irish people have come for centuries, each year on the last Sunday in July, in numbers exceeding 60,000, to visit his shrine and seek his blessings. But the tradition of the Irish going up to the mountaintops to pray is older than St. Patrick. A cult of mountains existed in pre-Christian Ireland, and megalithic cairns have been found on the summits of many Irish mountains, such as Slieve Donard. The annual pilgrimage to the top of Croagh Patrick preserves a religious tradition whose roots go far deeper in Irish history than those of Christianity.

Croagh is an ancient Gaelic word meaning "hill" or "mountain" and is related to the English *crag*, the Welsh *craig*, and the Scottish *creag*. Locally, Croagh Patrick is known simply as the Reek (see MacGillycuddys Reeks).

CUILLIN HILLS
Scotland

Highest elevation, 3,309ft/1,009m, Sgurr Alasdair.

The mountain names of Britain can be deceptive. The Peak District of Derbyshire has no peaks, while the Cuillin Hills of the Isle of Skye are not hills but mountains. Indeed, more than one writer has called them Britain's finest mountains, and the well-known British mountaineer and writer Wilfred Noyce called them "perhaps the closest approach to Alpine climbing in Britain."[95] But the character of the Cuillin Hills was probably best described by the mountaineer who knew them best, J. Norman Collie: "The Cuillin are never inferior mountains, unless we measure them by the number of feet they rise above the sea. 'Comparative bulk and height,' says the late Sheriff Nicolson [see Sgurr Alasdair], 'are of course important elements in mountain grandeur, but outline and features are, as with human beings, even more important.' It is the atmosphere that adds both dignity and charm to these Scottish hills, making them appear far bigger than they would in the clearer air of larger mountain ranges, and giving them all the softened color and perspective so necessary to emphasize the real beauty of true mountains."[149]

True mountains they are, not hills—especially the Black Cuillin, a spiky chain of gabbro peaks, some of whose summits can only be reached by genuine rock climbing. (The nearby Red Cuillin are different geologically, smaller and gentler, and of little mountaineering interest.) Yet despite their ruggedness, climbing came relatively late to the Cuillins, and thus we usually know who made the first ascents, unlike most British mountains. Indeed, the highest peak in the group, Sgurr Alasdair (see entry), was both unnamed and unclimbed until 1873 when it took the name of the man who first reached its top.

As for the name of the range itself, legend says the Cuillins of Skye—often called "the Coolins"—are the mountains of Cuchulain, the hero of Gaelic mythology. But despite a tantalizing, if superficial, resemblance between their names, any connection is unlikely. According to the English place-names scholar C.M. Matthews: "Scholars reject these tales but have nothing definite to put in their places ... with early Scottish names one is seldom on firm ground."[87]

The place-names of western Scotland are among the oldest in Britain. In the *Geographia* of Ptolemy, A.D. second century, appear the names Hebudes, Malaios, and Sketis, which survive as the modern names Hebrides, Mull, and Skye. Their original meanings have long been lost, however, and even the language in which they originally were spoken is only a conjecture. The name Cuillin is a similar enigma.

**D**

DEMAVEND *18,603ft/5,670m*   *Iran*
First ascent, 1837, W.T. Thomson.

Certain major mountains, because of the history and folklore associated with them, assume special significance in the nations in which they are located. Fuji-yama in Japan, Croagh Patrick in Ireland, and the sacred mountains of China are examples, and so is Demavend in Iran, located 50mi/80km northeast of Tehran. In the *Shah Nama*, the tenth century epic by the Persian poet Firdausi, the tyrant Zohak is imprisoned inside Demavend after being overthrown by the ideal king Feridun; local legend says Zohak's moans still can be heard from caverns within the mountain. The legendary ruler Jamshid is said to have lived on Demavend's slopes, as did Rustam, another hero from the *Shah Nama*. It even has been said that the Ark of Noah came to rest not on Ararat but on Demavend.

But despite these associations, Demavend's name comes not from folklore but from its being a volcano. Although Demavend has not erupted in historical times, hot springs and sulfurous vents on the mountain, as well as its great, symmetrical cinder cone, indicate volcanic activity relatively recently in the geologic past. *Dema* is a very old Persian word associated with "heat," and *-vend* is merely a suffix indicating this.

Since W.T. Thomson's first ascent in 1837, Demavend has been climbed countless times, and the normal route is not difficult, except for the elevation and occasional noxious sulfur fumes. In fact, legends and national significance, not technical problems, prevented an earlier ascent of the mountain; early Persians discouraged climbing on Demavend just as Tibetans today prohibit climbing on many Himalayan peaks in their territory.

DENT BLANCHE *14,295ft/4,357m*   *Switzerland*
First ascent, 1862, T. Kennedy, W. Wigram, J. Croz, and J. Konig.

The name Dent Blanche is French and means "white tooth." It's an appropriate descriptive name for this peak in the Pennine Alps, but it is only one of many "tooth" names found not only in the Alps but throughout the world. The Dent Blanche is a major Alpine summit, and its first ascent in 1862 via the south ridge was one of the great achievements in the "Golden Age of Mountaineering" (1855–1865). Almost as important were subsequent ascents, including that in 1882 of the east-northeast ridge by T. Stafford Anderson. Since then the ridge has been known as the Arête des Quatre Anes—the "ridge of the four asses"—a name born in a remark by one of the guides during the climb: "*Nous sommes pourtant quatre ânes d'être montes par ici,*" "We're four asses to have climbed this way."[110] On the west ridge of the Dent Blanche the famous British rock climber Owen Glynne Jones was killed in 1899.

DENTS DU MIDI   10,965ft/3,342m   *Switzerland*
First ascent, 1784, J. Clement.

Before watches and clocks became widely available, people living in mountainous areas often used the mountains as crude chronometers, approximating the time of day by the sun's position relative to a prominent summit. Thus, the curious name "noon mountain" is more common than one might suspect, appearing as Noon Peak in the White Mountains of the northeastern United States, and as Dents du Midi ("teeth of noon") in this mountain group in the western Alps, over whose summits the midday sun streams down the long Rhone Valley to Lake Geneva.

The Dents du Midi, with a rocky summit ridge rising to several pinnacles, are especially beautiful mountains, so much so that they have been called the Parthenon of the Alps. The names of the individual spires indicate something of their appeal: Haute Cime (10,695ft/3,260m), "high summit"; the Dent Noire (10,433ft/3,180m), "the black tooth"; the Cathedrale (10,387ft/3,166m); the Dent Jaune (10,456ft/3,187m), "the yellow tooth"; Les Doigts (10,538ft/3,212m), "the fingers"; and the Forteresse (10,381ft/3,164m), "the fortress."

DEVILS TOWER   5,110ft/1,558m   *Wyoming, USA*
First ascent, 1893, W. Ripley and W. Rogers.

To the Indians of northeastern Wyoming, the formation now known as Devils Tower would have been a dark enigma, an object of superstitious fear and awe. Believed to be the core of an extinct volcano (though many questions remain about its origin), Devils Tower rises abruptly nearly 900ft/274m above the surrounding plains. With its volcanic rocks crystallized into vertical columns, the formation as a whole more closely resembles the stump of a titanic tree than a mountain. One tribe is reported to have called the tower *Malo Tepee*, but the accuracy of this transliteration or its meaning cannot be determined. It is known that many Indians regarded the mysterious peak, whose summit had never been explored, as the abode of evil spirits, and from this has come the mountain's English name.

The first ascent of Devils Tower required attaching wooden ladders to its sides. The mountain was not climbed free until 1937. Since then it has been climbed often, even on its most difficult north and west faces. During a "Mountaineers Week" in 1956, eighty-one ascents were made.

DHARAMSURA   21,148ft/6,446m   *India*
First ascent, 1941, J.O.M. Roberts.

The peaks of the Himalaya bear some of the most poetic of mountain names and nowhere more so than in the Himachal Pradesh of the Punjab. There, for example, is Dharamsura, better known in translation as White Sail. Immedi-

76

ately southwest of Dharamsura is Papsura (21,165ft/6,451m) whose name means "peak of evil" (see entry).

Despite what would seem an obvious and appealing similarity between the soaring white flanks of many mountains and the sail-draped masts of ships, mountain names based on this resemblance are rare. In the Haast Range of New Zealand are several mountains each named for the topsails of a square-rigged ship (see Mount Aspiring), and on the coast of New Zealand there is a hill early English settlers called Main Topsail, but other examples are difficult to find, something made more curious by the comparative frequency of names based on other resemblances, such as to a cathedral or a castle. Perhaps this is because a ship's sails, while sharing shape and color with many mountains, lack the quintessential qualities of substance and solidity and thus have failed to inspire the imaginations of mountain-living peoples, particularly those with limited contact with the sea.

DHAULAGIRI 26,811ft/8,172m Nepal
First ascent, 1960, K. Diemberger, P. Diener, E. Forrer, A. Schelbert, and N. Dorji.

Dhaulagiri in western Nepal bears a name that traced to its Sanskrit origins means "white mountain" (*dhavala*, "white," *giri*, "mountain"). "White mountain" is the world's most common mountain name, usually appearing on very big, snow-capturing peaks, but Dhaulagiri has the distinction of being the biggest "white mountain" of them all. Indeed, the Dhaulagiri massif—30mi/48km long and including no fewer than fifteen summits topping 22,700ft/7,000m—is one of the biggest and highest mountain systems anywhere. This, coupled with the relatively late and incomplete exploration of the Himalaya, resulted in Dhaulagiri for thirty years being considered the highest mountain in the world.

Robert Colebrooks, Surveyor General of Bengal, as early as 1802 recognized Dhaulagiri as a major mountain, and in 1808 he sent his lieutenant, W.S. Webb, to make measurements. Webb, using observations from four different stations, in 1809 reported Dhaulagiri's elevation at 26,882ft/8,194m, a remarkably accurate estimate, but his report initially was ridiculed by geographers who long had believed Chimborazo in the Andes to be the world's tallest mountain. Webb's report eventually was accepted, however, and Dhaulagiri reigned unchallenged until 1848 when Kanchenjunga was measured.

West of the main summit of the Dhaulagiri massif are five other summits, ranging in elevation between 25,420ft/7,750m and 23,780ft/7,250m. Each of these is identified by the letter D followed by a Roman numeral (DI, DII, and so forth). This is a common means of identifying subsidiary peaks in little-known, sparsely populated areas of the Himalaya. (Lhotse, long regarded as a subsidiary peak of Everest, for many years was identified merely as EI.) In time these other peaks almost certainly will acquire more individual names as the region becomes better known, and this process already has begun; DII also is known as Mula Kang.

The topography of the Dhaulagiri massif is extremely complex and confusing. Most approaches to the mountain are difficult, a fact indirectly responsible for the first ascent of Annapurna, Dhaulagiri's eastern counterpart across the Kali Gandaki gorge. In 1950 Maurice Herzog and his party, intending to attempt Dhaulagiri but lacking reliable maps or directions, made a reconnaissance around Dhaulagiri's very difficult east side. Discouraged by what they found, they climbed Annapurna instead.

LES DIABLERETS   10,531ft/3,210m   Switzerland
First ascent unknown.

If someone in the eighteenth century had asked a Swiss peasant about the origin of the name of the westernmost major massif of the Bernese Alps, the peasant likely would have recounted a legend in which some demons (*diablerets*) used the mountains to play at ninepins. With boulders as bowling balls, the demons aimed to topple the spire known as the Tower of St. Martin. When they missed, their balls would send avalanches crashing into the valleys below. After all, was this not what had triggered the infamous rockslides of 1714 and 1749?

Actually, the name Diablerets predates the landslides, for in 1665 we find the mountain complex called the Sex de Diableyres. Before that the complex was called the Sex de Champ, a rather peculiar name for a mountain as *de champ* in French is "of the field." One writer has explained this by saying: "*Champ*, or 'field,' speaks of that which is horizontal. It is in its relationship with the valley that the Sex de Champ is positioned vertically and forms the horizon for the people of Ormont-Dessus, who continue to refer to the massif as Les Rochers de Champ, 'the rocks of the field,' as they first did in 1809. It is in this sense that we must understand it." A more easily understood local name for Les Diablerets is Bekka Monte, which in the local dialect means "weathered peak."

Within these mountains are other intriguing names. One is the Pas du Lustre, "pass of the chandelier," a rock wall immediately below the summit. The wall takes its name from an incident in 1857, when the botanist Jean Muret was being led down toward Anzeindaz by the aging guide Marletaz. When they arrived at the top of the wall, the guide forced Muret to pass a rope under his armpits to descend to the bottom. Later the scientist recounted his experience, saying, "Everything went well, even if at a rough spot these rascals suspended me like a chandelier!"

DOLOMITES   Italy
Highest elevation, 10,965ft/3,342m, Marmolata.

The Dolomites of northern Italy owe both their name and their fame to the distinctive type of rock composing them. The mineral dolomite was named for the French geologist Deodat de Gratet, Marquis de Dolomieu (1750–1801), who first described its unique properties. Although dolomite is a form of limestone, its magnesium (rather than calcium) carbonate makes it more resistant to chemical weathering than are other limestones. This has given the Dolomites an

A fall in the Alps, which the climber lived to recount. From Edward Whymper, Scrambles Amongst the Alps 1860-1869 *(Philadelphia: 1873).*

appearance strikingly different from most limestone mountains, indeed, different from most mountains of any composition, and the names of many of the peaks reflect something of the region's unique character. For example, Marmolata, the Dolomites' highest summit, derives its name from the Italian *marmo*, "marble." For centuries painters and architects have been inspired by the unusual colors and shapes of the Dolomites, and nearby towns have become popular resorts.

But it is to rock climbers, who often refer to the group as the Dollies, that the Dolomites truly belong. Snowfields and glaciers are few because of the range's relatively low elevation, but the region's great beauty and unique character of rock offer delights and challenges found nowhere else. The rock has been described as resembling a petrified sponge, full of holes, although most cliff faces are smooth. Ascending the peaks themselves can be easy, but the region's myriad crags, faces, pinnacles, and chimneys offer climbing of the highest standards.

DOM   *14,913ft/4,545m*   *Switzerland*
First ascent, 1858, J.L. Davies, J. Zumtaugwald, J. Kronig, and H. Brantschen.

The Dom is the second highest summit of the Pennine Alps and the highest mountain entirely within Switzerland. (Switzerland shares Monte Rosa, 15,203ft/4,634m, with Italy.) The name Dom, given to the mountain by the Abbe Berchtold of Zermatt, means "cathedral" in German, making this mountain one of many world-wide having this name. The cathedral image of the Dom probably was enhanced by the massif where it is located having many summits, of which the Dom is the highest. The others include the Taschhorn (14,744ft/4,494m), the Nadelhorn (14,206ft/4,330m), and the Lenzspitze (14,098ft/4,297m). Collectively they are known as the Mischabel.

The name Mischabel is particularly intriguing. According to local tradition in the Saas-Fee, the people of the district are descended from Saracen invaders of the tenth century. The Arabs—Moors, as they were known then—certainly invaded the Valais in 939 and later were employed by Hugo, king of Arles, to hold the Valaisian passes against rivals. To support this tradition, many people point to local place-names—Monte Moro ("Mount Moor"), the Allalin Glacier, and Mischabel—that seem clearly of Arabic origin. For example, the latter part of the name Mischabel is pronounced almost exactly the same as the Arabic *jebel*, "mountain." The difficulty here is that Arabic naming patterns would require *jebel* to be a prefix, not a suffix. Still, as the names scholar Isaac Taylor has pointed out, Mischabel could be a hybrid formation, akin to Mongibello in Sicily.[136] Other scholars, however, have questioned an Arabic origin for these names. Mischabel, they say, is simply a corruption of Mittlere Gabel, "middle peak," and Monte Moro was named for the Arab invaders, not by them.

DRAKENSBERG MOUNTAINS   *South Africa*
Highest elevation, 11,425ft/3,482m, Thabantshonyana.

To the Zulus of southern Africa, the great palisade extending 800mi/1,100km from the Tropic of Capricorn southwest to the Cape of Good Hope was known as *Khualamba*, "the barrier of spears." It's an appropriate name for the rock rampart of the Drakensberg, whose spear-like spires and precipitous faces, rising as much as 4,500ft/1,372m, form an effective barrier between the coastal lowlands and the high plateau of the interior. Most of the escarpment's upper portion is basaltic lava, whose weathering and linear faulting have given the mountains their rugged character and made their faces and pinnacles so appealing for climbers. One of these pinnacles, Devils Tooth, is known for its extreme difficulty.

Underlying the basalt is a sandstone formation containing many caves; the formation is known as Cave Sandstone. According to legend, a dragon once dwelt in these caves, and this accounts for the name by which the mountains are best known; Drakensberg is a Dutch word meaning "dragon mountain," and the name was given by South Africa's Dutch settlers, known as Boers. The basis for the legend is unknown—perhaps it's linked to the drawings the bushmen left in the caves—but as late as 1877 an old Dutch farmer and his son were reported to have seen a dragon in flight.

E

MOUNT EARNSLAW   9,250ft/2,819m   New Zealand
First ascent East Peak, 1890, H. Birley.
First ascent West Peak, 1914, H.F. Wright and J. Robertson.

Mount Earnslaw is a large massif whose twin peaks dominate this part of the Haast Range on New Zealand's South Island. The name Earnslaw was given by the surveyor J.T. Thomson, whose father came from the village of Earnslaw in Berwickshire, England. The name's meaning, too, can be traced to Old English origins; it comes from Anglo-Saxon elements meaning "eagles hill."

ECRINS   13,461ft/4,103m   France
First ascent, 1864, E. Whymper, A.W. Moore, H. Walker, C. Almer, and M. Croz.

With *ecrin* being the French word for "jewel box," the name of this massif containing the highest peaks of the Dauphine Alps is reminiscent of the name of the Kanchenjunga massif in the Himalaya, which means "five great treasuries of the snow" (see Kanchenjunga). The Alpine group, located entirely within France, sometimes is called variously Barre des Ecrins, Pointe des Ecrins, Pic des Ecrins, or most simply Les Ecrins.

The Ecrins are mostly hidden by surrounding peaks, and the group's separate identity was not confirmed until the explorations in 1862 of the British mountaineer Francis Fox Tuckett. The first ascent by Edward Whymper two years later sparked one of the more heated controversies in the Golden Age of Mountaineering in the Alps. Whymper claimed his guide, Christian Almer, was forced to make a bold and dangerous leap across a wide gap while negotiating the summit ridge. W.A.B. Coolidge challenged the claim, saying no such gap existed. Coolidge resigned from the Alpine Club when he felt its members believed Whymper, who had published 4,300 copies of lengthy correspondence on the subject to help substantiate his position. The issue eventually expired without ever being fully resolved. Subsequent climbers found no gap, but they conceded that such a feature might have existed and then been obliterated by natural forces.

MOUNT EDITH CAVELL 11,033ft/3,363m Alberta, Canada
First ascent, 1915, A.J. Gilmour and E.W. Holway.

After 1918, many previously unnamed Canadian mountains were given names honoring persons and events associated with World War I. One of these was Mount Edith Cavell, a peak in Jasper National Park near the Alberta–British Columbia border, named after an English nurse who was shot by the Germans in 1915 for helping convalescent prisoners to escape. A monument commemorating Cavell stands in Trafalgar Square in London.

Place-names, including many mountain names, honoring persons involved in World War I or World War II are particularly common in Canada. As the Canadian place-names scholar William B. Hamilton has pointed out: "A source frequently tapped for previously unnamed features in some sections of the country has been casualty lists of Canadian servicemen who paid the supreme sacrifice in the Second World War. More than 9,000 new names have been added to the map of Canada as a result of the decision to honor the memory of fallen servicemen."[58] Many of these names, doubtless, will eventually lapse into disuse, erased by fading memories or eclipsed by local usage, but Mount Edith Cavell will likely endure, for both she and the mountain named for her are memorable indeed.

TORRE EGGER 9,800ft/2,987m Chile
First ascent, 1976, J. Bragg, J. Donini, and G. Wilson.

Although most mountaineers now discount claims that Cerro Torre, highest of the "towers" in the Fitzroy group, was first climbed by Cesare Maestri and Toni Egger in 1959, Egger's achievements in Patagonia nonetheless are commemorated by having had his name placed on this nearby neighbor of Cerro Torre. Egger was killed on the descent from Cerro Torre, while Maestri, delirious from the ordeal, was able to recall few details of their desperate and courageous attempt.

MOUNT EGMONT 8,260ft/2,517m New Zealand
First ascent, 1839, E. Dieffenbach and party.

When Captain James Cook, exploring the southwest coast of New Zealand's North Island in 1770, saw this beautiful snow-clad volcanic peak rising more than 8,000ft/2,438m in a nearly perfect cone, he named it for the Earl of

Egmont, who had preceded Edward Hawke, Cook's sponsor, as first lord of the admiralty. Cook named better than he probably knew. The name Egmont comes from the Norman French meaning "pointed hill"; so nearly symmetrical is Egmont's volcanic cone that the mountain has been called "the Fujiyama of New Zealand."

The Maoris of New Zealand know Mount Egmont as Taranake, a name that survives not only on the mountain but also on the district encompassing the peak. The home of a legendary ancestor, Taranaki was taboo to the Maori, and they personified it in a legend relating Taranaki to Ruapehu and Tongariro, two other major mountains on North Island. In it, Taranaki was the husband of the beautiful Ruapehu. One day, while her husband was away hunting, Ruapehu was wooed and won by Tongariro. When Taranaki returned at the end of the day he surprised the pair. A titanic battle ensued in which Taranaki was defeated. He retreated toward the west coast, carving out the course of the Wanganui River as he went. When he reached the coast he moved northwards to the western extremity of North Island, where he rested. There his great weight made the shallow depression, afterwards filled with water, that became Te Ngaere Swamp. Taranaki now sits in silence, looking toward his wife and his rival. But despite Ruapehu's infatuation with Tongariro, she still loves her husband and sighs occasionally as she remembers him, while the mist drifting eastward from his head is the visible sign of his undying love for her. Tongariro, despairing of ever possessing her again, smokes and smolders in anger. And for the Maoris, corroboration of the legend is to be found in Tongariro National Park, where there is a large basin they call Rua Taranaki, "the pit of Taranaki," created when Taranaki departed from Ruapehu.

EIGER   13,039ft/3,974m   Switzerland
First ascent, 1858, C. Barrington, C. Almer, and P. Bohren.
First ascent, EIGER NORDWAND, 1938, A. Heckmair, H. Harrer, W. Borg, and F. Kasparek.

Rarely if ever have a mountain and its name been better matched—the Eiger is a difficult, exceedingly dangerous peak in the Bernese Alps; its German name means "ogre." By 1977 more than forty persons had died on the mountain, including some of the best mountaineers of their times. And though improved climbing and rescue techniques and equipment have made the mountain less dangerous than in the 1930s, when it was the object of several do-or-die attempts, it has by no means outlived its reputation as a "mountain of death."

Curiously, the mountain acquired its ominous name long before anyone gave any serious thought to climbing it. The peak was known by its present name as early as 1252, when the name appears in a Latin document describing a piece of land as running to the foot of the "Egere," the Eiger. (The American historian of the Alps, W.A.B. Coolidge, reports an 1817 source suggesting that the whole Bernese chain was formerly called the Innere Eiger, or Hintereiger, or simply, the Eiger.) Given the name's antiquity, we can only speculate as to what inspired it among the medieval Swiss villagers.

When the first ascent of the Eiger's mile-high north face (the Eiger Nordwand, the greatest face in the Alps) in the 1930s became the "last great Alpine problem," and when the death toll mounted, sensationalized press reports inspired other names. The German press circulated a grim pun, calling the Nordwand the Mordwand, "murder wall." One journalist described the Eiger as the White Cobra, building on the image of the Eiger's broad, flared shoulders arching around the concave north face like a cobra's hood, the small, dark summit the reptile's head. Persons—and they were many—who opposed attempts on the north face called the climb the Imbecile Variant, while mountaineers who saw the face as the ultimate mountaineering challenge called it the Final Exam.

Because of the Eiger's dramatic and well-publicized history, many areas of it are endowed with names reminding us of the mountain's tragic past. The Hinterstoisser Traverse, a key section, was named for Andreas Hinterstoisser, who pioneered the traverse during an attempt that killed him and his three companions. The Death Bivouac, an important overnight camp on the 1938 route, was named because a missing climber's body was found there. The White Spider is a snowfield high on the Nordwand whose entrance and exit cracks resemble a spider's spindly legs. (This name, popularized by Heinrich Harrer's book *The White Spider*, has become almost a synonym for the north face itself.) The Gotterquergang, "the traverse of the gods," was named for the awesome views its dizzying exposure gives of the valley below. The Longhi Ledge, near the summit, was named for Stefano Longhi, who died on it. The Harlin Direct Route, the first direct route on the Nordwand, was named for John Harlin, the American climber who conceived it, organized it, and died on it.

Because of the Eiger's notoriety, one would expect its name to be borrowed often (as has been the Matterhorn's), but this hasn't happened. The most likely reason is that the Eiger became famous—or infamous—relatively recently, when few mountains were still nameless. A peak in the Karakoram also is called the Ogre (23,900ft/7,285m), but it's possible that its English name has no connection with that of the Alpine peak; it often appears on maps under its local name, Baitha Brakk.

But perhaps the name hasn't been more widely imitated because the Eiger's history and the connotations of its name are unique, defying imitation. As Arthur Roth concluded in his book about the Eiger: "The Eigernordwand, 'the meanest mountain on earth,' as a writer for *Reader's Digest* once called it, will always be sui generis, the Final Exam for most Alpine climbers, the ultimate mental and physical test of a mountaineer's potential as a human being."[98]

MOUNT ELBRUZ   18,841ft/5,743m   USSR

First ascent, east peak, lower, 1868, D. Freshfield, A.W. Moore, C. Tucker, F. Devouassoud, and two local porters.
First ascent, west peak, 1874, F. Gardiner, F.C. Grove, H. Walker, and P. Knubel.

If asked to name Europe's highest summit, the overwhelming majority of people would say Mount Blanc. Technically, however, they would be wrong. Mount Elbruz, 3,070ft/936m higher, is located 12mi/19km north of the watershed officially marking the boundary between Europe and Asia. But Elbruz doesn't *seem* a European mountain. Thus when European mountaineers, having climbed almost all the major peaks in the Alps, began looking outside Europe for new mountains, the first peak to which they turned their attention was Elbruz. That's why Douglas Freshfield's first ascent of Elbruz, by a quirk of geography, was ironically a landmark in mountaineering outside Europe.

Elbruz's non-European character is reinforced by the mountain's name. Though etymologies and translations differ, *Elbruz* generally is accepted as coming from Persia. Some writers have said that it comes from *alburz*, "high snow," which likely appears in the name of the Elburz Mountains in Iran. Other writers have said Elbruz comes from *aitibares*, "high mountain," also plausible. But the most common explanation is that the Persian name for the peak means "shining, or sparkling, mountain." The Armenian name for Elbruz is Alberis, but though at least one writer has suggested a possible connection between this and the name of the Alps, any links more likely are with the Persian name.

Mount Elbruz, U.S.S.R. From Frederic Zurcher and Elie Margollé, Les ascensions célèbres *(Paris, 1867).*

EMEI SHAN   9,957ft/3,035m   *China*
First ascent unknown.

Most Chinese mountain names are descriptive, but because the Chinese language is particularly rich in homonyms, these descriptive names often have a poetic, metaphorical quality that distinguishes them from most descriptive names. Surely few mountains anywhere have had their names explained more fancifully than Emei Shan, located south of Chengtu in Szechuan Province and one of the best known and most venerated mountains in China.

Actually, the name Emei Shan (often spelled Omei Shan) is applied to multiple summits facing each other. As the Chinese names scholar Zhu Bin explains, *shan* means "mountain," while Emei actually is two words, *e* and *mei*, that together have two possible interpretations: "female beauties" and "delicate eyebrows."[14] Given these meanings, it was perhaps inevitable that folk etymologies would appear, and Zhu Bin relates them thus: "Once a painter drew a picture of four beautiful girls and presented it to his monk friend. Instead of following the painter's advice to hide the picture in a box, the monk hung it on a wall. One day the four girls came down from the picture and ran out of the temple. Being chased by the monk, the four sisters turned into four mountains, which became the four mountains of Emei. In this way, Emei Shan should be translated as 'mountain of beauties.' Nevertheless, many people noticed that the first and second mountains, which are located on two sides, are more like two delicate eyebrows. Thus Emei has its second origin: 'mountain of delicate eyebrows.'"

The first appearance of these metaphors has been lost in time, so it is difficult to determine which came first. The Buddhist name for Emei Shan is Guangming Shan, "bright mountain," inspired by the phantom-like images on the mountain caused by reflected sunlight. A stone path leads to a temple on Emei Shan's summit.

MOUNT EMIN   15,740ft/4,798m   *Zaire*
First ascent, 1906, the Duke of the Abruzzi with J. and L. Petigax.

All six Ruwenzori peaks exceeding 15,000ft/4,572m were named for persons prominent in the exploration of east and central Africa. Although Emin is a Turkish name, the mountain bearing it honors the German Eduard Schnitzer (1840–1892).

Schnitzer traveled extensively in East Africa, exploring the equatorial region for Germany and serving the Turkish government for nine years. During that time he adopted the Turkish name by which he is best known—Mehmed Emin Pasha—but though he was profoundly influenced by the Arab presence in East Africa, he did not convert to Islam. He served as governor of the Sudan and worked to suppress the slave trade. His eccentric and exotic career ended in 1892 when he was murdered by slave traders.

The peak bearing Emin Pasha's name lies north of the main Ruwenzori group. It has been visited relatively little since the Duke of the Abruzzi's tour de force in the Ruwenzori that resulted in first ascents of all six major summits.

MOUNT EQUINOX   3,816ft/1,163m   Vermont, USA
First ascent unknown.
See TACONIC MOUNTAINS.

MOUNT EREBUS   12,450ft/3,795m   Antarctica
First ascent, 1908, E. David and party of the Shackleton expedition.

When Sir J. Clark Ross in 1841 discovered the great Antarctic sea beyond
McMurdo Sound, he also discovered the continent's two great volcanoes. A
member of the expedition later wrote: "We were startled by the most unexpected discovery, in this vast region of glaciation, of a stupendous volcanic
mountain in a high state of activity."[69] Nearby rose "a sister volcano . . . but now
extinct, though having the same general outline, which also doubtless belched
forth at no distant period its volumes of smoke and flame."

The sea and the volcanic island later were named for Ross, but he himself
named the volcanoes. He called the active one Erebus and the extinct one Terror. The names certainly seem fitting for Antarctic volcanoes. In Greek
mythology Erebus was the place of darkness—like Antarctica for half the
year—through which spirits of the dead had to walk on their journey to Hades,
and terror is an emotion long associated with volcanoes. But though Ross surely
was conscious of these connotations when he gave the names, in fact he named
the mountains for the two tiny ships, the *Erebus* and the *Terror*, that had carried
his party to Antarctica and in which he was to spend eight years there
(1834–1843).

Though both mountains have now been climbed several times, the unexpected juxtaposition of fire and ice still causes people to associate their names
with the unknown terrors of the underworld—and with some reason. The
members of the Shackleton expedition who in 1908 made the first ascent of
Erebus found a steaming cauldron in its crater, and the members of the second
ascent party in 1912 had to retreat hastily from the mountain because of a minor
eruption.

MOUNT ETNA   10,741ft/3,274m   Sicily
First ascent unknown.

The most massive mountain in Europe still bears today the name by which it
was known to the ancient Greeks. They called it Aitne, from the Greek *aitho*,
"to burn" — a logical name for this great volcano, still active, which dominates
the island of Sicily.

Thucydides wrote of eruptions on Etna as early as the eighth century B.C.;
since then more than 260 eruptions have been recorded. The Greek
philosopher Empedocles (490–430 B.C.) is said to have climbed the mountain,
and while scholars question whether he actually committed suicide there by
hurling himself into the crater, there's no reason to doubt his ascent. The

Mount Etna, Crete, from Taormina. From William H.D. Adams, Mountains and Mountain Climbing *(London: 1883).*

Roman emperors Hadrian (A.D. 76–138) and Trajan (A.D. 53–117) both climbed it, reportedly to view the sunrise from its summit.

Because of its frequent eruptions, the most recent in 1974, Etna is an agglomeration of volcanic structures. The present eruptive center bears the name by which the Sicilians know the mountain, Mongibello. This name, like the mountain, is a layering of similar components; the Italian *monte* and the Arabic *jebel* both mean "mountain."

EVEREST   29,028ft/8,848m   Nepal–Tibet
First ascent, 1953, E. Hillary and T. Norkay.

The world's highest mountain was named for one of nineteenth-century Britain's finest colonial surveyors, Sir George Everest. Few people have ever heard of George Everest, and at first glance the man seems grotesquely less significant than the mountain named for him. The honor is deserved, however, because George Everest made a genuine contribution to mountain measurement that eventually led to recognition of Mount Everest as the world's highest summit.

George Everest, born in England, first journeyed to Asia as a young geodesist and surveyor, and by the age of twenty-four he was working with the survey of Java. Because of his successes there, he was chosen to assist in the survey of India. By the time he was thirty-three he was superintendent of the project, and ultimately he became surveyor general. He reorganized the survey, and by introducing the most accurate instruments then available he was able to increase markedly the standards and reliability of the survey's measurements.

That was very important to Himalayan exploration, because everywhere there was confusion as to which actually was the world's tallest peak. Many thought it was Chimborazo in Ecuador, but in the 1850s British surveyors exploring in the Himalaya were encountering mountains they knew could challenge the South American mountain. The problem was accurate measurement. It wasn't easy to get close to some of the Himalayan giants, and sightings from afar ran into problems of atmospheric disturbance, reducing accuracy. But because of George Everest's high standards and sophisticated methods, the stage had been set by 1852 for the final "discovery" of the world's highest mountain.

Observations of Mount Everest first were recorded in 1849, but at that time it was only one of many unnamed peaks, and surveyors identified it merely as Peak XV, no local name being known. That obscurity ended one day in 1852 when the head of the computing office of the Survey of India, Radhanath Sikhdar, burst breathlessly into the office of the surveyor general, Sir Andrew Waugh, and announced, "Sir, I have discovered the highest mountain in the world!"[76] A check of the six stations from which Peak XV had been observed confirmed this judgment; the mean height was 29,002ft/8,840m, later corrected to the present figure.

Three years later Waugh formally proposed to the Royal Geographic Society of London that the giant mountain be given the surname of his predecessor in office. A man named Brian Hodgson objected to this name on the grounds that the Nepalese already had names for the peak, and he cited Deva-dhunga, "seat of God," and Bhairava Langur, "terrible pass." On 11 May 1856 the Geographic Society met to discuss this objection—with Sir George Everest himself present. The society's members decided it was doubtful whether any of the Nepalese names could really be applied to the mountain, and they therefore approved the name Everest, which has since been widely accepted.

But the geographers had been wrong in thinking the mountain had no native name. To the Tibetans the peak is Chomolungma, sometimes spelled Jomolungma. (The transliteration preferred by the Chinese is Qomolungma.) Although confusion exists as to exactly how this name should be pronounced or exactly what it means, the most widely accepted translation is "goddess, mother of the world." Other meanings of approximately the same sounds also are possible: "goddess of the district," "goddess of the wind," and "bird of the wind." To the Nepalese, the mountain is Sagarmatha, "goddess of the sky." This is the name of the Nepalese national park created in 1976 that includes Everest, Lhotse, and Cho Oyu.

The accurate measurement of Everest did not halt the search for a peak that might be higher still. As late as World War II there were rumors that a group in the Kun Lun system of China might surpass Everest, but the reports were proved wrong. Even following the historic ascent of Everest in 1953 by Sir Edmund Hillary of New Zealand and the Sherpa Tenzing Norkay, speculation persisted that some peaks might be discovered in Antarctica that would top Everest, but with more and more surveys of that continent, hopes of Everest being dethroned faded forever. Sir George Everest and his surveyors may not have been famous, but they did know how to measure mountains, and they did discover the world's highest summit.

EVGENIA KORZHENEVSKAYA PEAK $\quad$ 23,310ft/7,105m $\quad$ USSR
First ascent, 1953, A. Ugarov and party.

Located near Peak of Communism in the Soviet Pamirs, Evgenia Korzhenevskaya Peak was discovered in 1910 by the Soviet geographer N.I. Korzhenevsky and named by him for his wife.

For an explorer to name a natural feature he discovered for his wife is less common than one might expect. One of the very few other examples is in Antarctica. Lincoln Ellsworth, following his 1935 trans-Antarctic flight, named a mountain in the northern part of the Sentinel Range for his wife, Mary Louise Ulmer (Mount Ulmer, 9,104ft/2,775m).

EXECUTIVE COMMITTEE RANGE $\quad$ Antarctica
Highest elevation, 13,717ft/4,181m, Mount Sidley.

Antarctica having had no history of human habitation, the task—and privilege—of supplying names for the continent's natural features fell largely to its explorers, many of whom followed a long tradition of using their naming

Mount Everest, Nepal-China. From William H.D. Adams, Mountains and Mountain Climbing (London: 1883).

prerogative to honor persons responsible for their expeditions. This practice accounts for numerous mountain names world-wide, such as Mount Hood in the Cascade Range of northwestern North America and Mount Hunter in the Alaska Range (see entries). Nonetheless, one has to go to Soviet mountain naming (see Peak of Communism) to match the grotesque banality of the name of this range in Marie Byrd Land; even the Matterhorn would be diminished by such a designation.

The five major mountains making up the Executive Committee Range trend north–south along the 126th Meridian. The range was explored in 1940 by the U.S. Antarctic Service expedition and named for the Antarctic Service Executive Committee, which was responsible for the expedition. Individual mountains in the range were named to honor individual members of the committee—with one exception. The highest and most imposing peak in the range had been discovered and named earlier, in 1934, by Admiral Byrd, who named it for Mrs. Mabelle E. Sidley, the daughter of William Horlick, a manufacturer who was partly responsible for Byrd's expedition.

MOUNT FAIRWEATHER   15,300ft/4,663m   Alaska, USA
First ascent, 1932, A. Carpe and T. Moore.

The peaks of the Fairweather Range, a southern extension of the St. Elias uplift, have been called "the most impressive coastal mountains on earth"[42]; the 15,300ft/4,663m summit of Mount Fairweather is only 14mi/23km from the ocean, and the entire range is bounded on three sides by the sea.

Mount Fairweather was sighted by Captain James Cook in 1778, and the ship's log he kept chronicles the origin of the name. The weather that spring had been nasty—nothing unusual for the southern coast of Alaska—and Cook's entry for 27 April 1778, speaks of the wind blowing very hard, then, "a perfect hurricane." But his entry for April 28 reads: "The weather now began to clear up; and, being able to see several leagues round us, I steered more to the Northward . . . with a fresh gale at South South East, and fair weather." The break in the weather allowed him to observe the mountain, which he mentioned in his log on May 3: "the most advanced point of the land, to the North West, lying under a very high peaked mountain, which obtained the name of Mount Fair Weather. . . . The point under the peaked mountain, which was called Cape Fair."[42] With time the name of the highest peak was transferred to the entire range.

Fairweather was not the first weather-inspired name Cook had bestowed during his voyage. On March 7, sailing along the coast of Oregon, Captain Cook was not lucky enough to find a break in the weather, so he gave to a cape he encountered there the name Foulweather.

The mountains that captured Cook's attention have impressed other observers—especially when the weather was fair. The naturalist John Muir, visiting Glacier Bay in 1890, wrote: "I also had glorious views of the Fairweather Range, Crillon, Lituya, and Fairweather. Mount Fairweather is the most beautiful of all the giants that stand guard about Glacier Bay. When the sun is shining on it from the east or south its magnificent glaciers and colors are brought out in most telling display. In the late afternoon its features become less distinct. The atmosphere seems pale and hazy...."[42]

CERRO FITZ ROY   11,073ft/3,375m   Argentina–Chile
First ascent, 1952, L. Terray and G. Magnone.

The peaks of Patagonia are known for their spectacular vertical walls and their almost surreal shapes, and nowhere are these characteristics better exhibited than on Cerro Fitz Roy, with its 6,000ft/1,829m diorite face. The first ascent of Fitz Roy in 1952 was a milestone in world mountaineering, requiring special bivouacs to overcome the region's notoriously bad weather. The mountain's name honors Robert Fitzroy, who commanded the HMS *Beagle* that carried Charles Darwin on his voyage around the world (1828–1836). On the journey Fitzroy explored and surveyed the coast of Patagonia and the Strait of Magellan.

MOUNT FORAKER   17,400ft/5,304m   Alaska, USA
First ascent, 1934, C.S. Houston, T.G. Brown, and C. Waterston.

The two highest peaks of the Alaska Range both were named for United States senators from Ohio: William McKinley and Joseph Benson Foraker. McKinley went on to become the twenty-fifth president of the United States, while Foraker was driven from public life in a corruption scandal. But in 1899, when Lieutenant Joseph S. Herron of the United States Army named the mountain, Foraker's political troubles were still in the future. He had served as governor of Ohio and in 1896 had been elected to the United States Senate. In 1902 he was reelected, but after being exposed for having accepted fees and loans from Standard Oil Company, he retired in disgrace. In 1914 Foraker attempted a comeback but was defeated in his bid for the Senate by Warren G. Harding, who like McKinley was to become another president from Ohio. The American mountain names scholar Francis P. Farquhar has written that the name Foraker has "not a very happy connotation for so great a mountain."[42]

Herron would have done better had he chosen one of the Indian names for the mountain. Although the Tanaina and Tanana Indians to the north perceived Mount Foraker and Mount McKinley as a single mass and gave them a single name, Denali, the Tanana Indians in the Lake Minchumena area were better able to distinguish the two summits and gave separate names to each. According to the Reverend Hudson Stuck, who made the first ascent of McKinley's true summit, the Indians had two names for Foraker: Sultana, meaning "the woman," and Menlale, "Denali's wife." If persistent efforts to change Mount McKinley's name to Denali ever succeed, perhaps consideration should be given to changing Mount Foraker's name as well.

FREMONT PEAK   13,730ft/4,185m   Wyoming, USA
First ascent, unconfirmed, 1842, J. Fremont with K. Carson and party; confirmed, 1878, the Hayden surveying party.

When young John Charles Fremont, not yet thirty, set out in June 1842 to lead an expedition searching for an overland route to the Pacific, the exploits that were to earn him national fame and the nickname "Pathfinder" were still before him. Among these exploits, vividly told in his widely read report, was the first ascent of this peak in the Wind River Range of Wyoming. That ascent has remained controversial over the years. No one doubts that Fremont climbed a peak in the range, and many people see no reason to doubt that it was this one. But Fremont himself gave the latitude and a good description of the peak he climbed, and according to Orrin Bonney, who did much research about the region and knew it well, Fremont's account more closely fits Mount Woodrow Wilson than Fremont Peak.

Even if Fremont did not make the first ascent, his name on this important peak would be fitting—his expedition was a milestone in the exploration of the West. In Arizona, where he served as governor for four years, is another Fremont Peak, 11,940ft/3,639m, but though Fremont built his reputation largely upon his personal knowledge of the West, he never saw the Arizona peak named for him.

FRONT RANGE   Colorado, USA
Highest elevation, 14,256ft/4,345m, Longs Peak.
See Introduction.

FUJIYAMA   12,388ft/3,776m   Japan
First ascent, A.D. 663, by monks.

Many of the world's mountains have religious significance, but only a few— Mount Sinai in Egypt, Croagh Patrick in Ireland, Adams Peak in Sri Lanka, and Fujiyama in Japan—have actually assumed the nature of major shrines, visited annually by thousands of pilgrims. Unlike the other shrine mountains, however, Fujiyama would be famous even without its religious importance. Located only 20mi/32km from the sea on the main Japanese island of Honshu, Fujiyama rises 11,000ft/3,353m above its southern base; it is the highest point in Japan.

Fujiyama is a singularly beautiful mountain. Its classic, near-perfect cinder cone is the standard to which all other volcanoes are compared. Lafcadio Hearn, the author who in 1897 climbed the mountain, wrote: "The most beautiful sight in Japan, and certainly one of the most beautiful in the world, is the distant apparition of Fuji on cloudless days—more especially days of spring and autumn, when the greater part of the peak is covered with late or with early snows. You can seldom distinguish the snowless base, which remains the same color as the sky; you perceive only the white cone seeming to hang in heaven, and the Japanese comparison of its shape to an inverted half-open fan is made wonderfully exact by the fine streaks that spread downward from the notched top, like shadows of fan-ribs."[137]

Fujiyama is a dormant volcano, but not extinct, and for this reason alone it would command attention. It has erupted eighteen times in recorded history, and the most recent eruption, in 1707, covered Tokyo 50mi/80km away with a layer of ash. From Fujiyama's volcanic nature most likely comes its name.

Or, to be more precise, the best known of its names comes from this, for Fujiyama has many names: Narusawa no takane, Tokiwa-yama, Hatachi-yama, Chiri-yama, Mie-yama, Nii-yama, Midashi-yama, and *many* more. Even its most famous name, Fujiyama, has several variations. Foreigners often refer to it merely as Fuji, but in Japan it's often called more formally Fuji-no-yama, and many Japanese refer to it as Fuji-san, giving to the mountain the same title of respect that would be accorded a venerable lady.

As for the name's meaning, *yama* simply means "mountain," but *fuji*, a very old name element, has caused names scholars considerable difficulty. *Fujiyama* has been translated variously as "mountain of immortality," "mountain of abundance," "big mountain," "There is no mountain like this one," and even "beauty of the long slope hanging in the sky." But most scholars, conceding the lack of a definitive interpretation, agree that the name probably refers to the mountain's volcanic nature and very likely could have come from an aboriginal Ainu word meaning "fire." Thus, "mountain of the goddess of fire" might be closest to the name's original meaning.

The name Fujiyama conforms to the standard Japanese (and Chinese) naming pattern of a specific term followed by a generic one. However, it's possible the name existed in some form in the Ainu language even before the Japanese people arrived in what is now Japan. The Ainu language, like that of the Basques in southwestern Europe, has remained a linguistic singularity; because of its antiquity, the exact meaning of the name Fujiyama probably never will be known.

G

GALDHØPIGGEN   8,097ft/2,468m   Norway
First ascent, 1850, L. Arnesen, S. Floten, and S. Sulheim.

A certain amount of confusion has existed as to which is Norway's highest mountain, Galdhøpiggen or Glittertinden, the peak that faces Galdhøpiggen, across the Visdalen Valley, in the Jotunheimen Mountains 150mi/241km northwest of Oslo. Because most persons do not regard Glittertinden's 100ft/30m snowcap as being legitimately part of the mountain, Galdhøpiggen is accepted generally as the highest. The early inhabitants of the region, however, were likely little concerned with such hair-splitting in the name of preeminence. To them, Galdhøpiggen was "the peak of the mountain side owned by the farms Galde," for that is what the name means, broken into its Norwegian name elements. As Tom Schmidt of the Institute of Name Research at the University of Oslo explains: "The name element *pigg*, 'pointed mountain peak,' is, in fact, fairly uncommon in names of mountains. It is believed to be related to the Old Norse *pikr*, ags. *pic*. Galdhøpiggen is the peak of the mountain Galdhøi probably an elliptic name from Gald-li-høi, the *hø* (cupola-shaped mountain) above Galdlii."[127]

Such a long, freight-train name as Galdhøpiggen is reminiscent of some North American Indian mountain names, but tourists and mountaineers refer to Galdhøpiggen simply as Piggen, much as English mountaineers affectionately call Ben Nevis "the Ben." With similar fond familiarity, nearby Glittertinden is called simply Tinden. Such nicknames probably are relatively recent; there's evidence that the name Galdhøpiggen originally incorporated the more common name element *tinden*, "mountain," instead of *piggen*, and the earliest tourists used the name Galdhøtinden.

GANESH I   24,298ft/7,406m   Nepal–Tibet
First ascent, 1955, R. Lambert, C. Kogan, and E. Gauchet.

In the Hindu mythology of Nepal, Ganesh is the child of Siva; he has an elephant's head atop a small, short-legged body with a potbelly, and the temptation is great to look for resemblances between his unusual appearance and the outlines of the Ganesh peaks. More likely, however, is that Ganesh Himal represents just one of many Siva names so common in Nepal (see Gaurisankar); the inspiration for the name probably was more religious than physiographic, especially as Ganesh, the lord of all the good and bad demons of Siva's train, is very popular in Nepal.

As for the mountains honoring Ganesh, they are nine large ice peaks in a group southeast of the Gurkha and Annapurna Himals. Ganesh I, the highest, straddles the Nepal–Tibet border, something that has impeded successful ascents, for attempts from the west have been uniformly unsuccessful, and access from Tibet has been discouraged. Most of the other Ganesh peaks are in Nepal, but these were added, with qualifications, to Nepal's permitted climbing list only in 1978. As is common in little known and sparsely populated regions of the Himalaya, most of the Ganesh peaks are identified merely as enumerations of the principal summit, though some are beginning to be known by more individual names: Ganesh II is known as Lapsang Karbo, Ganesh IV is Pabil, and Ganesh V has been dubbed the Bat.

The leader beckons. From the Alpine Journal, *Vol. 2, 1864-1866.*

GANNETT PEAK   13,785ft/4,202m   Wyoming, USA
First ascent, 1922, A. Tate and F. Stahlnaker.

While still in his twenties, Henry Gannett (1846–1914) became a leading topographer with the United States government surveys of Colorado and Wyoming headed by Ferdinand V. Hayden. Thus, Gannett surely would have noticed the snow-capped whaleback of a mountain in the Wind River Range that is the highest point in Wyoming, but neither he nor any other member of the survey climbed it, and the peak apparently was unnamed when William Henry Holmes, another topographer with the survey, sketched it—without labelling it—from the top of Fremont Peak. Gannett went on to become in 1882 chief geographer of the United States Geological Survey (USGS), and later he was founder and president of the National Geographic Society. With good reason he often is called "the father of American mapmaking," and it was fitting that when members of the USGS in 1906 determined the altitude of this mountain, they named it after him.

Gannett's preeminence in American geography also resulted in a 10,000ft/3,048m peak in Alaska's Chugach Range being named for him. And in 1922 an attempt was made to change the name of Mount Massive (14,421ft/4,396m), the second highest peak in Colorado, to Mount Gannett; not only did Gannett play a prominent role in mapping Colorado, he also was probably the first person to climb Mount Massive. But the new name would have duplicated the name in Wyoming, there affixed to an even more prominent peak, and the name Mount Massive had become so firmly established by local usage that the attempt failed.

GASHERBRUMS   *Pakistan*

GASHERBRUM I, *26,470ft/8,068m*
First ascent, 1958, P. Schoening and A. Kauffman.
GASHERBRUM II, *26,360ft/8,035m*
First ascent, 1956, F. Moravec, S. Larch, and H. Willenpart.
GASHERBRUM III, *26,090ft/7,952m*
First ascent, 1975, A. Chadwick, W. Rutkiewicz, J. Onyszkiewicz, and K. Zditowieki.
GASHERBRUM IV, *26,000ft/7,925m*
First ascent, 1958, W. Bonatti and C. Mauri.

The region around the Baltoro Glacier in northern Kashmir is perhaps the greatest assemblage of high peaks in the world. Contributing greatly to this distinction are the four Gasherbrums—all 26,000ft/7,925m or higher—located on the ridge enclosing the Upper Baltoro Glacier on the north. Gasherbrums II, III, and IV are grouped rather closely together in an east–west alignment, while Gasherbrum I is three miles southeast along the ridge, where it is partially blocked from view from the west by surrounding peaks. This has resulted in Gasherbrum I often being referred to as Hidden Peak. This name, while still widely used, is not gaining acceptance, and as some people have pointed out, Gasherbrum I is highly visible from the north, south, and east.

The name Gasherbrum has been translated as "shining wall," a name attributed to the 10,000ft/3,048m pale limestone walls of Gasherbrum IV, but H. Adams Carter, a linguist who visited the region in 1974 and queried local informants about place-names, reports that the name comes from the Balti rGasherbrum, from *rgasha*, "beautiful," and *brum*, "mountain."

The Gasherbrums have had considerable significance for mountaineers. The first ascent of Gasherbrum III in 1975 by a Polish women's party was the highest first ascent by women. Also in 1975, Reinhold Messner and Peter Habeler, in making the second ascent of Gasherbrum I, for the first time successfully employed alpine tactics on a 26,248ft/8,000m mountain, opening important new possibilities for big-mountain mountaineering.

GAURISANKAR   *23,440ft/7,145m*   Nepal–Tibet
No first ascent.

Of the deities in the Hindu pantheon, probably none is more revered among the Hindus of the Himalaya than Siva, who along with his associated deities is honored by many Himalayan mountain names, such as Shivling, Nanda Devi, Trisul, and Ganesh. The twin summits of Gaurisankar, standing at the head of the Rowaling region, honor both Siva and his consort. *Sankar* refers to Siva, while *Gauri* is one of the myriad names assumed by his consort (see Nanda Devi); here *Gauri* is interpreted as "the brilliant."

Gaurisankar also is considered sacred by other peoples of the region. To the Buddhist Sherpas living south of the mountain, who can see only its lower, southern summit, 23,000ft/7,010m, the peak is considered the most holy of all in the Himalaya; they know the mountain as Jomo Tsringma. It is holy as well to the Tibetans to the north and east; they call it Trashi Tsering.

The first name by which English-speaking peoples knew the mountain was Peak XX, a designation applied by the Survey of India when the peak's height and location were first determined in 1850. (For a brief time, Peak XX was confused with Peak XV—later known as Everest.)

Gaurisankar's status as a holy mountain is among the reasons the Nepalese government in the past has restricted climbing access to the mountain, and that, combined with severe technical difficulties, has resulted in the mountain being one of very few unclimbed 22,966ft/7,000m peaks in the Himalaya. Before 1964 six expeditions tried unsuccessfully to climb Gaurisankar. In 1959 a strong Japanese party attempted the mountain, and they concluded from their reconnaissance that it cannot be climbed from the south. In 1964 a small British team led by Don Whillans attempted the mountain from the northwest and reached 22,000ft/6,706m before avalanches forced them to retreat. All attempts from the east would have to pass through Tibet, which presents formidable political and logistical difficulties.

GIBRALTAR 1,398ft/426m   Iberian peninsula
First ascent unknown.

In ancient times the two huge rock formations flanking the Strait of Gibraltar were known as the Pillars of Hercules, and they were conspicuous landmarks to the numerous armies using the strait as an invasion route bridging northern Africa and southwestern Europe. The rocks' modern names come from one of the most successful of these invasions. In 711 the Arab general Musa ibn Nusayr, fresh from Islamic victories in North Africa, sent his officer Tariq ibn Zayid across the strait to establish what was to become the beachhead in the Moorish conquest of Spain. Tariq's campaign succeeded, and the Spanish Pillar of Hercules where he landed came to be called by the Arabs Jebel al-Tariq, "mountain of Tariq," soon corrupted by Europeans into Gibraltar. The African Pillar of Hercules was named Jebel Musa for Tariq's commander, who later joined Tariq in Europe.

GLITTERTINDEN 8,045ft/2,452m   Norway
First ascent, 1841, a survey party.

The summit snowcap that has made Glittertinden in the Jotunheimen Mountains a contender for being Norway's highest mountain (Norwegian mapmakers, accepting the peak's 100ft/30m snowcap, show Glittertinden three feet/one meter higher than nearby Galdhøpiggen) also has been said to be the inspiration for the mountain's name. Many persons believe that Glittertinden takes its name from its glittering mantle of snow and ice. This certainly is an attractive and plausible interpretation, one whose appeal led the poet and pioneer tourist A.O. Vinje (1818–1870) to write:

> Though not the highest
> He (Glittertinden) is the fairest.
> Next to Gaustod he is the most beautiful mountain I ever saw.
> Over his shoulders
> He has just thrown his sheer white coat,
> And on his head put a shawl/shroud
> Just like the girls of Gudbrandsdalen (the valley),
> And down his breast and bosom
> Glaciers float to his knees,
> And then this matchless, vivid name.[66]

But like so many poetic explanations for beguiling names, this one probably is more fancy than fact. Because the name Glittertinden is fairly old, despite not appearing in records before circa 1800, definitive determination of the name's origin is not possible. However, Tom Schmidt, of the Institute of Names Research at the University of Oslo, says that the name most likely is derived not from the glittering glaciers but rather from the river Glitra. As he has written: "The names of most Norwegian mountains are given in relation to nearby valleys, farms, lakes, rivers, etcetera, locations which were more important to the mainly agrarian communities than the uninviting peaks. Thus mountain *areas* may often have fairly old names (Dovrefjell, Rondane), but the individual peaks may have names of a modern, tourist type."[127] The name Glittertinden may not be of a "modern, tourist type," but the most popular explanation for the name most likely is.

Just as mountaineers often refer to Galdhøpiggen simply as Piggen, so they often call Glittertinden by the familiar nickname Tinden.

GOING-TO-THE-SUN MOUNTAIN   9,603ft/2,927m   Montana, USA
First ascent unknown.

The poetic name of this mountain in Glacier National Park is a translation from the language of the Blackfoot Indians. This name is not the Blackfoot name for the mountain, however; like most Indian mountain names, the name the Blackfoots had for this mountain was a simple descriptive name, here meaning "lone, high mountain." Rather, the present name, given in 1885, refers to a mythological chief of the Blackfoots who, according to legend, disappeared into the sky by ascending this mountain.

GOSAINTHAN   26,398ft/8,046m   Tibet
First ascent, 1964, Chinese expedition headed by Hsu Ching.
See SHISHA PANGMA.

GRAIAN ALPS   France–Italy
Highest elevation, 13,323ft/4,061m, Gran Paradiso.

The Graian Alps are a northern division of the western Alps, extending from Mount Cenis to the Little St. Bernard Pass and straddling the French–Italian border. The mountains were named by the Romans for the Graiae, three sentinels who, in Roman mythology, watched over their terrifying sisters, the Gorgons. Correspondingly, three mountain sentinels in the Graian Alps are said to watch over the French Savoy and the Italian Piedmont. One of these sentinels is believed to be Rochemelon, 11,608ft/3,538m, the peak first ascended in 1358 by the knight Rotario d'Asti, who had vowed to erect an oratory on the mountain upon his release from imprisonment by the Muslims.

GRAMPIAN MOUNTAINS   Scotland
Highest elevation, 4,406ft/1,343m, Ben Nevis.

The name of this ill-defined mountain group that includes the highest summits of Britain has been very troublesome not only to toponymists but also to geographers, some of whom wish it simply would disappear. For one thing, they say, the name obscures the real topography of the region, which consists of two mountain systems, not one. One is the Drumalban, a central mountain ridge stretching from Ben Lomond to Ben Hope in Sutherland. The other is the Monadh, or Mounth, a transverse ridge running along the south side of the Dee valley and eventually dwindling eastward to end at Tullos Hill opposite Aberdeen. As W. Douglas Simpson has put it: "These two ranges, Drumalban and the Mounth, constitute the real geographical and historic structure of the Central Highlands." Of the single term Grampian he has said: "It is as if I were to present to you, at the level of your eyes, my outstretched hand with the fingers close together. You get the impression of a continuous line, but of course you know that it is composed of separate members. The appearance of continuity is false."[130]

Equally troublesome has been the name's origin. Most persons say it resulted from an error in the transcription of *Life of Agricola*, wherein Tacitus described the victory of his father-in-law in A.D. 84 over the Caledonian confederacy at a place called Mons Graupius. By changing a single letter (u to m), the name Grampian was born. But many place-name experts say this possibility, while tempting, is not the name's origin. Rather, they say, the name's origin and meaning, like those of many Highland mountains, are unknown.

Because of this situation—topographic imprecision and onomastic uncertainty—many persons would agree with Simpson, who concluded: "It is greatly to be wished that the word 'Grampian' should disappear from our atlases, and from books dealing with the Central Highlands."[130]

GRAND TETON
Wyoming, USA
See TETON RANGE.

GREAT SMOKY MOUNTAINS
North Carolina–Tennessee, USA
Highest elevation, 6,642ft/2,024m, Clingmans Dome.

The hazy atmosphere that makes the heavily forested mountains of the Appalachian chain appear blue from a distance and gave the Blue Ridge Mountains their name also is responsible for the name of the Great Smoky Mountains further south. At the time of their settlement by colonists from Europe, the Great Smoky Mountains were home to numerous tribes of Indians, and the smoke from their campfires, as well as that from the hearths of the settlers, doubtless mingled with the heavy, humid air to reinforce the name by which the mountains were known.

GREEN MOUNTAINS
Vermont, USA
Highest elevation, 4,393ft/1,339m, Mount Mansfield.

The Green Mountains of Vermont are the only mountains in the United States that have given their name to an entire state, for that is what Vermont means—"green mountain." The state was named by Dr. Thomas Young, who

102

apparently was exercising Yankee individualism in his choice because he reversed what would be the normal order of the French words making up the name, *mont vert*.[135] Be that as it may, the state and the mountains are aptly named; the long, low chain of forested hills running north–south the length of the state are Vermont's most conspicuous geographical feature, and it is indeed appropriate that the Green Mountains are in the state of "green mountain." (The name also recalls the Revolutionary War heroes, the Green Mountain Boys.)

As for Mount Mansfield, the highest point in the Green Mountains, the Abenaki Indians inhabiting what is now Vermont saw in this peak a resemblance to the head of a moose, and their name for the mountain, Mozodepowadso, means just that, "mountain with a head like a moose." Although the region's white settlers supposedly saw not the profile of a moose but that of a man, the mountain's name has nothing to do with "man" but rather comes from Mansfield, Connecticut, the original home of some of the grantees of the township where Mount Mansfield is located.

MOUNT GREYLOCK   *3,505ft/1,068m*   *Massachusetts, USA*
First ascent unknown.

The highest point in the Berkshire Hills of Massachusetts is said to take its name from its hoary aspect in winter, its top capped with snow and cloaked with trees shorn of leaves. Though many mountain names were inspired by mountain colors, references to gray are rare, surely because a mountain's grayness rarely would be its most distinguishing characteristic, especially when the grayness is due to the mountain being low enough to be covered by deciduous trees. Had Mount Greylock been higher, its summit bare, it very likely could have become one of the world's multitudinous "white mountains," but its name would have been less interesting.

GROSSGLOCKNER   *12,457ft/3,797m*   *Austria*
First ascent, 1800, Count von Salm-Reifferscheif-Krantheim, Bishop of Gurk, and his party of sixty.

Two things distinguish Grossglockner: it is the highest mountain in Austria, a very mountainous country, and it was the first Alpine summit to be climbed by a bishop. A clue to the mountain's character is found in its name. Grossglockner means "big bell" in German, and the gently sloping, bell-shaped configuration of the peak, the highest point on the long ridge of the Hohe Tauern, made the mountain a rather easy ascent for the Bishop of Gurk, who set his mind to climb it at a time when climbing high mountains was considered eccentric behavior, even for the less conventional laity. The bishop took with him a retinue that included a botanist, porters, carpenters, nineteen guides, and his chef. Now an auto road, the Grossglocknerstrasse, takes visitors to the summit.

GUNNBJORNSFJELD   12,139ft/3,700m   Greenland
First ascent, 1935, L.R. Wager, A. Courtland, J.L. Longland, and E. Munke.

Appropriately, the highest mountain in Greenland—and in the Arctic—bears the name of the man credited with discovering Greenland. Toward the beginning of the tenth century a Norwegian named Gunnbjorn returned from a voyage claiming to have found some islands to the west of Iceland, and he may have seen, without landing there, the southern part of the east coast of Greenland. In 982 another Norwegian, Eric the Red, sailed from Iceland to find the land Gunnbjorn told of. He spent the next three years exploring the coasts of the great island he euphemistically was to call Greenland. For many years Gunnbjornsfjeld, located not in the ice-burdened interior but near the coast, was not recognized as Greenland's highest peak, that distinction going instead to Mount Forel, 11,023ft/3,360m, further south.

GURLA MANDHATA   25,355ft/7,728m   Tibet
No first ascent.

Because it is located entirely in Tibet, little is known about this ice peak, and no attempts have been made in recent years to climb it. Dr. Tom Longstaff was in the area in 1905, and it was on Gurla Mandhata that he and his two guides survived an avalanche that carried them 3,000ft/914m down the mountain in two minutes. The best explanation available for the name Gurla Mandhata is that it is a corrupted combination of the Sanskrit word *guru*, "mentor," and Mandhata, a mythical Hindu ruler.

MOUNT GUYOT   6,621ft/2,018m   North Carolina-Tennesee, USA
First ascent unknown.

When Arnold Henry Guyot proposed circa 1860 that the highest summit in the Great Smoky Mountains be named for Thomas Lanier Clingman (see Clingmans Dome), he eliminated the possibility that the region's tallest mountain honor the man who towered above all others in the scientific study of the Smokies—Guyot himself. Thus, when the United States Geographic Board many years later affixed new names to many peaks in the mountains, they honored Guyot by placing his name on the peak northeast of Clingmans Dome that is the second highest in the Smokies.

Guyot certainly wasn't physically towering. Of medium height, lean, bespectacled, he instead looked like what he was, a university professor. Moreover, his command of English was halting, at best. Yet when Guyot's close friend Louis Agassiz in 1847 asked him to come to the United States from their native Switzerland, Guyot brought with him both ideas and zeal that were to transform not only the discipline of geography but also how it was taught in America's schools.

Guyot devoted much of the latter part of his long life to the problems of the Appalachian Mountains, which before him had been studied sporadically and unscientifically. Season after season Guyot came to the Appalachians, especially the Great Smokies, there to tramp tirelessly through the often trailless, jungle-thick vegetation to make barometric measurements and record his observations. After one season he wrote, "I camped out twenty nights, spending a night at every one of the highest summits, so as to have observations at the most favorable hours."[50]

Because of his authority as a preeminent geographer, Guyot's effect on the nomenclature of the region was enormous. Before him, many places were nameless, while many others had several, competing names. Through his own naming and through his maps, Guyot attempted to bring rationality, or at least consistency, to the region's names, and his thoughts on naming mountains remain valid today: "When more than one name has been given to the same point, as happens when it is seen from the valleys on two different sides of the mountain, it seems proper for the observer to adopt the name which appears most natural or more euphonic. When the choice lies between the name of a man and that of a name which is descriptive and characteristic, I should choose the latter. In regard to points without established names, but recently named by scientific observers, and not by residents of the country, the right of priority ought to be respected. . . But it is evident that popular usage will decide in the last resort and that the name universally adopted will, in time, become that which geography ought to accept."

Drawing upon these principles, Guyot successfully supported the highest point in the Smokies being named Clingmans Dome and not Mount Buckley, a minor controversy at the time. But much more significantly, it was Guyot who, by choosing On the Appalachian Mountain System as the title for his great work, helped determine that the name of the range would be Appalachian and not Allegheny, a matter previously not settled (see Appalachian Mountains).

Guyot had come to the Smokies from work in the White Mountains of northern New England, and when he felt his work was done in the Smokies he sought other mountains to explore and study, visiting the Rockies and California's Coast Range. The scientific exploration of mountains was his life's work. Six weeks before his death he wrote to an old friend in Switzerland, "Even last year I could have told you of my seventy-six years and my ability still to climb our mountains, but unhappily it is not so now."[50]

In addition to this peak in the Great Smokies, Guyot's name appears on a peak in the White Mountains of New Hampshire, 4,589ft/1,399m, and on one in Sequoia National Park in California, 12,305ft/3,751m. Few men's names confer more honor on the mountains that bear them.

 **H**

HALEAKALA   10,023ft/3,055m   Hawaii, USA
First ascent unknown.

What a mountain Haleakala must have been! The top of this mammoth
shield volcano dominating the Hawaiian island of Maui vanished long before
human memory in some cataclysmic explosion that left a caldera that begs
wonder at the size of the original mountain. Even today the enormous, gently
sloping mass of Haleakala rises more than 10,000ft/3,048m directly from sea
level, and the caldera is 8mi/13km in diameter, covers 18 square miles/47 square
kilometers, and is ringed by a wall 2,600ft/792m high.

Haleakala is only one of three huge shield volcanoes in the Hawaiian archi-
pelago. South of Maui, forming the island of Hawaii, are Mauna Loa and
Mauna Kea, and all three volcanoes have figured in Hawaiian mythology.
Haleakala, however, is the only one whose name comes from this association;
the other two have simple descriptive names. Haleakala was believed to have
been where the demigod Maui lassoed the sun so that the day might be
lengthened and his mother thereby might have more time to dry her tapa cloth.
The name Haleakala can be translated literally as "house used by the sun."

HALF DOME   8,937ft/2,724m   California, USA
First ascent, 1875, G. Anderson.
First ascent, northwest face, 1957, R. Robbins, J. Gallwas, and M. Sherrick.

In 1865 the Geological Survey of California described Half Dome as "a crest of
granite rising to a height of 4,737ft/1,444m above the valley, perfectly inaccessible, and probably the only one of all the prominent points about the Yosemite
which never has been, and never will be, trodden by a human foot..."[27] They
were wrong, of course; just ten years later G. Anderson scaled the southeast side
using eyehooks he bolted into the rock. (The second ascent was made by lasso-
ing the bolts!) But it was the great northwest face that was the real challenge.
Pleistocene glaciers moving down the Yosemite valley sheared away half of the
granite dome—whence the name—leaving behind a vertical 2,000ft/610m wall
that was unscaled until new techniques were developed in the 1950s, and when
the successful ascent finally was made, it was the first Grade VI climb in North
America. Since then, other routes have been put up the face, one of them
preserving in its name, Tis-sa-ack, an Indian legend concerning Half Dome.
According to Royal Robbins, who along with a climber named Peterson
pioneered the route, Tis-sa-ack was an Indian maiden whose tears of sorrow for
a lost lover became the black streaks on Half Dome's face.[121]

MOUNT HARVARD 14,420ft/4,395m Colorado, USA

First ascent, 1869, members of Whitney surveying expedition.
See COLLEGIATE PEAKS.

HEKLA 4,747ft/1,447m Iceland

First ascent unknown.

For approximately one thousand years farmers in the Southern Lowlands of Iceland have looked with apprehension toward the middle of the mountain crescent half surrounding their sprawling rural district. They have looked toward Hekla, best known and most destructive of Iceland's many volcanoes. Yet unlike the names of many menacing volcanoes, that of Hekla carries rather benign connotations. *Hekla* in Icelandic refers to a kind of cowled or hooded frock, and the volcano's name probably alludes to the cap of clouds, smoke, or snow it often wears.

This is an appealing and plausible explanation, but it's possible it derives more from folk etymology than from fact. One writer has pointed out that the name Hecla appears on three mountains in the Hebrides, where it means "serrated" rather than "hooded." Thus, it's possible the name of the Icelandic mountain

Mount Hekla, Iceland. From William H.D. Adams, Mountains and Mountain Climbing *(London, 1883).*

originally referred to serrations along the mountain's ridge, the cowl meaning having evolved later. (It's interesting to speculate that *hecla*, meaning "serrated," might have some remote connection with the name of a mountain four miles east of Oakridge in Oregon, USA. There a woman in 1872 named the mountain Heckletooth because the tall rocks surrounding its summit reminded her of the teeth of a "heckle," an instrument used for handling flax.)

Local people around Hekla, however, refer to the volcano by another name that leaves no doubt as to its meaning. They call it "the gateway to hell"—and with good reason. When the Reverend Frederick Moore explored the mountain in 1860 he found "gaping ice holes, and great masses of snow side by side with sulphureous steam jets."[138] Moreover, unlike most other volcanic fissures in Iceland, Hekla has erupted not once but often. The first mention of an eruption occurs in the *Hungrvaka*, a history of the conversion of Iceland written circa 1200. It says: "During the episcopate of Bishop Gizur (1082–1118) were many great events: the death of King Knut the Saint on Fyn...the coming up of fire in Hekla, and many other great events, although they are not included here."[138] Early annals speak of this as the "first" eruption of Hekla—it wasn't—but many more were to follow, in 1158, 1206, 1222, 1300, and so on. The eruption of 1300 rent the mountain, creating a deep, rugged valley still visible today, and the word *geyser* comes from the actual Icelandic name for a volcanic spout of steam and water northwest of Hekla.

MOUNT HERMON   *9,232ft/2,814m*   *Lebanon–Syria*
First ascent unknown.

In a region where a long and complex history has endowed even minor natural features with religious significance, it was perhaps inevitable for the prominent Hermon massif comprising the southern end of the Anti-Lebanon Mountains to encompass numerous religious sites. The ancient Phoenicians and Canaanites considered the summit the seat of Baal, and they conducted sacrifices in temples on the mountain as late as the fifth century A.D. On Hermon's slopes the Greeks and the Romans built their own temples, on the sites of still earlier temples.

The ancient Sidonians called the mountain, or part of it, Sirion, a name of uncertain meaning. The ancient Amorites called it Senir, a name that in its Hebrew form means "breastplate" or "body armor," probably referring to the mountain's steep, bare eastern slopes. But to the Jews of the Old Testament it was Hermon, and they expressed their reverence for the mountain in the Psalms, praising God for having created it.

In the Old Testament the mountain is mentioned once using the name's plural form, *hermonim*, most likely a reference to the mountain having three distinct summits, clustered near the middle of a 20mi/32km summit ridge. In addition to being a sacred mountain to the ancient Jews, Mount Hermon also was for them a prominent landmark, marking the northern limit of Joshua's victorious campaigns, and it was part of the dominion of Og.

108

Christians have suggested that Mount Hermon was the site of Christ's Transfiguration. This obviously can never be verified, but the mountain's elevation and location are consistent with Biblical accounts of the mountain Christ ascended.

The original meaning of the name Hermon has been lost. Today the mountain is known locally by its Arabic names, Jebel eth-Thilj, "mount of snow," and Jebel esh-Sheikh, "mount of the elder" or "mount of the chief." The former name refers to Hermon retaining snow even into the summer, long after it has disappeared elsewhere. And the latter name doubtless preserves some of the reverence that ancient people had for the mountain and that led them to believe it was a place sacred to their gods.

HIDDEN PEAK   26,470ft/8,068m   Pakistan
First ascent, 1958, P. Schoening and A. Kauffman.
See GASHERBRUM I.

HIMALAYA MOUNTAINS   Central Asia
Highest elevation, 29,028ft/8,848m, Mount Everest.

If mountains are giants, then the Himalaya are titans. Of the fourteen mountains in the world higher than 26,248ft/8,000m, ten are in the Himalaya, and the range contains more than thirty summits exceeding 25,000ft/7,620m. When Rudyard Kipling's Kim saw the Himalaya he exclaimed: "Surely the gods live here. This is no place for men."[137]

In a sense, Kim was right. The gods are everywhere in the Himalaya, their names affixed to mountains that themselves are regarded as sacred: Nanda Devi, "the goddess Nanda"; Gaurisankar, "Siva and his consort"; Annapurna, "the bountiful goddess"; and many, many more. Even the name Himalaya implies a place above and apart from the human world. Most authorities agree that Himalaya is a joining of two Sanskrit words—*hima*, "snow," and *alaya*, "abode"—to form the poetic and appropriate "abode of the snow."

This translation, accepted by most people, is accurate as far as it goes. But Sanskrit is among the oldest of the Indo–European languages, and when the Aryan invaders introduced Sanskrit into the Indian subcontinent approximately 3,000 years ago during the Indo–European dispersal, they brought with them words that linguists millennia later would use as clues to the vocabulary of the original Indo–European language. Why is it, then, that the Sanskrit *hima* bears no resemblance to the presumed Indo–European root meaning "snow," *snigh* or *snoigh*? Nor, in fact, does it resemble the words for snow in any of the other Indo–European languages, such as English, Latin, Greek, German, Russian, Gaelic, and so forth; the words for snow in those languages clearly are derived from the Indo–European root. Why is the Sanskrit word different?

The answer is that *hima* in Sanskrit means not only "snow" but also "winter," and when the Indo–European words for that season are examined it becomes clear that this is closer to the original meaning of *hima*. The presumed Indo–

109

European ancestor word for winter is *gheim* or *ghyem*, and its offspring include the Slavic *zima*, the Lithuanian *ziema*, the Latin *heims*, the Gaelic *gam*, and, of course, the English *winter*. Thus, the name Himalaya means not merely "abode of the snow" but more fully "abode of the season of snow."

Semantic niceties aside, the name, beautiful in its simplicity, is appropriate. As one writer has observed: "The snowline is to be seen everywhere along this incredible range; the snowcap is the point toward which your eye is drawn no matter in which direction you look."[137] But while Himalaya is almost universally accepted as the name for this great range, many Hindus prefer the name Himachal, also from two Sanskrit words: *hima*, "snow, or winter," and *achal*, "mountain," together meaning "snow mountains."

The immensity and complexity of the Himalaya have resulted in various taxonomic subdivisions. One system divides the range into four mountain groups: the Punjab, the Kumaun, the Nepal, and the Assam. The range also is seen as three roughly parallel lines, called the Great Himalaya (containing the high peaks), the Lesser Himalaya, and the Outer Himalaya. And in the southern crest of the mountains, deep transverse valleys separate the peaks into huge, isolated massifs known as *himals*.

Regarding the pronunciation of the name Himalaya, most references say accenting either the second or the third syllable is acceptable. Because the issue of "correct" pronunciation provokes ire or distress among some people, it's worth repeating the words of the famous nineteenth century explorer of Central Asia, Sir Francis Younghusband: "I ought to be able to pronounce the name of the mountains in which I was born, but I doubt if I can. Himalaya is short for Himal-laya, 'snow abode.' And Indians pronounce it in a flowing, rhythmic way without any very decided accent on either of the first two a's."[157]

HINDU KUSH   Central Asia
Highest elevation, 25,230ft/7,690ft, Tirich Mir.

The mountains of the Hindu Kush, mostly in northeastern Afghanistan, are part of the great Central Asian complex of ranges that includes many of the world's highest peaks. In addition, the Hindu Kush encompasses some of the great trade—and invasion—routes of Central Asia, a fact linked with many of the names the mountains have borne during the centuries. When Alexander the Great crossed the range in 328 B.C., his soldiers called it Parapamissus, "the mountains over which no eagles can fly." Most Greeks, however, referred to the range as the Caucasus because the Caucasus Mountains to the west were the highest mountains known to them and they naturally applied the name to high ranges elsewhere (just as we now refer to mountain flora the world over as alpine). For example, the Greek historian Arrian applied the name Caucasus to the Himalaya, and map-makers later labeled the Hindu Kush as the Indicus Caucasus to distinguish the range from the Colchian Caucasus to the west, the mountains bearing the name today.

The transfer of a name from one mountain range to another is a common if often regrettable practice (consider how many mountain areas world-wide have been called the Alps), and the Hindu Kush many times has borne names originally bestowed elsewhere. Aristotle knew the Hindu Kush as the Asiatic Parnassus, and even into modern times the mountains have been labeled the Paropamirs on some maps.

As for the present name, folklore for generations has translated Hindu Kush to mean "Hindu killer" or "Hindu death." This explanation goes back as far as Baber (1483–1530), founder of the Mongol empire. According to this folk etymology, Hindu slaves, captured in the Indus Valley and marched to market across these mountains, often died from the altitude and cold. Certainly both Genghis Khan and Tamerlane crossed the passes of the Hindu Kush and returned with Hindu slaves.

The true origin of the name, however, is less romantic. Hindu Kush is derived from the Sanskrit, Hindu coming from *sindhuh* meaning "river"—originally applied to the Indus on the western edge of the Indian subcontinent—and Kush from a Sanskrit root related to the Persian *kuh* meaning "mountain." Thus, the name Hindu Kush shares its origin with such names as the Indus, India, Hindustan, the Indian Ocean, the East and West Indies, and the U.S. state of Indiana.

HÖHE TAUERN

Austria

Highest elevation, 12,457ft/3,797m, Grossglockner.

According to legend, the peaks of the Höhe Tauern were the home of ice dwarfs. The basis of the legend is easy to understand. The mountains are the highest in Austria—their name in German means "high towers"—and their upper slopes hold snow and ice much longer than other Austrian mountains. The Höhe Tauern, despite their elevation, present few technical difficulties for mountaineers, and the highest of the peaks, Grossglockner (see entry) was climbed in 1800 by a local bishop whose sixty-member party included nineteen guides, as well as porters, carpenters, and even the bishop's chef.

MOUNT HOOD   11,234ft/3,424m

Oregon, USA

First ascent, 1857, H.L. Pittock, L. Chittenden, W. Cornell, and T.A. Wood.

When the British navigator Captain George Vancouver, exploring the western coast of North America, sailed south from Puget Sound in October 1792, he left behind his lieutenant, William R. Broughton, to explore the entrance to the Columbia River, which had been discovered earlier that year. Vancouver also asked Broughton to investigate a very high, strikingly symmetrical peak they had seen from their ship *Discovery*. Vancouver estimated the peak's height at 25,000ft/7,620m and thought it might be the tallest mountain

111

in the world. Later, Vancouver recorded Broughton's description of the mountain: "A very distant high snowy mountain now appeared rising beautifully conspicuous in the midst of an extensive tract of low, or moderately, elevated land." In his journal entry the next day Vancouver again recorded observations of the mountain and mentioned its naming: "Mr. Broughton honored it with Lord Hood's name; its appearance was magnificent; and it was clothed with snow from its summit, as low down as the high land, by which it was intercepted, rendered it visible."[43]

The naming was an honor indeed, for Lord Hood was the distinguished British seaman and naval hero who as a member of the Board of Admiralty had authorized Vancouver's voyage. Viscount Horatio Nelson, who served under Hood, wrote that he was "the best officer, take him altogether, that England has to boast of, great in all situations which an admiral can be placed in."[43]

When Lewis and Clark saw the mountain in 1805 during their expedition, they called it "falls mountain or Timm Mountain." They noted that "falls mountain" was how local Indians referred to the peak, probably because of numerous cascades nearby, and it has been suggested that the name Timm was derived from the Chinook words *tum tum*, which imitated the sound of a beating heart and thus meant "brave." (Tumwater Falls, which empties into the south end of Puget Sound, was named because its falling water sounds like a beating heart.) Not long after Lewis and Clark's observations, the mountain was named Mount Adams, but this name soon was transferred to the higher peak to the north, and frequent references to the mountain in journals and diaries kept by the early pioneers make clear that the peak was widely known by the name Mount Hood by the 1830s.

The beautiful volcanic cone of Mount Hood is a familiar sight to the residents of Portland, Oregon, only 45mi/72km to the west, and the Mazamas mountaineering club of Portland was organized on Mount Hood's summit in 1894. Until the 1980 eruption of Mount St. Helens, each summer the Mazamas climbed to the summits of Mounts Hood, Adams, and St. Helens—the "three Guardians of the Columbia River"—all visible from Portland.

The Indians of the region also saw the three peaks as related, and the mountains figure in several Indian legends. Fred Beckey tells one of them thus: "The best known of the tribal myths concerns the creation of the Bridge of the Gods and the Columbia River Gorge. Romantic legends were told about two brothers who were the sons of Soclai Tyee (the Great Spirit). Known as Wy'east (Mount Hood) and Klickitat, or Pah-to (Mount Adams), the brothers fought over a beautiful maiden, Loo-wit (Mount St. Helens). During the battles the opposing forces had formed a tunnel through the base of the mountain range. The inland sea drained away and formed a natural bridge above the Columbia River. The destructive warfare continued; finally, great stones were hurled so vigorously onto the bridge that it collapsed; the fallen stones became the Cascades. The lovely Loo-wit belonged to Pah-to, the victor, but her heart was with Wy'east—so she became a sleeping beauty."[12]

HUANDOY 20,980ft/6,395m   Peru
First ascent, 1932, E. Hein and E. Schneider.

Huandoy, a massif of four peaks around a high glacial plateau, like many
Peruvian mountains takes its Quechua name from another natural feature near-
by. Huandoy has been translated by César Morales Arnao, a fluent speaker of
Quechua, to mean "filled with overflowing," and according to him, "This name
most likely comes from the ice-choked glacial lake at the head of the Quebrada
Ancash, which has in past centuries overflowed and caused floods."[2]

HUASCARAN 22,205ft/6,768m   Peru
First ascent of Huascaran Norte, 21,834ft/6,655m, 1908,
A. Peck, R. Taugwalder, and G. Zumtaugwald.
First ascent of Huascaran Sur, 22,205ft/6,768m, 1932,
P. Borchers, W. Bernhard, H. Hoerlin, E. Hein, and E. Schneider.

The temptation is great to find a connection between the names Huascaran
and Huascar, the one belonging to the highest summit in the Cordillera Blanca,
the other to the son and legal heir of the Inca ruler Huayna Capac. Despite a
strong coincidence in sound between the two names, however, the likelihood of
any connection is remote. The Quechua-speaking Incas simply did not name
mountains for individuals, however significant.

Huascaran's name, like most Quechua mountain names, has more humble,
undramatic origins. Most authorities derive the name from two Quechua
words: huasca, "rope," and uran, "down," although they disagree as to how a
combination of these two words came to be applied to the mountain. According to César Morales Arnao, member of the Club Andino Peruano and fluent
speaker of Quechua who has studied Peruvian mountain names, the name
Huascaran first appeared in 1850 as Huascan. "The name was doubtless given
by the local people because the mountain rises above the village of Huashco
...; Huashco gets its name from the word for rope... At the beginning of this
century, during the explorations by the Englishman Enock and the American
Annie Peck, the name appeared as Huascaran, a form which has not changed.
When the mountain was mentioned, it was thought of in connection with the
village and was called Huashco-uran, or 'beyond and down from the village of
Huashco.'"[2]

Other scholars, however, have given a different explanation for the name,
based upon the same two words. The Toponimia Quechua explains it thus:
"Because of (the mountain's) steepness, descent is possible only with the help of
a strong rope. The word uran does not appear in any dictionary but in the very
oldest, that of Fray Domingo of Santo Tomas, and only in it is found uraman,
meaning 'downward.' Because of this, we will dare to presume that uran is a
corruption of uraman. Then the true meaning of Huascaran would be 'mountain so steep that descent is only possible with a rope."[52] Arnao is skeptical of
this explanation, and its plausibility would be bolstered by evidence showing
that the Incas actually used ropes in their mountain travels.

113

Huascaran's name is typically Quechuan in having an ambiguous origin; it is also typical in having a poignant legend associated with it. The descendents of the Incas tell that Huascaran once was a woman with numerous children. Her husband, Canchon, was seduced by a woman named Sutoc, who was a better cook. Consumed with rage and jealousy, Huascaran castrated her husband, then fled, followed by her children, the strongest and biggest closest to her and the smallest farther away; on her back she carried her favorite. When they stopped their flight, they were transformed into the mountains of the Cordillera Blanca, and their tears became the streams flowing into the Rio Santa and the Rio Maranon. Huascaran, of course, became the dominant peak, while the child on her back presumably became Huascaran Norte, the smaller of the twin summits. Canchon, too, turned to stone, and became the most beautiful mountain of the Cordillera Negra, where a peak still bears his name.

CORDILLERA HUAYHUASH
Peru

Highest elevation, 21,759ft/6,632m, Yerupaja.

Why a range as formidable and impressive as the Cordillera Huayhuash of Peru bears the name of an insignificant weasel-like creature is only one of the many mysteries of Andean mountain naming. Finding authoritative translations of Quechua mountain names is relatively easy, but explaining why a particular peak bears a particular name probably is more difficult here than in any other mountain region of the world. To be sure, the little animals known as huayhuash do inhabit the mountains named for them. But as the names scholar George R. Stewart has pointed out, places have not often been named for an animal simply because many of them live there—many bears do not, necessarily, a Bear Mountain make. Rather, a specific incident involving a specific animal usually is required. And since there is no evidence of either an extraordinary abundance of huayhuash in the mountains or a specific incident involving them, speculation about the name's origin is only that.

More easy to understand would have been a name derived from one of the range's distinctive topographic features, such as the numerous turquoise tarns nestled among the peaks. One of these lakes, Ninakocha at the base of Jirishanca, is believed to be the source of the Amazon, known in the region as the Nupe or the Rio Maranon. Also noteworthy are the range's snow and ice formations, rivalling in beauty and challenge those of the Cordillera Blanca to the west. But as to the little creatures known as huayhuash...

HUGIHORN *11,883ft/3,622m*
Switzerland

First ascent, P. Montandon.

Franz Josef Hugi (1796-1855) was a Swiss geologist whose pioneer cold-weather explorations in the Alps caused him to be called "the real father of winter mountaineering." He was the first to penetrate the high Alps in winter, and in January 1832 he spent two weeks in a hut in the mountains. From his observations there Hugi was able to disprove the theory then common that glaciers do not move in winter. The Hugihorn, a peak in the Schreckhorn group, was first climbed and named, appropriately, by another pioneer of winter mountaineering, Paul Montandon.

HUMPHREYS PEAK   *12,633ft/3,851m*   *Arizona, USA*
First ascent unknown.
See SAN FRANCISCO PEAKS.

MOUNT HUNTER   *14,570ft/4,441m*   *Alaska, USA*
First ascent, 1954, F. Beckey, H. Harrer, and H. Meybohm.

To persons who believe a mountain's name should somehow reflect its identity and history, the name of the third highest mountain in the Alaska Range will be a disappointment. Not only does Mount Hunter bear the name of someone who never saw the mountain—not very unusual—it also bears a name that originally was applied to another mountain. In 1903 Robert Dunn, a reporter with the *New York Commercial Advertiser*, journeyed to Alaska, and while there he named a high mountain for the person who had financed his trip, his aunt, Anna Falconnet Hunter. Three years later R.W. Porter with the United States Geological Survey took the name of Dunn's aunt and mistakenly applied it to the peak where it still appears.

Hunter is not the only name that has been proposed for the mountain near the head of the Tokositna Glacier in Denali National Park. In 1906, the same year the name Hunter was applied by mistake, some members of an exploring party referred to the mountain as Little McKinley. And prospectors in the Yentna district to the south were calling the mountain Roosevelt in honor of Theodore Roosevelt. But Hunter is the name that has survived.

INNOMINATE

The name Innominate is a deliberate paradox, similar to the sentence, "This statement is false." Innominate is simply a sesquipedalian way of saying "no name," yet Innominate clearly *is* a name, with all the features and functions of any other name. In fact, Innominate has become a fairly common mountain name. Its first appearance, most likely, was in the English Lake District, where the Innominate Crack has become a popular rock-climbing route. But names such as this seem to catch the fancy of mountaineers, and they have applied it to a mountain (the Innominate) in the Big Horn Mountains in Wyoming, to one of the towers of Patagonia (Torre Innominata), and even to a peak in the Himalaya. Nor does this complete the list of the world's "no-name" mountains; the Trango Tower John Cleare has called "the most elegant" is the Nameless Tower, while a peak in the Dauphine Alps is the Pic Sans Nom, and other examples surely could be found. All these illustrate that even if humans decide not to decide upon a name, a distinctive mountain usually will acquire a name nonetheless, and usually the name will be inspired by one of the mountain's distinguishing characteristics—even if the distinguishing characteristic is the absence of a name!

IXTACCIHUATL   *17,343ft/5,286m*   Mexico
First ascent, 1889, J. de Salis.

South of Mexico City are Mexico's three great volcanoes, the highest mountains in North America outside of Alaska. Of the three, two are still alive; both Popocatapetl (17,887ft/5,452m) and Orizaba (18,700ft/5,700m) have erupted in historic times and still emit steam and gas. Ixtaccihuatl (or Iztaccihuatl), however, is dead, its cone and crater long since having eroded beyond recognition into the mountain's present long, irregular ridge. It's this ridge that is responsible for the mountain's name. The Nahuatl-speaking Aztecs of the region saw in the ridge the shroud-covered body of a woman, dead like the volcano, and they used two Nahuatl words to identify it: *iztac*, "white," and *cihuatl*, "woman." (English-speaking visitors to the mountain, intimidated by the unfamiliar consonant clusters of Nahuatl, often refer to the mountain by its nickname, "Ixty.") The inspiration for the white-woman image is obvious. As the writers O.D. von Engeln and Jane McKelway put it: "The bottom of this mountain is invisible at twilight, and the shape of its snowy top looks like a woman in a white robe lying down; hence, at twilight the mountain appears as a shining, ghost-like figure floating in the air."[39]

This image found expression in Aztec legend. Ixtaccihuatl is closely related to nearby Popocatapetl (see entry) not only in geology but also in myth. Richard Hughes of New Mexico knows the tales well: "There are several beautiful Aztec legends about the mountains, all having to do with love, death, and grief. The best of them tells of an aging Aztec emperor, possessed of a beautiful daughter, Ixtaccihuatl, and many fierce enemies. He offered his daughter's hand to the warrior who could vanquish his foes, and among those who took up the challenge was Popocatapetl, the bravest of all, and the true love of the princess. After a long and bloody war, Popocatapetl was preparing to return in triumph, but his rivals sent back word that he had been slain. The princess languished at the news, and soon died. Finding his beloved dead, at the moment of his triumphant return, Popocatapetl was overcome with irremediable sorrow. He swore

116

never to leave her. He constructed a great pyramid, on which he lay her lifeless body, and by it another on which he stood, holding a torch to illuminate her eternal slumber. Just as the snows could not extinguish his torch, so Popocatapetl's love for his princess has endured through the ages."[68]

MOUNT JACKSON   4,052ft/1,235m   *New Hampshire, USA*

First ascent unknown.
See Introduction.

MOUNT JEFFERSON   10,495ft/3,199m   *Oregon, USA*

First ascent, 1888, by unknown climber.
See MOUNT ADAMS.

JIRISHANCA   20,099ft/6,129m   *Peru*

First ascent, 1957, T. Egger and S. Jungmeier.

Even in west-central Peru's Cordillera Huayhuash, a range of high and impressive mountains, the distinct and dramatic form of Jirishanca impresses itself upon the imaginations of visitors. It has been called "the Matterhorn of Peru" and described as both "a most imposing fang" and "an ox horn sticking from a skull of black rock."[27] Jirishanca has a Quechua name that like many other Quechua mountain names is difficult to translate [*jirish*, "hummingbird," *samca*, "glimmering dream"], but the most common translation is "the hummingbird's beak of ice."[27] The appropriateness of this name was noted by a member of a party that visited the mountain in 1954, three years before the first ascent: "'The Hummingbird's Bill' was topped by a really fantastic structure of neve and cornice on surrealistic lines, about 100 to 130 feet (30 to 40 meters) high. Only a bird could have attained the summit."[73]

JOTUNHEIMEN MOUNTAINS   *Norway*

Highest elevation, 8,097ft/2,468m, Galdhøpiggen.
See Introduction.

Early mountaineers on the Jungfrau. From Francis Gribble, The Early Mountaineers *(London: 1899).*

JUNGFRAU 13,642ft/4,158m   *Switzerland*
First ascent, 1811, J.R. and H. Meyer and party.

The high peaks of the Bernese Oberland—the Mönch, the Eiger, the Finsteraarhorn, and the Jungfrau—form a great wall overlooking the Swiss town of Interlaken to the north. There, Augustinian monks looking at the snow-covered peak dominating the southern skyline were reminded of the town's Augustinian nuns, whose white robes, like the mountain's white slopes, were a familiar sight. The monks reverently called the mountain the Jungfrau, a name that in German means "maiden."

The Jungfrau was among the first of the high Alpine peaks to be climbed. In 1811, before many Englishmen were interested in climbing in the Alps, two Swiss brothers, Johann and Hieronymus Meyer, made the ascent accompanied by chamois hunters.

K2 28,253ft/8,611m   *China–Pakistan*
First ascent, 1954, A. Campagnoni and L. Lacedelli.

Is K2 a name? Some persons have suggested that it's not, that it remains a mere surveyors' notation, and that its presence on the world's second highest mountain is inappropriate and demeaning. (One writer grudgingly called K2 "reminiscent of a sneeze but better than no name at all."[76]) But the Balti porters of the area, who are familiar with the mountain and not with surveyors' symbols, know better. To them the mountain at the head of the Baltoro Glacier in the Karakoram is Ketu, among other names, and they are not bothered at all by the rather unconventional origin of these syllables. Moreover, the name K2 does everything a good place-name should do: it designates a specific place and distinguishes it from other places; it has achieved widespread acceptance, even among persons of different languages; and it has preserved close associations with the mountain's history. In fact, the name K2 serves its mountain far better than many mountain names serve theirs.

The name's history began in 1856 when Lieutenant T.G. Montgomerie, an assistant of Henry Godwin-Austen, director of the Great Trigonometrical Survey of India, designated the mountain on his survey maps with the surveyors' symbol K2, *K* standing for Karakoram and *2* designating the second peak listed. Montgomerie is reported to have remarked to his native assistant on the day they sighted the mountain, "Babu, we have shot the giant." In his notebook

119

Montgomerie wrote, "It was across the plains of Haramukh that I took the first observation to K2, a distance of 137 miles."[76]

Montgomerie was justifiably proud of sighting K2. It is located in one of the world's wildest and least visited regions, so much so that the mountain had no local name when Montgomerie designated it K2. Several names have been put forward as native names for the mountain, but none has been authenticated. Chogori (more properly Ch'ogo Ri, Balti for "great mountain") has been the most common, but H. Adams Carter, a linguist who queried local people in the area about place-names, reports that Chogori and P'alchan Kangri "are synthetic names given by Europeans to K2 and Broad Peak which are not used in Pakistan or by the Baltis, who live closest to the region. In fact, I have heard angry protests by Pakistanis over the use of these names."[22] Other purported but undocumented native names include the Tibetan Mch'og, Skinmang, Dapsang, Lanfafahad, Lamba Pahar, and Chiring. But visitors such as Carter report hearing the Balti porters calling the mountain Ketu or one of its variants, such as Kechu and Kechu Kangri. Thus K2 seems well-established and likely to become even more so.

Still, attempts have been made to change the name, either to confer an honor or in agreement with the person who wrote, "The capital letter with its numeral is all the name we have—quite as meaningless as the hieroglyphics upon a Chinese laundry check."[76] The most nearly successful renaming has been the attempt to name K2 by analogy with Everest, giving it the name of the man who as director of the Survey of India was responsible for its identification and measurement—Godwin-Austen. This name was proposed in 1888 by General J.T. Walker, himself a former surveyor general of India, at a meeting of the Royal Geographical Society. The appeal of the parallel with Everest has been so strong that K2 still is occasionally called Mount Godwin-Austen. Earlier, it was proposed to name the mountain for Sir Andrew Waugh, who in 1843 succeeded Sir George Everest as surveyor general of India. Montgomerie, who made the actual sighting, was proposed as an eponym, as was Prince Albert, Queen Victoria's husband. But none of these names has had the appeal, or the acceptance, of K2, demonstrating that a great mountain, through its size and presence, its history and reputation, can imbue the most obscure of names with meaning and significance—even when the name is a surveyors' symbol.

Actually, many names on and around K2 recall some of the persons prominent in its history. Godwin-Austen's name is on the glacier at the southeast base of the mountain, while Savoia Glacier and Savoia Saddle recall Luigi Amedeo di Savoia, better known as the Duke of the Abruzzi, who in 1909 made an important reconnaissance of K2 and succeeded in reaching 20,000ft/6,096m on the mountain's southeast ridge, the ridge by which the first ascent was made. The ridge since then has been known as the Abruzzi Spur. And De Filippi Glacier honors the geographer in the Abruzzi party.

KAILAS   *22,028ft/6,714m*   *Tibet*
No first ascent.

The Himalaya include many mountains regarded as sacred, most related in some way to the Hindu god Siva (see Gaurisankar, Ganesh, and Nanda Devi), but Kailas in southwestern Tibet is said to be among the most holy of the Himalayan holies. The name, whose original meaning has been lost, appears in ancient Sanskrit literature as the paradise of Siva and Parvati. The Hindu *Mahabharata* refers to the mountain as Kailasa, and Tibetans, who also regard the mountain as sacred, know it as Kang-rim-poche.

Much of this veneration, certainly, is due to the fact that four great rivers—the Indus, the Ganges, the Sutlej, and the Brahmaputra (Tsang Po)—all have their sources within 40mi/64km of the peak. Pilgrims attempt to circle the mountain in three days, traveling along a trail that takes them 25mi/40km through very rugged mountain terrain, including passes as high as 18,000ft/5,486m. Some zealots make the circuit by measuring the distance with their bodies, lying on the ground, extending their arms, marking their reach with metal-tipped gloves, and then rising to repeat the process. The entire ordeal, taking at least three weeks, is said to require more than 20,000 prostrations.

The nineteenth century Swedish explorer Sven Hedin called Kailas the most famous mountain in the world. No one today would say that, a reminder that the mountain's location in Tibet made it better known to early explorers from the West than to later ones. The first westerners to see the mountain most likely were the Portuguese Jesuits who founded a church in 1626 near the headwaters of the Sutlej. In 1735 the mountain appeared on D'Anville's map of Tibet as Kontaisse, and subsequent publications listed it variously as Gang-dis-ri and Tisre—all said to be corruptions of an old Tibetan name. In the nineteenth and early twentieth centuries, western visitors to Tibet mentioned the mountain, and in 1926 Hugh Ruttledge, his wife, and Colonel R.C. Wilson became the first Europeans to walk the sacred circumference. Now, however, westerners are denied access to the mountain, and though Wilson reported the east ridge as offering a possible route to the summit, permission to climb Kailas is not likely to be granted.

KAMET   *25,447ft/7,756m*   *India*
First ascent, 1931, F. Smythe, E. Shipton, R.L. Holdsworth, and L. Sherpa.

The giant Himalayan mountain Kamet was discovered in 1848 by the British surveyor Richard Strachey, who was measuring the peaks visible from a point near the Indian hill station of Naini-tal. One of the peaks, he found, topped all its neighbors by more than 1,000ft/305m, rising to an elevation of more than 25,000ft/7,620m and dominating that portion of the Garhwal Himalaya. The mountain was called Kamet, for reasons unknown, but it was known to Tibetans as Kangmen, a name reported to mean, appropriately, "huge grandmother of the sacred snow chain."

Later, it was discovered that Nanda Devi (25,645ft/7,817m) was the highest summit in British territory. That mountain was guarded, however, by its seemingly impregnable "Sanctuary," a ring of peaks — twelve more than 21,000ft/6,401m — 70mi/113km in diameter, with no known entrance under 17,000ft/5,181m except the formidable Rishiganga Gorge, not penetrated until 1934. Thus, much British mountaineering in the Himalaya was focused on Kamet, including reconnaissances and attempts by T.G. Longstaff, A.M. Slingsby, and C.F. Meade. The successful ascent in 1931 by a strong British party made Kamet the first Himalayan giant over 25,000ft/7,620m to be climbed.

KANCHENJUNGA 28,168ft/8,585m   Nepal–Sikkim
First ascent, 1955, G. Band and J. Brown.

The Tibetan-speaking people of Sikkim call this, the world's third highest mountain, by a series of Tibetan words—*kang-chen-zod-nga*—that together mean "five great treasuries of the snow." The name reflects something of the religious significance the mountain has for the Sikkimese, who believe it to be the abode of a goddess, but this beautiful, poetic name also has significance for western mountaineers and others interested in the mountain's history and character. Although Kanchenjunga actually has seven major summits rather than five, the apellation "treasuries of the snow" certainly is accurate. The avalanches Kanchenjunga throws down have been described as the world's largest, and the mountain's climbing history is replete with disaster or near-disaster caused by avalanches. In 1905 an avalanche killed four members of the first serious international attempt on the mountain, and an avalanche nearly wiped out the 1930 international expedition headed by G.O. Dyhrenfurth. Similar instances have been common on Kanchenjunga.

In a sense, the mountain's "treasuries of the snow" have remained sealed and inviolate, despite several successful assaults. When George Band and Joe Brown made the first ascent in 1955, they did not stand on the actual summit but stopped slightly short of it, thus keeping a promise made by the expedition's leader, Dr. R.C. Evans, to the Maharajah of Sikkim. Subsequent expeditions similarly have respected the Sikkimese people's veneration of the mountain.

KARAKORAM   Central Asia
Highest elevation, 28,253ft/8,611m, K2.

Of the fourteen peaks in the world whose elevations exceed 26,248ft/8,000m, the four not found in the Himalaya are found in the sister mountain range, the Karakoram. These peaks include K2, the world's second tallest; the others are Gasherbrum I (26,470ft/8,068m), Broad Peak (26,400ft/8,047m), and Gasherbrum II (26,360ft/8,035m). The Karakoram also feed the world's longest mountain glaciers—the Siachen (45mi/72km), the Hispar (38mi/61km), the Biafo (37mi/59km), the Baltoro (35mi/57km), and the Batura (35mi/57km). Everywhere, travelers in the range see a wilderness of white; rivers of ice, and white mountains stacked into the distance seemingly without end. Why, then, does the name of the range come from Altaic words meaning "black pass" or "black earth"?

The generally accepted answer is that the name originally was applied not to the mountains but was transferred to them from Karakoram Pass, 18,550ft/ 5,654m high, the crest of an ancient and well-known trade route connecting India and Pakistan with Central Asia. Unfortunately, at least some travelers to the pass report that the color of the earth and rocks there is not black, but yellow.

Because of this, some writers have suggested that the pass, in turn, took its name from Karakorum, capital of the Mongols under Genghis Khan. While the Mongols were overlords of most of Europe and Asia, the name of their remote capital would have become well known, and the name easily could have been transferred to the important pass along one of the main routes leading to the city. According to tradition, the sands surrounding the city Karakorum were black.

Whatever the name's history, the identification with black is clear. *Kara*, "black," is common in both Turkish and Mongolian, both Altaic languages. The Mongolians call the mountain range the Kara-kherem, "the black barrier." (They call the Great Wall of China Tsagaan-kherem, "the white barrier.") *Korum* means "pass" in Mongolian, and names such as Takta-korum and Ak-korum are found in the Kun Lun Range. *Korum* is said to mean "earth" or "gravel" in Turkish.

Just as opinions have differed regarding the name's origin, so they have differed regarding its spelling. The name appeared as Kurrakooram on an 1808 map; it was spelled Kara-Kurum in 1842 and later was Karakoorum. The present spelling, with *a* in the final syllable, seems to be winning general acceptance, even though the Committee on Geographic Names of the Royal Geographic Society, called upon to act as an arbiter, decided in favor of *u*.

Even the very use of the name has been challenged. Some writers have preferred to call the range the Muztagh Mountains. *Muztagh* is an Altaic word meaning "snow-ice mountain," seemingly an appropriate alternative to Karakoram. But Eric Shipton reports that throughout much of Central Asia *muztagh* already is applied generically to any snowy mountain or range and that, strictly speaking, *muztagh* means not icy peaks but high pastures, just as the word *alpen* originally meant high mountain meadows to the Swiss and not the peaks surrounding them.

The remoteness and sparse population of the Karakoram have influenced the names found there. The caravans crossing the two main trade routes through the mountains didn't bother to name the surrounding peaks; of the four 26,248ft/8,000m Karakoram peaks, two were nameless until relatively recent European explorations, and even the peaks of the Gasherbrum group are distinguished from each other by Roman numerals. Although the journeys of Father Ippolito Desideri brought Europeans to the Karakoram in 1715, true geographical explorations began only in the nineteenth century. When British surveyors finally explored the range, they found many of even the tallest peaks without local names. Thus, K2 (see entry), the world's second highest mountain, is designated only by a surveyors' symbol.

KARL MARX PEAK   22,068ft/6,726m   USSR
First ascent, 1946, V. Abalakov, A. Sikorenko, and Y. Ivanov.
See LENIN PEAK.

MOUNT KATAHDIN   5,268ft/1,606m   Maine, USA
First ascent, 1804, C. Turner.

The first European to see Mount Katahdin in what is now northern Maine was the French explorer Samuel de Champlain, who sighted the mountain in 1605. The highest point in Maine, Mount Katahdin, rises dramatically above an ocean of dense forest and is the only land above timberline for more than a hundred miles. The mountain's name reflects its prominence; it comes from an Abenaki Indian word meaning simply "main mountain." (Attempts to approximate the Indian word have resulted in numerous variant spellings of the name Katahdin. Henry David Thoreau, for example, spelled the name Ktaadn in his book describing his journey to the mountain.)

The region's Indians regarded mountains such as Katahdin and the highest peaks of the White Mountains to the west as the abode of evil spirits, and Pamola, Katahdin's eastern summit, was said by the Indians to be the name of the mountain's fierce, avenging spirit. When the pioneer Charles Turner in 1804 made the first recorded ascent of Katahdin, he did so despite strong Indian warnings that spirits such as Pamola would harm him.

MOUNT KENYA   17,058ft/5,199m   Kenya
First ascent, 1899, H. Mackinder, C. Ollier, and J. Brocherel.

Mount Kenya, the second highest mountain in Africa, has a dramatic two-horned summit and poses a greater mountaineering challenge than Kilimanjaro. As William Bueler has remarked, "Mount Kenya well deserves the distinction of being the only mountain in the world that has given its name to an entire country."[20]

But while the distinction of the name is easily established, its origins are not. Like many mountain names derived from native words, Kenya has suffered from confusion and distortion by non-native speakers. The best explanation of the name has been presented by Marshall A. McPhee in his book *Kenya*. He says problems with the name began in 1849 with the first European sighting of the mountain, by the German missionary Dr. Johann L. Krapf. Seeing the peak from the Kamba village of Kitui, Krapf called the mountain Kima ja Kegnia, which he took to be the Kamba name for "mount of whiteness." But as McPhee explains: "Krapf seems to have misunderstood the local dialect for there is no such word as *kegnia* in the Kamba vocabulary. However, the name Kegnia has persisted and developed by common usage into Kenya, which is similar to *erukenya*, the Masai description of a mountain shrouded in mist. The Kikuyu name for Mount Kenya is Kere-Nyaga, the 'mountain of mystery.' One theory

124

of the misunderstanding by Krapf of the Kamba description of the mountain is that the Kamba have neither the letter R nor the letter G standing alone in their language and therefore they pronounce Kere-Nyaga as Kiinyaa. The Kamba, of course, are closely related to the Kikuyu, and their venacular is similar."

The night after Krapf first saw Mount Kenya he wrote about it in his journal: "It appeared to me like a gigantic wall, on whose summit I observed two immense towers, or horns, as you might call them."[85] His reports, however, were not believed in Europe; a snow-capped mountain on the equator simply was not credible.

When Sir Halford Mackinder led a large expedition to the mountain in 1899, he found the mountain as Krapf had described it, including the two horns making up the summit. These Mackinder named Batian (17,058ft/5,199m) and Nelion (17,022ft/5,188m) after two well-known Masai chiefs. (Point Lenana, a secondary summit, is named for the son of one of the chiefs.) The gap separating the two horns is called the Gate of the Mists.

KHAN TENGRI   22,949ft/6,995m   USSR–China
First ascent, 1931, expedition of M.T. Pogrebetsky.

For seventy-five years, from its sighting in 1857 by the Russian geographer P.P. Semenov until 1932, Khan Tengri was believed to be the highest mountain in the Tien Shan Range. And it was not until 1946 that the location of a higher peak, first suspected fourteen years earlier, was confirmed. Now Khan Tengri is recognized as the second highest summit in the Tien Shan, after Pobeda Peak (24,406ft/7,438m), but Khan Tengri's name is a reminder that the mountain's reputation rested not solely on its elevation. *Khan Tengri* is two Khirgiz words that have been translated as "prince of the spirits" and "lord of the skies," fitting metaphors for a lordly, pyramid-mountain, removed from human habitation by nearly 100mi/161km and guarded, as if by a moat, by deep gorges. The Russian traveler Alexander Inonoff called Khan Tengri "the throne of the Almighty," and he wrote that its snows reflect the sun "in myriads of sparkles, sometimes with the red shade of rubies, sometimes with the tender light of opals."[76]

KICHATNA SPIRES   8,985ft/2,739m   Alaska, USA
First ascent, 1966, R. Millikan and A. Davidson.

Because of their dramatic appearance and the climbing interest focused on them in recent years, it's easy sometimes to forget that the Kichatna Spires actually are only part of a larger mountain group, the Kichatna Mountains, stretching in a 40mi/64km range 70mi/113km southwest of Mount McKinley in the Alaska Range. Moreover, the name Kichatna originally did not apply to the mountains at all but rather to the river whose headwaters are at the Caldwell Glacier near the spires. Lieutenant J.S. Herron of the United States Army was exploring in the region in 1899, and he adopted the Indian name of the river, writing it "Kee-chat-no," meaning "Kichat River."[100]

As for the spires themselves, the names Kichatna Spires and Cathedral Spires increasingly are used interchangeably. Although time and usage will determine which name prevails, the purpose of identification will be best served if it is Kichatna, even though the name Kichatna is shared by the mountains and the river. The *Dictionary of Alaska Place-Names* lists more than twenty places named Cathedral in that state alone, and Cathedral occurs frequently elsewhere as well; moreover, the name Cathedral Spires is duplicated on a formation in Yosemite National Park in California. As the mountaineer Andrew Embick has summarized the situation: "Because of the plethora of mountaineering place-names involving 'cathedral,' it is urged that the area be generally referred to as the 'Kichatna Spires,' recognizing that to be strictly accurate one should say 'Cathedral Spires of the Kichatna Mountains.'"[37]

KILIMANJARO   19,340ft/5,895m   *Tanzania*
First ascent, 1889, H. Meyer and L. Purtscheller.

For as long as people have explored and traded along the east coast of Africa, they have been cognizant of Kilimanjaro, Africa's highest peak and the continent's greatest landmark. With its base measuring 30 by 50 mi/48 by 80 km, and its great bulk rising as much as 16,000ft/4,877m above the surrounding plain, Kilimanjaro has been called the most visible mountain on earth; it can be seen from the Indian Ocean 160mi/257km away and from Mount Kenya 200mi/322km away. Mention of the peak goes back nearly as far as the recorded history of East Africa. In his *Geography*, written in the second century A.D., Ptolemy spoke of a "great snow mountain" lying inland from the since-lost city of Rhapta. More than a thousand years later a Spanish geographer, Fernandez de Encisco, wrote in 1519 that "west (of Mombasa) stands the Ethiopean Mount Olympus, which is exceedingly high, and beyond it are the mountains of the moon, in which are the sources of the Nile."[131]

By the time Europeans began exploring Africa in earnest in the nineteenth century, then, the mountain already was well known, if not explored. Even a name for it already was in place; inhabitants of the coast called it Kilima Ndscharo, a name that in its Anglicized form the mountain has borne ever since. But as to the origin of that name, there is only confusion.

In 1848 two German missionaries, Johannes Rebmann and Ludwig Krapf, became the first Europeans actually to visit the mountain. They ascribed the name to two Swahili words meaning "great mountain" or alternatively "mountain of the caravans," from its serving as a landmark for traders, but the Swahili words *kilima* and *njaro* also have been translated as "mountain of the god of cold" and "mountain of the cold demons." The Chagga people, whose homeland includes the mountain, have another explanation for the name. According to an oral tradition of the Kilema branch of the Chagga, one of their ancestors was called Kilema and he was the son of Njaro, thus providing a tidy explanation for the names of both the tribe and the mountain. Some anthropologists, however, have been skeptical of this folk etymology, and most other branches of the Chagga know the mountain not as Kilimanjaro but as Kibo, a name western geographers have adopted for Kilimanjaro's main summit. Other tribes in the region have had their own names for the mountain. The Kamba call it Kimaja Jeu, "white mountain," and the Masai and Wakuavi call it Ol Donyo Eibor, also meaning "white mountain."

The Chagga people, while viewing Kibo as a benign force and innocent of the witchcraft and magic most primitive peoples associate with high mountains, nonetheless had no interest in exploring its cold upper slopes. Probably the first to do that were the members of an exploratory party sent in the early nineteenth century by the coastal king Rungua; he had been told that the white glistening on the mountain was silver, and he wanted some. According to the legend, usually regarded as apocryphal, only one member of the party survived, with frostbitten hands and feet turned inward from the cold.

KINABALU   13,455ft/4,101m   Borneo
First ascent, 1851, H. Low.

Kinabalu, located at Borneo's northern tip and rising 5,000ft/1,524m higher than any other mountain on the island, is regarded with superstitious awe and fear by the local tribesmen. Its name, which comes from their language, means "mountain of the dead," and they believe that a species of grass on the peak is grazed by spectral buffaloes following their dead masters into the spirit world.

Mountaineers venturing to the mountain have encountered no supernatural obstacles, however; their main difficulties have been bushwhacking through dense tropical forest to get to the peak and confronting almost daily fog and rain on the mountain itself. The first person to climb Kinabalu was Hugh Low, an English colonial official, and the main summit, Lows Peak, was named for him, as was a 4,000ft/1,219m gully incising the mountain from the north.

KINGS PEAK   13,528ft/4,123m   Utah, USA
First ascent unknown.
See WHEELER PEAK.

MOUNT KOSCIUSZKO   7,316ft/2,230m   Australia
First ascent, 1839, P. de Strzelecki.

In 1839 the map of Australia still contained substantial blank areas, but these rapidly were being filled in by explorers. One of these was a forty-two-year-old Pole named Paul Edmund de Strzelecki, who had undertaken to do a geological survey of the uncharted country. The field work for his geological map took him to New South Wales and eventually to the Great Dividing Range, where he ascended alone what he correctly considered to be the continent's highest peak. He named it for another Pole, Tadeusz Kosciuszko (1746–1817).

Kosciuszko and Strzelecki had much in common. Although both were born in Poland, both left their homeland early to find honor and recognition elsewhere. Kosciuszko at age thirty came to the New World to serve liberty as a colonel of engineers in the American Revolutionary Army. He returned to Poland to fight for Polish independence from Russia, but he was defeated in battle and disappointed in diplomacy. He served the cause of liberty all his life, and France conferred citizenship on him. But he never was able to win freedom for Poland, and he spent most of his later life away from his native country.

Strzelecki too spent most of his adult life far from Poland. A self-taught geologist, his surveys took him to Canada and the islands of the South Pacific before he arrived in Australia, where he eventually became a citizen. Like Kosciuszko, Strzelecki was a valiant idealist; he opposed the slave trade and administered famine relief funds in Ireland with unprecedented efficiency. Like Kosciuszko, he had a keen and adventurous mind. But he was passed over for an important surveying commission, and in his later years he grew resentful of earlier poor treatment by his fellow Australians. He died in 1873 disappointed and pessimistic, leaving behind, like Kosciuszko, the sadness of ideals and expectations unfulfilled.

Strzelecki's ascent of Mount Kosciuszko was not an outstanding mountaineering achievement. Australia is the least mountainous of the continents, and the only one with no mountains high enough to support glaciers. Mount Kosciuszko, the site of a popular resort, is not a difficult climb. A motor road once led to the summit, but it has since been closed to protect the mountain's wilderness values.

KUH LALEH-ZAR   14,350ft/4,374m   Iran
First ascent unknown.
See Introduction.

KUN LUN MOUNTAINS   China
Highest elevation, 25,340ft/7,724m, Ulugh Muztagh.

Very likely no mountains on earth are less known to westerners than those of the Kun Lun Range in Central Asia. Just as the Himalaya form the southern battlement guarding the Tibetan plateau, the Kun Lun Mountains form the northern battlement, and like the Himalaya, the Kun Lun Range consists of linear, roughly parallel subranges, the Astin Tagh on the north and the Arka Tagh on the south. Not only are the Kun Lun peaks geographically remote, reached only by crossing vast distances of very sparsely populated deserts and steppes, the mountains also are politically inaccessible; the range forms the border between western China and northern Tibet, both regions traditionally off-limits to visitors.

Just as the mountains of the Kun Lun are alien to most westerners, so are the origin and meaning of the range's name, which comes from the time of the ancient Chinese emperors and is very old, appearing in records about 2,000 years ago, and then out of use. According to Lin Ziyu, who has researched the origin of this name, the noun *kun lun* refers to a structure in an imperial hall where the emperor held various grand ceremonies, such as court meetings and sacrificial rites.[158] In *The Records of History* by Si Ma-qian (145B.C.–?) of the western Han Dynasty, the author described a *kun lun* thus: "In the draft of the imperial hall there is a temple-like wall-less, two-story structure roofed with thatch. The lower story is the passage of water running around in the moat of the hall; the upper story is used as the passage for men, with its entrance at the southwestern side. This structure is called *kun lun*."[158] A slightly later work, *A History of the Han Dynasty* by Bangu (A.D. 32–92) elaborates: "Kun Lun is the name of a mountain located in the southwestern part of Jiu Quan ("wine spring") County, Gansu Province, and was once a frontier fortress. The mountain is so named because it looks like a *kun lun*." For the name to spread from a single, well-known mountain to encompass eventually the entire range is merely one more example of the natural evolution of many mountain names throughout the world.

According to the Chinese place-names scholar Zhu Bin, the Kun Lun Mountains, while little known to westerners, are very important to the Chinese and are regarded as "the Chinese Olympus, where all the Chinese gods live." But as to the origins of the name, most Chinese are ignorant.[14]

 *L*

LASSEN PEAK   *10,457ft/3,187m*   *California, USA*
First ascent unknown.

Until the eruption in 1980 of Mount St. Helens, Lassen Peak, the southernmost major peak of the Cascade Range, was the most recently active volcano in the contiguous United States, with minor eruptions as late as 1914–21. Since then, however, Lassen Peak has remained dormant, and each year thousands of tourists visit the national park named for the mountain. The peak itself was named by local residents for Peter Lassen, a native of Denmark who came to California in 1840 and became a prominent pioneer in northeastern California; Lassen County also is named for him. Before Peter Lassen's time, the volcano was known as Mount Joseph, a name given in 1827, or one of the variants that evolved from it: Mount St. Joseph, Mount St. Jose, or Mount San Jose. By 1851 the peak was called Lassens Butte, and the present name gradually replaced earlier names.

"*The whirling snow mocked our efforts.*" *From Edward Whymper,* Travels amongst the Great Andes of the Equator *(London: 1883).*

LAURENTIAN MOUNTAINS
Quebec, Canada
Highest elevation, 3,905ft/1,190m

The Laurentian Mountains of southern Quebec owe their distinction among mountains not to their elevation but to their age. They are among the oldest mountains in the world—and certainly in North America—and appropriately their name is among the continent's oldest too. On 7 August 1535, the French explorer Jacques Cartier sought refuge from bad weather in a small bay, and he gratefully named it after St. Lawrence, whose day it was. From the bay the name spread to include the gulf, then the river, and eventually the mountains.

The oldest rocks of the Laurentians have been estimated at 2,500 million years. Because of their great age, the mountains have been eroded to a hummocky peneplain now better known for its lakes—at least 70,000—than for its summits. The best known of the Laurentian peaks is Mont Tremblant (3,150ft/960m), French for "trembling mountain," a name most likely derived from earthquake activity at some time.

LEBANON RANGE
Lebanon
Highest elevation, 10,131ft/3,088m, Qurnet es Sauda.

For nearly half the year the high slopes of the Lebanon Range are white with snow, the precious meltwater from them nourishing the famed cedars of Lebanon that still grow on the mountain's slopes, and bringing to springtime bloom the red anemones that reminded the ancient Greeks of the blood of the slain god Adonis. The ancient Aramaic-speaking Phoenicians of the region looked at the snowy mountains and were reminded of the whiteness of milk. The name they gave the range means "white as milk" or more simply "white," and in various forms it has persisted to the present, appearing in Latin as Mons Libanus and in Arabic as Jebel Liban.

In the Lebanon Range, as in mountains elsewhere, people facing ethnic or religious persecution have found sanctuary, and for more than a thousand years the Lebanon Range has been the refuge of the Maronite Christian and the Druse Muslim sects. The mountains also are the last redoubt of the cedars for which Lebanon was famous throughout the ancient world. On the slopes of Qurnet es Sauda a few small groves survive, the only remnants of the forests that once yielded the lumber to build cities and form the hulls of the vast Phoenician merchant fleet.

LENIN PEAK   *23,382ft/7,127m*   USSR
First ascent, 1928, E. Allwein, K. Wein, and E. Schneider.

Until it was renamed by the Soviet government, the third highest peak in the Soviet Union, located in the northern Pamirs, was called Mount Kaufmann, a name honoring Constantine Petrovich Kaufmann, the conqueror and governor-general of Russian Turkestan from 1867 until his death in 1882. The present name, like many in the Pamirs (such as Karl Marx Peak, 22,068ft/ 6,726m), was given to commemorate a leading figure of the Russian Revolution and Communist ideology, and until 1933 Lenin Peak was believed the highest in the USSR. In that year, however, Stalin Peak (24,590ft/7,495m) was discovered, and later Pobeda Peak (24,406ft/7,439m) also was determined to be higher than Lenin Peak. But while the elevation of Lenin Peak has been eclipsed by subsequent events, the stature of its eponym has not. When Joseph Stalin's reputation darkened after his death, Stalin Peak was renamed Peak of Communism, but Lenin Peak has continued to honor Vladimir Ilyich Ulyanov, better known as Lenin.

LHOTSE   27,890ft/8,501m   Nepal–Tibet
First ascent, 1956, E. Reiss and F. Luchsinger.

Only by being located next to Everest could a mountain such as Lhotse— fourth highest in the world—have been so neglected for so long. Indeed, for many years Lhotse was not thought to be a separate mountain at all but rather a subsidiary summit of Everest, and no attempts were made to climb it until after the conquest of Everest in 1953. This subordinate relationship to its higher neighbor is reflected in Lhotse's name: it's Tibetan and means "south peak"— south of Everest, that is.

Actually, Lhotse is only one of several features that owe their names to their relation to Everest. West of Everest is Nuptse, 25,850ft/7,879m, "west peak." North is Changtse, 24,764ft/7,548m, "north peak." The cols connecting these peaks to Everest also have directional names: Chang La, "north col," joins Changtse with Everest, while Nuptse and Everest are connected by the Lho La, "south col." The famous South Col between Everest and Lhotse has no Tibetan name. This situation has caused considerable confusion and controversey, and the Swiss particularly, led by Marcel Kurz and G.O. Dyhrenfurth, have felt that the names of the cols should be consistent with the names of the peaks. Thus they unilaterally took the name Lho La from its present location near Nuptse and applied it to the South Col. Although Nup La, "west col," would seem a logical new name for the west col, the Swiss called it Khumbu La.

This attempt by the Swiss to establish consistency among the names in the Everest region was well-intentioned, and it has received considerable support. As Louis C. Baume, chronicler of the Himalaya, has written: "There is indeed some force in their point of view; it is more symmetrical and much tidier." But Baume goes on to say, "It ignores the origins of names and the important historical associations that lie behind them."[11] And Professor N.E. Odell, in a letter to the *Alpine Journal*, has pointed out that the name Lho La is not as illogical as it might seem, the Lho La being indeed a "south col" to persons traveling up the Rongbuk Glacier from Tibet, the route of early explorers.[11]

The controversy remains unresolved. Baume's own sympathies clearly are with preserving the established usage, and he quotes Fosco Mariani, who wrote in *Karakoram: the Ascent of Gasherbrum IV:* "In this whole matter, nothing is worse than systematization. System is the catalog, the tags and labels; it is a museum, death; and place names are too important, too charged with spiritual magnetism, to be left in the hands of bureaucrats and commissions. They need the touch of life!"[11] There is a practical argument, too, against altering established names to achieve consistency. As examples such as Mount McKinley in Alaska, Mount Massive in Colorado, K2 in the Karakoram, and many others show, changing the name of even a single mountain is difficult enough, but reshuffling an entire complex of names usually is as easy and successful as transplanting a forest of trees, and such attempts inevitably result not in less confusion but more.

LOCHNAGAR   *3,786ft/1,154m*   *Scotland*
First ascent unknown.
See CAIRNGORM MOUNTAINS.

MOUNT LOGAN   *19,850ft/6,050m*   *Yukon, Canada*
First ascent, 1925, A.H. MacCarthy, H. Lambert, W. Foster, L. Lindsay, N. Read, and A. Carpé.

Two mountains in Canada bear the name Mount Logan; one is the peak in the St. Elias Range of the southwestern Yukon, and the other is a 3,700ft/ 1,128m summit in the Shickshock Mountains of eastern Quebec. Both were named for William E. Logan, pioneer geologist and first director of the Geological Survey of Canada. But there the resemblances cease. The Yukon mountain not only is the second highest mountain in North America and the highest in Canada, but it also has been called the most massive mountain in the world, its summit plateau 20mi/32km long and its myriad outliers and ridges rising from a glacier system nearly as large as Switzerland.

The enormous scale of this mountain mass, barring easy access or exploration, resulted, ironically, in the mountain's existence not even being suspected until 1890, and thus the mountain was not named until relatively late. The mountain's size similarly posed gargantuan problems for the party that made the first ascent, more than a quarter of a century later. To prepare for the assault, Captain A.H. MacCarthy and a sourdough guide named Andy Taylor spent seventy days during the winter establishing and stocking a series of camps, combating some of the world's worst weather. The actual ascent the following spring required a 93mi/150km approach via the Chitina Valley, followed by a 93mi/150km trek across glaciers. For forty-four consecutive days the party did not set foot on rock or earth, and during a ten-day period spent above 14,764ft/ 4,500m the temperatures ranged between minus 18 and minus 33 degrees centigrade.

LONGS PEAK   14,256ft/4,345m   Colorado, USA
First ascent unknown.

In 1820, a young U.S. Army officer named Stephen H. Long led twenty-two men on horseback along Colorado's Front Range. The botanist and geologist for the expedition was twenty-three-year-old Dr. Edwin James. The journal James kept, published in 1823, mentioned a high peak to the northwest. Although James labeled it Highest Peak on his map, it appeared as Longs Peak on an 1829 map, and in 1842 the explorer John C. Fremont noted that the name Longs Peak was being used among the fur traders of the region.

Long's expedition did not really discover Longs Peak. The Arapaho and Ute Indians of central Colorado knew the mountain well, as did white trappers and mountain men. Although John Wesley Powell in 1868 made the first recorded ascent of Longs Peak, evidence exists indicating that Indians had climbed it earlier, either to light signal fires or to search for eagle feathers. The Indians probably had a name for Longs Peak itself, but usually they lumped it with nearby Meeker Peak and called the two "the two guides." (The French recorded the Indian name as Nesotaieux.) French-speaking trappers, like the Indians, had a single name for both peaks; they called them Les Deux Oreilles, "the two ears."

Thousands of persons have climbed Longs Peak, including at least one person on crutches. Yet the mountain's 1,700ft/518m vertical east face known as the Diamond was not climbed until 1960 and still poses formidable big-wall challenges.

MOUNT LUCANIA   17,147ft/5,226m   Yukon, Canada
First ascent, 1937, B. Washburn and R. Bates

Two peaks in the mountain ranges of southeastern Alaska and the Yukon were named for ships, and both were named by the same person. On 28 May 1897 the Cunard liner *Lucania* docked at New York harbor after completing a six-day voyage from Liverpool. On board was the Duke of the Abruzzi and the party he had assembled to explore and climb the high peaks of the St. Elias Range. The party proceeded to the Pacific Northwest, where they traveled north along the coast to the mountains. In his book describing the expedition, Filippo de Filippi wrote: "On the far horizon, somewhere between fifty and one hundred miles off, a broad summit towered up behind the western corner of Mount Logan. ...H.R.H. [the Duke] named this peak Lucania, in remembrance of the ship that had brought us to America."

Mount Bona (16,550ft/5,044m) in the Wrangell Mountains received its name at the same time, and in the same manner. Again, de Filippi described the naming: "Finally, to the northwest, some two hundred miles [322km] off, a conical peak soared up ... apparently of even greater height than the other two [Lucania and Bear]. This was christened the Bona after a racing yacht then belonging to H.R.H."[42]

Given that ships have been named for virtually everything else, it's not unlikely they have been for mountains, but Mounts Bona and Lucania are perhaps the only mountains named for ships.

134

 **M**

MOUNT McKINLEY   *20,320ft/6,194m*   *Alaska, USA*
First ascent north summit, 19,470ft/5,934m, 1910, P. Anderson and W. Taylor.
First ascent south summit, 20,320ft/6,194m, 1913, H. Stuck, W. Harper,
R. Tatum, and H. Karstens.

Throughout the years several attempts have been made to change the name of the highest summit in North America from McKinley to Denali, an Indian word widely accepted to mean "the great one." These attempts, like most others to retrofit mountains with titles more appropriate or poetic, thus far have failed, but it must be conceded that if ever a name does not match its mountain, it is this one.

The name McKinley, of course, honors William McKinley, twenty-fifth president of the United States who was assassinated in 1901 as he was about to enter his second term in office. President McKinley had many noteworthy achievements during his administration, but he had no interest either in mountains or mountaineering, and it's certain he never saw—nor cared to see—the mountain named for him. What's more, the name was given to the mountain even before McKinley became president, while he was only a candidate—and then only as an act of spite.

The mountain was named by W.A. Dickey, a Princeton graduate who had come to Alaska during the gold rush. According to the telling of the story by Grant Pearson, longtime Alaska wilderness ranger and superintendent of McKinley National Park, Dickey and a friend were prospecting on the Susitna River, where there are excellent views of the mountain, when they fell in with a couple of other prospectors. It was 1896; the presidential campaign was underway; and the most hotly debated issue was whether the nation should abandon gold as the basis for its currency. For days the new prospectors had burdened Dickey with harangues favoring *their* candidate, William Jennings Bryan, a Democrat and an advocate of a free silver monetary policy. Dickey and his companion supported a gold standard, so when the other prospectors departed, Dickey defiantly named the mountain after *his* candidate—William McKinley.

Dickey wrote a newspaper article describing the mountain, and he used the name he had assigned. Most people of the time treated the naming as a joke; after all, William McKinley was nothing but a politician back in the States. But when McKinley became president—and especially after he was assassinated—the name began to gain acceptance and has been encrusted on the mountain ever since.

Actually, the name McKinley superseded an earlier name, a name lacking in presidential presence and also regarded jocularly by Alaskans but one at least honoring someone who cared about the mountain. He was Frank Densmore, a prospector, who first saw the mountain from Lake Minchumina to the north in 1889. The mountain made a deep impression on him, and he spoke so enthusiastically about it among other prospectors that for years many of them referred to the mountain as Densmore's Peak.

Densmore was not the first white man to see the mountain. The English navigator and explorer, George Vancouver, was the first to mention it. Seeing it from Cook Inlet in 1794, he wrote of "the stupendous snow mountains."[69] In 1878 two pioneer Alaska traders, Alfred Mayo and Arthur Harper, journeyed up the Tanana River and returned to report an enormous ice mountain to the south, but they didn't name it. The Russian explorers and colonizers of Alaska also had been aware of the massive white mountain. They called it Bolshaya Gora, meaning simply "big mountain." That corresponded with the Indian designations of the peak. The Tanana Indian name has been widely reported as Denali; the Tanaina Indian name is given as Doleika, or Traleika. All these names have been translated to mean "the big one" or "the high one." Most Indian names for mountains are simply descriptive, and unlike other peoples, notably English-speaking peoples, Indians never have been addicted to bestowing commemorative names, such as McKinley.

Indians do, however, tend to wrap great mountains in legends and to place them in their cosmology. An Alaskan Indian legend tells that the snow and ice on McKinley (or Denali) were created to keep the mountain sheep from escaping the wolves; another says flying geese crash into the mountain's sides so that the ravens might feed.

The Indians had no interest in climbing the mountain, and it was not until the white men arrived that anyone attempted an assault. Appropriately, the first verified ascent was by two prospectors, Peter Anderson and William Taylor, who on 10 April 1910 reached the north summit (19,470ft/5,934m). The south summit (20,320ft/6,194m) was first climbed on 7 June 1913 by Archdeacon Hudson Stuck, Walter Harper, Robert Tatum, and Harry Karstens, later park superintendent.

Together, McKinley's two summits are known as the Churchill Peaks, a name proposed by the National Park Service in 1965 to honor Sir Winston Churchill, British prime minister during World War II. The prime minister, like the president, never saw the mountains named for him—nor cared to.

The issue of Mount McKinley's name refuses to die. Most recently, in 1975, the state of Alaska sought to have Mount McKinley renamed Denali and for Mount McKinley National Park to become Denali National Park. In 1977, the day before the United States Board on Geographic Names (USBGN) was to make its decision on Alaska's request, the congressional delegation from Ohio, McKinley's home state, introduced a resolution in the 95th Congress to block the name change. The USBGN then was forced to sit out the dispute, as it cannot rule on matters before Congress. The Alaska initiative died when that Congress ended. The attempt was not entirely in vain, however; in 1980, when

Congress added land to the national park, it also exercised its naming preroga-tive and renamed it Denali National Park, even though the mountain still is McKinley.

BEN MACDHUI   *4,296ft / 1,309m*   *Scotland*
First ascent unknown.

The second highest summit in Britain provides a good reminder that charac-teristics or incidents inspirational to early namers will not necessarily have mean-ing for later peoples. To contemporary Scots, the most notable aspects of Ben Macdhui are its elevation, its wild ruggedness, its romantic legends, and its hav-ing the highest lake in Britain, Loch Etchachan (3,058ft/932m). But the early Gaelic-speaking peoples of the region gave Ben Macdhui a name translated vari-ously as "hill of the black pig," "boar hunting ground," and "dark hills," and the incidents or features that inspired these meanings have long been lost in time.

Not all the mountain's early history has been lost, however. In 1963 a leaf-shaped arrowhead, carefully worked in flint, was found on Ben Macdhui, a relic from the time when neolithic men hunted red deer among the Cairngorms. And early legends about the mountain persist as well, especially that of the Ferlas Mor, the giant Gray Man who sometimes stalks mountain travelers. In 1925 the Scottish mountaineer J. Norman Collie reported an incident that had happened to him several years earlier on Ben Macdhui. As he climbed toward the summit in a thick mist, he heard footsteps behind him in the snow, slowing when he slowed and hastening when he hastened. When he reached the sum-mit and stopped, the steps continued drawing nearer. Said Collie: "I was seized with an intolerable fright, and I ran my hardest down the mountainside. No power on earth will ever take me up Ben Macdhui again."[111]

THE MAC GILLYCUDDYS REEKS   *Ireland*
Highest elevation, 3,414ft / 1,041m, Carrauntual.

The highest elevations in Ireland are found in the MacGillycuddys Reeks, an east–west ridge of hills in the Kerry Mountains. Highest of these hills is Carraun-tual, whose name is generally accepted as coming from the Gaelic *corran tuathail*, "the inverted reaping hook." The name also is said to be a corruption of Gaelic words meaning "Toole's cairn."

The origin of the name of the mountain group is more certain. MacGillycuddy was a local chief whose name comes from the Gaelic Mac Gilla Mo-chuta, "the son of the servant of St. Mo-chuta." The name, like the mountain, is of Kerry. St. Mo-chuta is the Irish name for St. Carthage, native of Castlemaine and founder of the great Celtic monastery at Lismore; he died in 637. As for the Reeks, D.D.C.P. Mould in *The Mountains of Ireland* explains the term: "The word Reek is used in Ireland for a mountain ridge. Perhaps the basic idea is a ridge shape. . . . Croagh Patrick in all the country round about it is always called The Reek."[90]

MACHAPUCHARE   22,958ft/6,998m   Nepal
First ascent, 1957, W. Noyce and D. Cox.

Machapuchare has been described as a "classic twin-headed 'Matterhorn' and
one of the world's most beautiful mountains."[27] The high crystal wall of the
Annapurna Himal is a scenic backdrop for this dramatic peak standing isolated
before it. But Machapuchare's Nepalese namers, who regarded the peak as
sacred, were even more impressed with another aspect of the mountain's appearance, that is, its striking resemblance to the tail of a fish, and that is what
the name Machapuchare means—"fish's tail." Some say that the inspiration for
the metaphor is a resemblance between the motion of a fish's tail and the waft-
ing of snow spume from the mountain, but more obvious is the resemblance
from certain angles between the mountain's shape and a fish's caudal fin,
Machapuchare's flanks appearing to narrow and then flare outward, the two
summits separated by a col as if by a caudal notch.

The first ascent of Machapuchare has not been universally accepted; the
climbers stopped 150ft/46m short of the summit because ice conditions were
too dangerous. Subsequent attempts have been prohibited by the Nepalese
government.

MAKALU   27,790ft/8,470m   Nepal–Tibet
First ascent, 1955, J. Couzy and L. Terray.

Makalu, fifth highest of the world's mountains and a neighbor of Everest, is a
four-sided pyramid that has been called the "most handsome" of Nepal's 8,000m
peaks.[27] Several explanations exist for the mountain's name, but the most likely
is that it was inspired by the dark granite comprising the mountain; *maha-kala*
in Tibetan means "the great black one." An alternative explanation is that the
name comes from the Sanskrit. Pierra Vittoz believes the name is a corruption
of the Sanskrit *Maha-kala*, a nickname of the Hindu god Siva. Thus, Vittoz
translates the name to mean "sublimity."[75] Others have said, however, that the
Sanskrit *maha-kala* refers not to Siva but rather means "great weather" and
possibly is an allusion to the storms generated by the mountain. Still another
explanation, one less probable, is that the name is derived from a transposition
in the Tibetan words *kama-lung.* This is the name of the valley to the north of
the Makalu massif, and it is close in sound to Khamba Lung, the name Rinzin
Namgyal of the Survey of India gave to the mountain when he explored the
region in 1884. This name was derived from the adjoining Khamba district in
Tibet.

MALADETA MASSIF   Spain
Highest elevation, 11,168ft/3,404m, Pico Aneto.

The Maladeta massif, located along the spine of the Pyrenees midway between
the Atlantic and the Mediterranean, is the highest mountain group in the
range, but that does little to explain the massif's name, which is Spanish and

138

Ascent of Maladeta, Spain. From William H.D. Adams, Mountains and Mountain Climbing *(London: 1883).*

means "accursed." (This meaning is mirrored in the name by which French speakers in the Pyrenees know the mountains—Monts Maudit.) Such gothic-sounding names as Maladeta are common in the southern Pyrenees, and the English writer Hilaire Belloc, who knew the region well, has suggested that the names were inspired by the mountains themselves: "The general character of the rocks is more savage and fantastic, and it is upon the south side of the range that one most feels creeping over one that sentiment of unreality, or of a spell, which so many travelers in the Pyrenees have been curious to note. The local names express it on every side. There are 'Mouth of Hell,' 'the Accursed Mountain,' 'the Lost Mountain,' 'the Peak of Hell,' 'the Enchanted Hill,' and hundreds of other legendary titles that express, as well as do the mountain tunes, the sense of an unquiet mystery."[13]

Actually, it's possible that the meaning "accursed" for Maladeta is a Spanish-French folk etymology and that the name's true meaning is much less romantic but much older. According to a French names scholar, *mala* is a very ancient, pre-Latin name element of obscure meaning that also appears in the name of another important Pyrenean peak, Vignemale, in which *mala* is prefixed by another ancient name element *vinia*, referring to "rocky heights."[123] The plausibility of this is increased by the Pyrenees being a linguistically complex region where such elements quite possibly have been preserved.

Regardless of how visitors choose to interpret the name, the Maladeta group invariably commands respect and attention. The traveler Amy Oakley wrote: "This revelation of Maladeta from Port de Vanasque I should call the climax of the Pyrenean experience. Its remoteness from the world of men, its aloofness, encircled as it is by a bodyguard of hills, have kept Maladeta a thing apart, not of our planet."[96]

MANASLU 26,658ft/8,125m   Nepal
First ascent, 1956, T. Imanishi and G. Norbu.

Many of the world's great mountains bear names that seem trivial or frivolous when measured against the mountains they identify. Fortunate it is, then, that many of the Himalayan giants were named by peoples who regard the mountains as sacred, embodiments of a transcendent natural order. Manaslu, located in the Gurkha Himal east of Annapurna in central Nepal, is an example. The name Manaslu is derived from the Sanskrit word *manasa*, meaning "intellect" or "soul," and thus the name can be translated as "mountain of the soul." (In southwestern New Mexico, USA, there is a minor range, the Animas Mountains, whose name can be translated from the Spanish as "mountains of the spirit.") Why Manaslu bears this particular name is unknown, and the mountain's other names are easier to explain. In the Sama language Manaslu is called Kambung, after a local god, while Tibetans refer to it as Kutan I, a name derived from *kang*, meaning "a flat place," descriptive of the mountain's summit.

The first ascent of Manaslu followed four years of intense interest in the mountain by the Japanese; they undertook two unsuccessful expeditions, one of them hampered by strong local hostility toward the climbers. When Gyalzen Norbu

140

accompanied T. Imanishi to the top in 1956, he became the first Sherpa to climb two 8,000-meter peaks, having participated in the successful first ascent of Makalu the year before.

MOUNT MANSFIELD   4,393ft / 1,339m   Vermont, USA

First ascent unknown.
See GREEN MOUNTAINS.

MOUNT MARCUS BAKER   13,176ft / 4,016m   Alaska, USA
First ascent, 1938, B. Washburn, P. Gabriel, N. Bright, and N. Dyhrenfurth.

The highest mountain in the Chugach Range, like many Alaskan mountains, was named by a geographer for a geographer. Alfred Hulse Brooks, for whom the Brooks Range was named (see entry), in 1924 proposed to the United States Geological Survey (USGS) that the mountain be named for Marcus Baker (1849–1903), who had gained prominence because of his involvement with the USGS, the Coast Survey, and the Carnegie Institution. Baker also was the author of the *Geographic Dictionary of Alaska* and was a member of the United States Geographic Board from its founding until his death. But James McCormick, who at the time of Brooks' proposal was director of the USGS, had reservations about this recommendation because Baker's name already appeared on several geographical features, such as Baker Island and Baker Point. Brooks pressed the issue, and later in 1924 the United States Geographic Board approved the name. (Brooks's case doubtless was strengthened by the mountain's proximity to the Baker Glacier, named for Marcus Baker in 1910.)

This was not the only time this mountain has been named by a man determined to press his personal preference—on maps it has appeared as both Mount Marcus Baker and Mount St. Agnes. In an *American Alpine Journal* article, Francis B. Farquhar retold Bradford Washburn's explanation of the St. Agnes name: "James W. Bagley, of the USGS, named this peak after his wife, but knowing that the name would not stick if the secret leaked out, he added the 'St.' for concealment. The secret never did leak out until this moment, unless Brooks possibly got wind of it. At all events, Agnes, whether saint or not, lost her peak to Mr. Baker."[42]

MOUNT MARCY   5,347ft / 1,630m   New York, USA
First ascent, 1872, V. Colvin.
See ADIRONDACKS.

MARMOLATA   10,965ft / 3,342m   Italy
First ascent, 1863, P. Grohmann with the Dimai brothers.
See DOLOMITES.

MAROON BELLS   14,156ft/4,315m   Colorado, USA
First recorded ascent, 1908, P. Hagerman.
NORTH MAROON PEAK, 14,014ft/4,271m
First ascent unknown.

What usually captures the attention of visitors to these twin peaks in Colorado's Elk Range is the mountains' striking sedimentary layers, the thin, parallel strata running like ghost lines across the mountains' steep faces; this, and the mountains' distinctive shapes, have made the Maroon Bells the most photographed mountains in Colorado. But what the surveyors of the Hayden Survey noticed when they visited the mountains in 1873 was their color. In his report, A.C. Peale wrote: "As we go toward Maroon Mountain the bright red sandstones become darker. Maroon Mountain derives its name from the color of its rocks. We did not ascend it but made a station on a high point a short distance south of it."[44]

Today, with two summits generally recognized, the peaks are popularly known as the Maroon Bells, and little imagination is needed to see in the peaks great bells frozen in their swinging (see Grossglockner). When seven persons lost their lives on the mountains during a nine-month period in 1965–66, newspapers called the Maroon Bells the "mountains of frozen death" and victims "those for whom the Bells tolled."[34]

MASHERBRUM   25,660ft/7,821m   Pakistan
First ascent, 1960, G. Bell and W. Unsoeld.

Masherbrum is one of the major Karakoram peaks flanking the Baltoro Glacier in northern Kashmir. Viewed from the north, the peak appears as a great rock tooth rising from a steep cone of ice, but what many Balti-speaking peoples of the region have noticed most about the mountain is the resemblance of the mountain's twin summits to an old muzzle-loading gun. According to H. Adams Carter, linguist and mountaineer who was in the region in 1974 inquiring about local place-names, that is one popular explanation for the name Masherbrum; the porters he questioned agreed that it comes from *mashadar*, "muzzle-loading gun," plus *brum*, "mountain." This certainly is a plausible explanation, and as Carter points out, "the dropping of final syllables in compound names is common."[22]

But the "muzzle-loading gun" interpretation is only one of several that have been proposed for the name Masherbrum, and it's possible the Balti porters Carter questioned had accepted this interpretation in ignorance of the name's true origins. For example, Carter mentions that the Raja of Khapalu derives the name Masherbrum from *masha*, "queen or lady," and *brum*, "mountain," thereby meaning "queen of mountains." This interpretation also has not been proved valid, but it certainly is plausible and would make Masherbrum similar in meaning to many other mountain names in the region (see Gasherbrums). Carter also mentions the possibility that the name has a connection with the

Arabic *mahsher*, "doomsday," so the name would mean "doomsday mountain," but even with an explanation why a mountain might bear this curious name, this origin is improbable because, as Carter points out, "It is highly unlikely that Arabic would appear in any Balti place name."[22]

MOUNT MASSIVE   14,421ft/4,396m   Colorado, USA
First ascent, 1874, H. Gannett.

The bulky, sprawling appearance of this huge peak in the Sawatch Range in-spired early prospectors and miners to give the mountain its current name. The peak is the second highest in Colorado, only twelve feet lower than its neighbor, Mount Elbert (14,433ft/4,399m). Successive measurements of Colorado's peaks have altered Mount Massive's status among the state's "Fourteeners," each time provoking outcries among partisans of different mountains. Mount Massive had been thought to be Colorado's highest peak, and when a survey showed Mount Elbert to be slightly higher, supporters of Mount Massive threatened to build a cairn on its top that would make it number one again. (When a survey showed Mount Massive higher than Mount Rainier in the state of Washington, the Tacoma Chamber of Commerce threatened to build up *their* mountain.)

Attempts to change Mount Massive's name have been no more successful than the attempts to change its elevation. The name Mount Gannett was pro-posed in 1922 to honor the surveyor Henry Gannett (see Gannett Peak), who made the first ascent of Mount Massive, but local opposition prevailed. Similarly, an unsuccessful proposal in 1965 to rename the mountain for Sir Winston Churchill, who had died that year, provoked outrage among the people of nearby Leadville.

MATTERHORN   14,690ft/4,478m   Switzerland
First ascent, 1865, E. Whymper, C. Hudson, D. Hadow, F. Douglas, with M. Croz and P. Taugwalder, father and son.

Perhaps more than any other mountain, the Matterhorn in the Pennine Alps exemplifies how a great and distinctive mountain can imbue even a common-place name with special meaning and appeal. The name Matterhorn is simple enough: it's a combination of two German words, *matt*, "meadow," and *horn*, "peak," that together mean "the peak at the meadow." (The name of the town at the base of the Matterhorn, Zermatt, means simply "at the meadow.") The French call the mountain Mont Cervin and the Italians Monte Cervino, both names derived from words meaning "deer" or "stag" and both referring to a sup-posed resemblance between the sharp, jutting peak and a deer's antlers. But English-speakers and climbers generally know the mountain by its German name.

It's not known when the name Matterhorn first settled upon the peak. W.A.B. Coolidge, the American who became an expert on the history of the Alps, reported: "It is worth noting that the name 'Matter' or Matterhorn was applied to the pass in Italy before it came to mean the peak exclusively. Sebas-tian Münster (1543) gives the name of 'Mons Matter' to the pass, marking it as

Rockfall on the Matterhorn, Switzerland. From Edward Whymper, Scrambles Amongst the Alps 1860-1869 *(Philadelphia: 1873).*

'Augstalbert-Mons Sylvius' on his map of the Valais, the former of these last two names referring, of course, to Aosta." Coolidge believed Mont Cervin was derived from Mons Sylvius. Other early names Coolidge found in his researches included der Gletscher, Mattenberg, and Austelerberg.[30] But the name that has endured and prospered is Matterhorn.

Given the meaning of the name Matterhorn, it could have been applied with equal sense to hundreds of Alpine peaks; but only the mountain above Zermatt could have bestowed on the name world-wide recognition. The mountaineering writer James Ramsay Ullman put it thus: "There are hundreds of mountains higher than the Matterhorn; there are hundreds that are harder to climb. But there is none, anywhere in the world, which has so consistently and deeply stirred the imagination of men. Rising in an immense isolated pyramid on the frontier between Switzerland and Italy, it possesses not only the dimensions but the stark simplicity of greatness, and its sprawling neighbor peaks, some of which actually exceed its 14,690-foot/4,478-meter altitude, seem to shrink into insignificance beside it. Through all the centuries that men have known the Alps, their eyes have been drawn irresistibly upward to its savage, soaring pinnacle. Other mountains were—well—mountains. This mountain was beauty and magic and terror."[140] The story of the dramatic race for the first ascent of the Matterhorn and the tragic descent that claimed the lives of four of the seven persons who reached the summit, is one of the best known in all mountaineering.

It's no wonder, then, that the name Matterhorn has traveled far beyond the Alps to be applied to other mountains, either as an actual name or as a generic term (Jirishanca in the Andes is known as "the Matterhorn of Peru"). In the United States, peaks bearing the name Matterhorn are found in California, Colorado, Oregon, Nevada, and even Vermont, where the gently contoured, forest-covered mountain there bears no resemblance to its namesake. Probably the best known American Matterhorn is in Yosemite National Park, where John Muir in 1877 applied the name to what had been called Banner Peak. The next year the Wheeler Survey adopted the name Matterhorn not only for the peak but also for a nearby canyon, and both peak and canyon continue to bear the name.

With but few exceptions, applying the name of one peak to another is unfortunate. Each mountain deserves a name that reflects its own individual identity, not one that encourages associations and comparisons with a mountain elsewhere. That such comparisons occur is seen in a comment by L. Hutchinson in the Sierra Club *Bulletin* about the California Matterhorn: "That the name is a poor one there can be no doubt...there is only the barest suggestion of resemblance to the wonderful Swiss mountain after which it is named."[56]

There is only one Matterhorn—or at least there should be only one.

MAUNA KEA   *13,796ft/4,205m*   *Hawaii, USA*
First ascent unknown.

If one measured Mauna Kea's elevation not from sea level but from the mountain's base beneath the Pacific Ocean, then at 32,000ft/9,754m it would be the world's tallest mountain. As it is, Mauna Kea is one of the world's highest island mountains, and together with its neighbor and close rival in elevation Mauna Loa (13,680ft/4,170m), it makes up the bulk of the island of Hawaii. This enormous mountain is a dormant shield volcano, born of fire and, like other shield volcanoes, composed of successive layers of lava and ash that have issued over time from several volcanic vents. The mountain's name, however, like that of so many major mountains, comes from the ice and snow on its summit. *Mauna* is the Polynesian word for "mountain," while *kea* means "white." Thus Mauna Kea joins literally dozens of other mountains throughout the world whose names mean simply "white mountain."

Not only did the Hawaiians give Mauna Kea the same name other isolated preliterate peoples have given to major mountains, they also invested Mauna Kea with similar legends. Throughout the world high mountains have been believed inhabited by gods and goddesses, often malevolent. Mount Olympus was the home of the Greek gods; Tibetan divinities dwell among the Himalaya; and the Jotunheimen Mountains of Norway are named for the dwelling place of the giants of Norse mythology. According to Hawaiian mythology, Mauna Kea is the abode of the goddess Poliahu, archenemy of the beautiful fire goddess, Pele, whose home is Mauna Loa. It is their quarrels and battles that cause the earth to tremble and fire to spew forth.

MAUNA LOA   *13,680ft/4,170m*   *Hawaii, USA*
First ascent unknown.

The huge shield volcano Mauna Loa is the world's largest volcanic structure. Its total height, including that beneath sea level, is approximately 30,000ft/9,144m; it has a base diameter of 400mi/644km; and its volume has been estimated at 54.9 million cubic yards/42 million cubic meters. Mauna Loa and its slightly taller neighbor, Mauna Kea (13,796ft/4,205m) together make up more than half the mass of the island of Hawaii, largest in the Hawaiian group, and they probably are the world's bulkiest mountains. Yet the impressiveness of Mauna Loa is obscured by it being a "shield volcano," an enormous, gently sloping mass built up by successive eruptions from several vents, not a "composite" volcano like Fujiyama, whose rather steep, symmetrical sides were built up by ejecta from a single, central pipe.

The massive, sprawling character of Mauna Loa is reflected in its name, which in the Polynesian language of Hawaii means simply "long mountain" (*mauna*, "mountain," *loa*, "long"). Not until one sees the fire pit Halemaumau inside Kilauea, a cinder cone on the east slope of Mauna Loa, and the huge active crater Mokuaweoweo on the summit of Mauna Loa itself does the mountain become truly awesome. The lava lakes that often form in these craters remind one that in Hawaiian mythology Mauna Loa is the domain of Pele, the beautiful goddess of fire (see Mauna Kea). Halemaumau, "everlasting home," is her abode, and fine filaments of lava, ejected during eruptions and stretched thin by strong winds, are called "Pele's hair" when they occasionally are found on Mauna Loa's upper slopes.

MOUNT MAZAMA *Oregon, USA*

Two things are notable about the name Mount Mazama. First, it possibly is the only mountain name given by a mountaineering organization to commemorate itself. And second, it is the only mountain name to be given posthumously, for Mount Mazama, once a mighty volcano, now exists only in people's imaginations.

Mazama is Spanish for "mountain goat," certainly an apt name for the well-known mountaineering organization based in Portland, Oregon, and at the Mazamas' annual meeting in 1896 they bestowed their name on the prehistoric volcano whose caldera now is occupied by Crater Lake. The mountain itself once was the highest in the southern part of the range, its height estimated at over 12,000ft/3,658m. But about 4500 B.C. the volcano collapsed, and all that remains of its once-proud cone is the high point on the rim of its caldera now known as Hillman Peak (8,156ft/2,486m).

LA MEIJE *13,081ft/3,987m* *France*
First ascent, 1877, B. de Castelnau and P. and J. Gaspard.

La Meije in the Massif du Pelvoux in the Dauphine Alps was the last major summit to be conquered by Victorian pioneer mountaineers. It is an east-west rocky ridge rising to three serrated summits, but what inspired its name was not its appearance, impressive though that is, but its location. The French name La Meije is a reference to the mountain's position in the middle of the region; *meije* is how the Latin root *media*, meaning "middle", would have appeared in medieval French, the *dia* becoming *je*. Edward Whymper, in his *Scrambles Amongst the Alps*, reported that earlier travelers had known the mountain as the Aiguille du Midi de la Grave, "needle-mountain of the middle of La Grave (the local district)," again, a reference to the peak's position.[154]

Such names are fairly common among mountains. Lhotse, "south peak," is named for its location relative to Everest. The Front Range of Colorado is at the front of the Rocky Mountains when approached from the east. North Sister in the Cascades in Oregon is, not surprisingly, the northernmost of the Three Sisters. Some persons may be disappointed to learn that the beautiful name La Meije has such a mundane meaning, but at least they should know La Meije, with its simple name, is in very good company.

PIC DU MIDI D'OSSAU *9,466ft/2,885m* *France*
First ascent, 1787, by a shepherd.

The English writer Hilaire Belloc knew the Pyrenees well. Of the Pic du Midi d'Ossau, the last major mountain before the Pyrenees meet the Atlantic Ocean, he wrote: "The Pic du Midi remains in one's mind more perhaps than any of the isolated mountains of Europe. It is quite savage and alone, and you must fatigue

147

Le pic du Midi d'Ossau, France. From Frederic Zurcher and Elie Margollé, Les ascensions célèbres *(Paris: 1867).*

yourself to reach it. There is no common knowledge of it, and yet it is as much itself as is the Matterhorn....I know of no hill which seems more to deserve a name or to possess a personality."[13]

Belloc's reference to the mountain's name—or rather lack of one—stems from Pic du Midi d'Ossau meaning in French simply "peak in the middle of the Ossau." That is an accurate, if greatly limited, description of the mountain; the peak, the gaunt core of an ancient volcano eroded into a distinctive mitten shape, dominates the Ossau Valley of the western French Pyrenees. But Belloc is right about the name: the mountain does seem to deserve more. And Belloc was not the only writer whose emotions were stirred by the Pic du Midi d'Ossau. The traveler Amy Oakley wrote: "There is something repellent about this peak, which is the personification of austerity. It is surrounded by dark and gloomy forests, the haunt of bears."[96]

But while the mountain's name reveals little about the mountain's character, it reveals much about the region in which the mountain is located. For though the name of the mountain is French, the name of the Ossau Valley is derived from the Basque *osca,* "gorge," and near Larun the valley does narrow into some deep gorges. Names such as Pic du Midi d'Ossau, a mixture of French and Basque

148

elements, epitomize the complex cultural history of the Pyrenees. Though the Pic d'Anie to the east marks the western boundary of the Basques, as Amy Oakley wrote: "Basque influence is everywhere apparent, a constant reminder of Ossau's proximity to the Pays Basque."[96]

MISCHABEL   14,913ft / 4,545m   *Switzerland*
First ascent, 1858, J.L. Davies.
See DOM.

MOUNT MITCHELL   6,684ft / 2,037m   *North Carolina, USA*
First ascent unknown.

Had not Dr. Elisha Mitchell died climbing this peak in the Black Mountains, the highest point in the eastern United States very likely would have been named Mount Clingman. Mitchell was a Connecticut Yankee who came to the University of North Carolina in 1824 as a professor of science, and by 1835 he was conducting scientific explorations in the mountains of western North Carolina. Using barometric readings, Mitchell was able to overturn the conventional notion that the highest point in the East was Mount Washington in the White Mountains of New Hampshire; rather, he determined, it was in the Black Mountains. In 1844 Mitchell returned to the mountains to make more measurements, aided by one Big Tom Wilson, a local bear hunter and guide. But that same year Thomas Lanier Clingman (see Clingmans Dome) also made measurements in the Black Mountains, and he announced that he had found a mountain higher than any measured by Mitchell. Soon there was little doubt which mountain in the range was the highest, so the controversy centered on which man had measured it first, Mitchell or Clingman. An intense rivalry developed between the two men, as each tried to muster support for his position.

The dispute came to a tragic resolution, of sorts, in 1857 when Mitchell set out to verify his measurements. En route to the home of Big Tom Wilson, Mitchell fell to his death in a pool beneath a cascade now called Mitchells Falls. Clingman, for all his conceit and contentiousness, was not mean-natured, and after Mitchell's death Clingman accepted the mountain being named for Mitchell. As Michael Frome has written: "Clingman, who may very well have deserved the honor, settled for a nearby mountain [Clingmans Peak, 6,520ft / 1,987m]."[50]

MITRE PEAK   5,560ft / 1,695m   *New Zealand*
First ascent, 1911, by unknown climber.

At least three of the world's mountains owe their names to their resemblance to a mitre, the liturgical headdress worn by bishops and abbots. The New Zealand mountain is a prominent peak on the south shore of Milford Sound on the southwestern coast of South Island. The peak rises almost sheer above the sound and consists of five closely grouped summits. The name most likely was given in 1851 by the surveyors on the ship *Acheron.*

In the Vilcabamba region of Peru there is a peak with the same name, Nevado Mitre (18,635ft/5,680m). Like the peak in New Zealand—and like a mitre—it has multiple tops, its summit consisting of three pinnacles. The circumstances of its naming are unknown, but the inspiration for the name is clear.

And in the Karakoram there is still another mitre mountain, Mitre Peak (elevation unknown), located west of the Gasherbrum group and, with them, among the great peaks flanking the Baltoro Glacier. This peak often appears on maps under its Balti name, Skilbrum. Again, the circumstances of the Mitre naming are unknown, but while one might expect a mountain metaphor based on a bishop's cap in New Zealand or Peru, one cannot help but wonder how such a name got onto a remote peak in Central Asia.

MONASHEE MOUNTAINS   *British Columbia, Canada*
Highest elevation, 10,650ft/3,246m, Mount Monashee.
See Introduction.

MÖNCH   *13,468ft/4,105m*   *Switzerland*
First ascent, 1857, S. Porges and C. Almer.

One of the major peaks of the Bernese Alps and the range's fourth highest, the Mönch, German for "monk," was named by the same Swiss folk who gave the Mönch's neighbors their names: Jungfrau, "maiden," and Eiger, "ogre." And also like its neighbors, the first ascent of the Mönch was among the great conquests of the Golden Age of Mountaineering. The peak was climbed in 1857 by a Viennese physician and the great Swiss guide Christian Almer, two years after a Russian princess, Helene Kozlow-Massalsky, with the pen name of Doria d'Istria, had announced that she and her three guides had reached the summit. Although the guides signed testimonials to that effect, the princess had actually abandoned the attempt at the foot of the final snow ridge.

The name "monk" also appears in the Tatra Mountains, on a small, spiky peak called the Minch.

MONT-AUX-SOURCES   *10,820ft/3,298m*   *Lesotho, Africa*
First ascent, 1836, T. Arbousset and F. Daumas.

Mont-aux-sources, with its 10,000ft/3,048m-long amphitheater known as the Sentinel, has been described as the most spectacular section of southern Africa's Drakensberg wall, and the elongated, rock-bastioned peak is a commanding feature of Royal Natal National Park. But when the two French missionaries Arbousset and Daumas explored the mountain in 1836 and made the first ascent, they noticed something besides the mountain's rock faces: at least three major rivers have their sources there. They gave the mountain its name, which in French means simply "mountain of the sources."

The three rivers are the Tugela, the Eland, and the Khubedu. The Tugela rises on the mountain's long, flat summit and falls in a spectacular cascade down the amphitheater's east face. Nearby begin the Eland and the Khubedu, separated only by a low, swampy ridge, but the rivers do not meet again until each has flowed nearly 600mi/965km.

MOOSES TOOTH 10,335ft/3,150m   Alaska, USA
First ascent, 1964, W. Welsch, K. Bierl, A. Hasenkopf, and A. Reichegger.

In Mooses Tooth two very common place-name elements have been combined to create a distinctive name for a distinctive peak. Wherever moose are found, their name tends to be applied to natural features, especially water bodies providing habitat for moose. The place-name dictionary of Alaska prepared by Donald Orth for the United States Geological Survey lists forty-six Moose Creeks and eighty names having *moose* as an element. And *tooth*, too, is a common name element, especially on mountains, appearing frequently in the Alps in the French form *dent* (Dent Blanche, "white tooth," Dent du Géant, "giant's tooth," and even Dent de Crocodile, "crocodile's tooth"). English-speakers also are fond of the tooth metaphor for mountains, and examples include Sharks Tooth in Colorado, the Beartooth Range in Montana, and, of course, Mooses Tooth in Alaska.

The Alaskan "tooth" is a long crest of ice near the head of the Buckskin Glacier southeast of Mount McKinley in the Alaska Range. The name Mooses Tooth, evocative of the peak's appearance, is a translation of the name the Athabascan Indians had for the mountain. The Browne-Parker Expedition to the region in 1910 called the peak Mount Hubbard for Thomas H. Hubbard, then president of the Peary Arctic Club, but the translation of the Indian name, obtained in 1953 by the USGS, has more popular appeal and has prevailed.

MOUNT MORAN 12,594ft/3,839m   Wyoming, USA
First ascent, 1922, L.H. Hardy, B.C. Rich, and B. McNulty.

The surveyor Ferdinand V. Hayden named this mountain, fourth highest in the Teton Range, for his friend Thomas Moran (1837-1926), a well-known artist of the time. Other members of Hayden's 1872 surveying expedition called the peak Mount Leidy for the prominent comparative anatomist Joseph Leidy, but the name Mount Moran appeared on an 1873 map, and a peak in the nearby Gros Ventre Range now bears Leidy's name. Moran saw the Tetons, including the mountain later named for him, only once, and then from the Idaho side. The visibility was poor, he wrote, the atmosphere "so very smoky that the

Tetons can scarcely be seen and at times are entirely obscured."[15] Nonetheless, the field sketches he made allowed him to produce his Teton landscape paintings, including studies of Mount Moran.

BEN MORE   3,843ft/1,171m   Scotland
First ascent unknown.

Certain mountain names have meanings so directly descriptive that their widespread use is inevitable; names meaning "white mountain" are found throughout the world, and the name Ben More, meaning "big mountain" in Gaelic, is found throughout Scotland. In the Outer Hebrides, the highest mountain of South Uist is Bheinn Mhor (2,034ft/620m), while the second highest mountain on Lewis is Beinn Mhor (1,874ft/571m). Further south, the summit capping the island of Mull is Ben More (3,169ft/966m). On the mainland, the name appears in Sutherland as Ben More Assynt (3,273ft/998m). But probably the best known of Scotland's "big mountains" is 3,843ft/1,171m Ben More in Argyll in the southwestern Highlands. This mountain has been described as "a huge sugarloaf and one of the most majestic and prominent mountains of Scotland."[111] It was while walking on this mountain in 1892 that W.W. Naismith conceived the formula that has become widely known as Naismith's Rule: in planning for mountain travel, allow one hour for every 3mi/4.8km on the map, plus an additional hour for every 2,000ft/610m of climbing. (Later generations reduced the climbing estimate to 1,500ft/457m an hour.)

MOURNE MOUNTAINS   Northern Ireland
Highest elevation, 2,796ft/852m, Slieve Donard.

In the extreme south of County Down in Northern Ireland is the "kingdom of Mourne," a mountainous triangle whose three lines of hills, like the prongs of a trident, point southeast toward the Irish Sea. Before the thirteenth century, the Irish knew the mountains as the Beanna Boirche, "the mountains of Boirche," a king whose seat was at Slieve Binnian (2,249ft/685m), "mountain of the sharp peak." But about the time of the Anglo-Norman invasion, the MacMahons assumed overlordship of the region, and their name was corrupted to the present name, Mourne.

As with the name of the mountain group, the names of individual peaks in the Mournes reveal much about their history, both verified and legendary. (The events of the *Tain Bo Cuailgne*, the Irish mythological epic, took place in the Mourne Mountains.) The mountains' highest point, Slieve Donard, takes its name from St. Donard, said to have been a convert of St. Patrick; St. Donard established a hermitage and oratory near the mountain before his death in 506. The name of 1,144ft/349m Knockshee, topped by a Bronze Age cairn, in Gaelic means "fairy hill." Slieve Commedagh, 2,512ft/766m, in Gaelic means "mountain of the watching," probably a reference to the mountain at one time being a lookout. And the name of 1,013ft/309m Knockchree, meaning in Gaelic "mountain of the heart," recalls the tale of a man named MacCremon who, dying abroad, asked that his heart be brought home and buried here.

MUNROS   *3,000ft/914m plus*   *Scotland*

The differences between a "mountain" and a "hill" are more subtle than one might expect, and especially so in a place like Great Britain where even eminences everyone agrees are mountains nonetheless have the gentle slopes and rounded contours usually associated with hills. There a criterion such as elevation becomes important. As Edward Pyatt has written: "There should be a difference in height too. Mountains should be higher than hills."[111] Thus it happens that in Scotland there are hills, and there are Munros.

The name, as virtually all British mountain enthusiasts know, comes from the tables compiled by Sir Hugh Munro listing all Scottish mountains 3,000ft/914m or higher, and any Scottish mountain meeting this criterion is a Munro. These tables were first published in the Scottish Mountaineering Club *Journal* in September 1891, and they listed 538 summits, of which 283 were separate mountains. (In 1921 the tables were revised to show 543 tops and 276 mountains.) It was inevitable that as soon as the list was published, some hikers would set as a goal reaching all the summits, and "Munro bagging" has continued to be popular. Munro himself was fond of climbing Scotland's 3,000ft/914m "mountains," and he died having ascended all but two of the Munros.

MULHACEN   *11,421ft/3,481m*   *Spain*
First ascent unknown.
See SIERRA NEVADA, Spain.

MUZTAGH ATA   *24,758ft/7,546m*   *China*
First ascent, 1956, three members of the Sino-Russian expedition led by E.A. Beletsky.

According to Sven Hedin, the Swedish explorer of Central Asia, the name of this, the third highest summit in the Chinese Pamirs, can be translated from the Altaic to mean "father of ice mountains." *Muztagh* is a generic term used throughout Central Asia for any high, ice-covered mountain, and *ata* means "father." Hedin in 1894 attempted to climb the mountain, and Bill Tilman, Eric Shipton, and Gyalzen Sherpa in 1947 almost reached the summit. But just as it remained for the Russians to make detailed explorations of the Muztagh Ata region after initial reconnaissances by others, so it remained for them to make the first ascent.

N

NAMPA   22,162ft/6,755m   Nepal
First ascent, 1972, F. Kimara and S. Takahashi.
See API-NAMPA.

NANDA DEVI   25,645ft/7,817m   India
First ascent, 1936, N.E. Odell and H.W. Tilman.

Highest peak in the Garhwal Himalaya, highest in India, and her most sacred
mountain, for fourteen years—from 1936 to 1950—the highest mountain ever
ascended, Nanda Devi above all else is the mountain that watches over the
sources of the sacred river Ganges. From all of India pilgrims for centuries have
come to worship at the infant Ganges, seeing above them, beautiful and inaccessible, the white form of the mountain they call Nanda Devi, "the bliss-giving
goddess." T.G. Longstaff, who explored the area in 1905, later wrote: "I have
always believed that Nanda Devi reigned over the most superbly beautiful part
of all Himalaya...."[69] But the veneration of Nanda Devi is due to more than
the mountain's proximity to the Ganges. According to Vasudha Rajgopalan of
the Center for the Study of the World's Religions at Harvard University, Nanda
"is a manifestation of the goddess Parvati—the Sanskrit word for 'mountain' is
parvata, and Parvati means 'from the mountains.' Parvati first came onto the
earth as the daughter of Himavan, the king of the Himalaya, and has, therefore,
always been associated with the mountains."

As for Nanda's presence in Garhwal, H. Adams Carter, mountaineer and
linguist, has visited the Nanda Devi region and has eloquently explained her
status: "Although the goddess Nanda ... does not appear in the ancient sacred
Hindu texts, that does not mean that she, a consort of Siva, is not one of the
important, if not the most important, of the Hindu deities in Garhwal. She
permeates the whole area. In the region drained by the Rishi Ganga and the
Dhauli Ganga, every nook and cranny seems in one way or another to be dedi-
cated to her. The highest and most impressive mount of the region, Nanda
Devi, bears her name. Other peaks too bear her name. Within the Inner Sanctuary rises her bed (Nanda Khat) and nearby her fortress (Nanda Kot) and her
headdress (Nanda Ghunti). But her own name does not always appear. The
name of the town of Lata has to do with 'leg.' Lata supports the small mountain, above the town, Jipur, Nanda's resting place. Thus, names which do not
seem to the casual observer to be connected to the goddess are closely linked to
her in the minds of the local people. They feel her presence everywhere."[23]

Longstaff was the first person ever to surmount the ring of mountains known
as the Sanctuary that surrounds Nanda Devi—70mi/113km in circumference,
with an average elevation of 20,000ft/6,096m and nineteen peaks over 21,000ft/

6,401m. But topping this still does not bring one to the base of Nanda Devi. Inside the Sanctuary is the Inner Sanctuary, a second mountain wall, thousands of feet high, allowing access only through the precipitous, mile-deep gorge of the Rishiganga, never penetrated even by local shepherds. Nanda Devi thus joined those few mountains whose approaches were more difficult and significant than their first ascents. The name Rishiganga comes from the Rishis, the seven saintly sages whose protectress was the goddess Nanda. They fled from demons to the upper reaches of the gorge, where they sought refuge at the Rishikot, "the Rishis' fortress."

For nearly thirty years after Longstaff's explorations, the mountains barred all access to Nanda Devi, the Rishiganga apparently impassable. Then in 1934 came Eric Shipton and Bill Tilman, and with three Sherpas they pioneered a passage to the base of the mountain in a reconnaissance that has become famous in mountaineering history. Tilman returned two years later with Noel Odell to make the first ascent. Tilman later wrote of the moments he spent on the summit: "The air was still, we could bask gratefully in the friendly rays of our late enemy the sun. . . . After the first joy in victory came a feeling of sadness that the mountain had succumbed, that the proud head of the goddess was bowed."[69]

Willi Unsoeld, who in 1963 made the first ascent of Everest by the west ridge, named his daughter for Nanda Devi. In 1976 she joined her father on an American expedition trying to climb Nanda Devi by the north ridge. Nanda Devi Unsoeld died in the attempt. Of her death her father wrote: "My final prayer was one of thanksgiving for a world filled with the sublimity of the high places, for the sheer beauty of the mountains and for the surpassing miracle that we should be so formed as to respond with ecstasy to such beauty, and for the constant element of danger without which the mountain experience would not exercise such a grip on our sensibilities. We then laid the body to rest in its icy tomb, at rest on the breast of the Bliss-giving Goddess Nanda."[143]

NANGA PARBAT 26,658ft/8,125m Pakistan
First ascent, 1953, H. Buhl.

The similarities between the Eiger in the Alps and Nanga Parbat, the westernmost major Himalayan mountain, are numerous and obvious: both are major summits in their ranges; both are characterized by frequent avalanches, making climbing extremely dangerous; and thus, both have acquired evil reputations. The events that have caused the Eiger to be called "the mountain of death" and Nanga Parbat "the killer mountain" have been chronicled often, probably out of proportion to the achievements on the mountains. But the mountains' formal names are very dissimilar. The "ogre" bodes ill, but Nanga Parbat has a rather unthreatening meaning: it comes from the Sanskrit *nanga parvata* and means "naked mountain." At first glance, this name would seem unexpected on a mountain that is anything but naked, its festooning glaciers among its most distinguishing characteristics, but winds so scour the gneiss ribs of Nanga Parbat that its surface appears exposed, naked.

Given this rather prosaic meaning behind the name of a very unprosaic mountain, many persons have expressed preference for the name by which the natives west of Nanga Parbat know the mountain: Diamir, "king of the mountains." Indeed, no one disputes, as John Cleare has written, that Nanga Parbat (or Diamir) is "one of the grandest peaks of the Himalayas." But the name Diamir already appears on the mountain's west, Diamir Face, and, however appropriate, seems unlikely to spread further, so in the future Nanga Parbat will continue to be Naked Mountain—naked or not.

BEN NEVIS 4,406ft / 1,343m   Scotland
First ascent unknown.

Ben Nevis, the bulky mountain mass whose summit is the highest in Britain, often has been likened to a whale—long, humpbacked, and enormous. Indeed, James Ramsay Ullman has stretched the simile further and compared Ben Nevis to Moby Dick[69], and perhaps that's the best comparison of all, for it alludes not only to the mountain's distinctive characteristics of length, shape, and size but also to the characteristic most likely responsible for the mountain's name—its snow-capturing height, making Ben Nevis white when other mountains are not.

According to most accounts, the name Ben Nevis evolved from the Gaelic *beinn-nimh-bhatais*, translated variously as "mountain with the cold brow" and "mountain with its peak in the clouds," both apt descriptions. *Beinn*, meaning "mountain" and Anglicized as *ben*, is found throughout Scotland and Ireland. Ben Nevis, highest mountain in the Gaelic world, sometimes is known as the "Ben of Bens," but climbers and hikers often refer to the mountain with affectionate familiarity as "the Ben."

As for *nevis*, more than one scholar has suggested, with good reasons, that its meaning has been irretrievably lost in time, something common among Scottish place-names (see Cuillin Hills). Scholars who believe that Nevis has meaning generally agree that the name describes the mountain's preeminent summit, white when nearby peaks are barren of snow. This characteristic was documented by one Clement L. Wragge, who from 1881 to 1904 made extensive meteorological observations on Ben Nevis's summit. He recorded snow cover for an average of 215 days per year, with snow or sleet falling an average of 169 days per year, for a total annual precipitation of four meters.

This snow is responsible for much of Ben Nevis's appeal for climbers. Merely reaching the summit is not difficult; it has been done by car and motorcycle, and there is an annual footrace to the top. But the mountain's northeast face is a 1,400ft/427m wall that especially in winter offers mountaineering challenges comparable to those found on much higher mountains. The British mountaineer J.E.Q. Barford, who compiled *Climbing in Britain*, has written: "Ben Nevis presents climbing problems as severe as or more severe than any usually encountered in the Alps with the additional handicap of limited daylight."[69]

NUPTSE 25,850ft/7,879m *Nepal*

First ascent, 1961, D. Davis and T. Sherpa.
See LHOTSE.

MOUNT OLYMPUS 9,570ft/2,917m *Greece*

First ascent, 1913, F. Boissonnas, D. Baud-Bovy, and Christos Kakalos.

Mount Olympus, highest summit in Greece, located on the Aegean coast between Thessaly and Macedonia, reminds us that the ancient Greeks, for all their snobbish sophistication, originated as a primitive people not too different in many ways from the barbarians they came to abhor. One characteristic they shared with other primitive peoples was making mountains the mythological home of their gods. It's a process that has occurred in the Himalaya, in Japan, in China, in the South Pacific, among the Indians of North and South America, and in Africa, and more complete records doubtless would show it at work elsewhere in Europe. Nor is this process to be regarded as merely a crude aberration in human history. Nothing could have been more common or natural than that our ancestors should have viewed high mountains as the abode of the powers that ruled their universe—powerful, remote, unpredictable, unassailable.

It's not known when Olympus first acquired religious associations, but as the region's conspicuously dominant mountain, it likely was the object of a cult early, prior to the Dorian invasion circa 1200 B.C. Successive invaders would have adapted the settings of local cults to their own mythologies. Certainly by the ninth century B.C. the mountain was well known to the Greeks; Homer's *Iliad* mentions Zeus addressing the other gods from the highest peak of "many-ridged Olympus." It's usually unclear whether such statements meant the mountain literally or whether the peak merely symbolized a divine realm high above the earth. Originally, however, the mountain was believed the actual home of the gods, and evidence that a mountain cult existed on Olympus even in Hellenistic times is shown by recent discoveries of an altar and Hellenistic coins on the summit of Agios Antonios (9,236ft/2,815m), a subsidiary summit of Olympus.

The original meaning of the name Olympus has been lost, though it has been suggested that it comes from a Caucasian word meaning "mountain." Plausible but only speculative—and in any case the name's original meaning long since has been eclipsed by the meaning given it by Greek mythology. Olympus has become so well known as the home of the gods that the name now is a synonym for lofty divinity, hence the adjective Olympian. Indeed, Olympus is perhaps

157

the best example of a mountain name better known than the peak itself; even mountaineers sometimes are surprised to learn that there really is a Mount Olympus and that it really is a big, formidable mountain.

It was inevitable that a mountain name as famous as Olympus would be imitated elsewhere. The best-known Mount Olympus outside Greece is the peak in the state of Washington, USA, that gave its name to the peninsula and range where it is located (see entry). But the Olympus in Washington, and even the one in Greece, impressive though they are, are not the highest or largest mountains to which the name has been given. A strong possibility exists that the largest volcanic mountain in the entire solar system is the gargantuan volcano on Mars that astronomers have named Olympus Mons. Discovered in 1879 by the Italian astronomer Schiaparelli, who called it Nix Olympica, it is a truly enormous volcano, with ten times the volume of Earth's largest volcano, Mauna Loa (see entry). Its elevation of 88,587ft/27,001m makes it slightly more than three times the height of Everest; it covers a circular area approximately 432mi/695km in diameter; and it's guarded by an escarpment that in several places rises as much as four miles/seven kilometers above the surrounding plain. If ever a mountain was Olympian, that one is.

MOUNT OLYMPUS   7,965ft/2,427m   *Washington, USA*
First ascent, West Peak, 7,965ft/2,427m, 1907, L. A. Nelson and party. Middle Peak, 7,930ft/2,417m, 1907, B.H. Browne, W.G. Clark, G.W. Humes, H.C. Parker, H. Sisson. East Peak, 7,780ft/2,371m, 1899, J. McGlone.

On 4 July 1778 the English explorer Captain John Meares looked from the deck of his ship in the Strait of Juan de Fuca toward the land mass later to be known as the Olympic Peninsula. Mists that earlier had obscured his view dissolved, and he beheld in the south a large, white mountain. He is reported to have exclaimed that this was a mountain fit to be the abode of the gods. With that in mind, presumably, he labeled the peak on his charts Mount Olympus. It was the first English place-name in the state of Washington and the name the mountain has borne ever since.

But Captain Meares was not the first non-Indian to view the mountain, nor to give it a name. In 1774 the Spanish explorer Juan Perez, coasting north along "California," sighted what appeared to be a whole range of mountains, the first range he had come to. He named the highest peak El Cerro de la Santa Rosalia, "Santa Rosalia Mountain." That name, however, like most the Spanish planted in the Pacific Northwest, proved ephemeral.

The first ascent of East Peak came in 1899 when a short Irishman named Jack McGlone, working on a government survey crew camped beneath the mountain, announced to his companions one evening, "I'll just be going up there to have a look around." Several hours later, after dark, he stood on the summit, where he stuffed a piece of newspaper into a tin can and built a cairn.[105]

The Olympic Peninsula where Mount Olympus is located took its name from the Olympic Mountains there, named in turn for Mount Olympus. For a range to be named for its dominant summit is uncommon but not particularly exceptional; the St. Elias Mountains in Alaska are another example. And as history records, what Captain Meares noticed most when looking toward the peninsula was not the mountains but *the* mountain—Olympus.

ONTAKE   *10,049ft / 3,063m*   *Japan*
First ascent unknown.

In a land where many mountains have religious significance, Ontake is second only to Fujiyama in commanding reverence among the Japanese. The mountain's name has been translated as "the august peak," and as W.H. Murray Walton has explained, it comes from a legend from the time of the foundation of the empire, more than 2,600 years ago: "Two great gods stopped on the mountain and made a solemn pledge that they would govern the world and the nations; that they would heal diseases, teach the use of medicines, and drive out false gods; that they would instruct man in the cultivation of rice fields . . . they would explain the right way man should walk, would strengthen his moral sense and would enable him to fulfill the duties allotted to him."[148] Walton further tells of another legend wherein a holy man, En-no-shokaka, banished to an island for three years, sent his spirit at night to worship on the mountain, holding communion with the gods of the mountain and receiving from them the command to "open the mountain." Later, when people neglected their shrines there, they were visited by a plague.

From this background of legend has come one of Japan's oldest cults, whose members in 1951 were estimated at more than three million. Among other activities, they form cooperative societies to enable members—as many as 70,000 annually—to make pilgrimages to Ontake's summit, where they pray and seek temporal blessings. The faithful who make thirty-three or more ascents are called *reijin*, and their devotion is marked by special stones on Ontake's summit.

ORIZABA   *18,700ft / 5,700m*   *Mexico*
First ascent, 1848, F. Maynard and G. Reynolds.

When the weather is clear, travelers aboard ships near Veracruz in the Gulf of Mexico can see the snowcapped cone of Pico de Orizaba, highest of Mexico's three great volcanoes and third highest summit in North America. Like the other two volcanoes, Popocatapetl and Ixtaccihuatl, Orizaba is not presently active, having last erupted in 1566. And also like Popocatapetl and Ixtaccihuatl, Orizaba has figured prominently in the mythology of the local Indian peoples (see entries). But Orizaba differs from Popo and Ixty—and from most mountains anywhere—in having borne two names, Orizaba and Citlaltepetl, throughout its long history. A mountain having two names is not in itself unusual; on the contrary, rare is the mountain that has had only one name during its past. But the typical pattern when two or more names exist for a single place is for one name eventually to become dominant and the others to wither. When multiple names do persist on a mountain, they usually are from different languages; the

159

Matterhorn, for example, is known to the French as Le Cervin, and many Central Asian peaks have both a native name and a European name. For two names—from the same language—to have survived together on Orizaba for several hundred years is unusual indeed.

As their origins indicate, the names Orizaba and Citlaltepetl are old, relics from the time when the Nahuatl language of the Aztecs was spoken throughout central Mexico. And while a few Nahuatl speakers can still be found in the Aztecs' former territories, their language faded rapidly after the Spanish Conquest in the sixteenth century; few places, if any, received Nahuatl names after that.

The most widely known of Orizaba's two names is, of course, Orizaba. It's a corruption of the Nahuatl word *ahuilizapan*, meaning "in the happy waters" and has no direct connection to the mountain but refers instead to the region's rapidly running streams. Thus Orizaba is just one of many mountain names worldwide that can be traced to a watercourse near the mountain. Very likely Orizaba was the name of the ancient Totonac Indian village that survived successive conquests by Toltecs, Chichimecas, Teochichimecas, Mexicas, and conclusively, the Spanish to become the modern city of Orizaba, located southeast of the volcano.

The volcano's other name, Citlaltepetl, is unique to the mountain. In Aztec mythology, Citlaltepetl is the abode of the spirit of Quetzalcoatl, the feathered serpent, watcher over the Aztecs, determiner of their destiny. His body, immolated on the volcano's summit by divine fire, became Venus, the evening star, and Citlaltepetl in Nahuatl means "mountain of the star." This name is much less widely known than Orizaba, but then Orizaba also is the name of the city, a large city with considerable historical and commercial importance. The name Citlaltepetl, however, is found only on the mountain. Moreover, such Nahuatl names are becoming increasingly popular among Mexicans, so the likelihood is great that the volcano's two names will continue to share the mountain in apparently noncompetitive coexistence.

OWEN STANLEY RANGE
Papua New Guinea

Highest elevation, 13,363ft/4,073m, Mount Victoria.

The Owen Stanley Range runs like a spine along the northwest-southeast axis of the huge equatorial island of New Guinea, helping to make the island among the world's most mountainous. Like many of the world's mountain ranges, the Owen Stanley Range bears the name of a man who likely never saw the mountains, or only from afar. Owen Stanley was skipper of the ship that from 1846 to 1850 sailed the South Seas, carrying on board young T.H. Huxley. Stanley, a tragic figure, committed suicide in Australia. Later, when Huxley was exploring the interior of Papua, he named the mountains he found there for his old shipmate.

The Owen Stanley Range's highest summit also has an interesting commemorative name. Though many persons in the United States might not suspect it, Britain's Queen Victoria is by far the world's most popular eponym. Her reign came to symbolize an age of exploration and discovery; it is neither inappropriate nor surprising that her name is found in many of the world's most remote and little-known places. In addition to two Australian states (Victoria and Queensland), the harbor of Hong Kong, the chief town of the Seychelles, and several other cities and towns throughout the world, her name has been given to a huge island in the Canadian Arctic, a major region in the Antarctic, an enormous desert in Australia, a major lake and a spectacular waterfall in Africa, rivers in Australia and Argentina—and at least three mountains, one in Canada, one in the jungle-covered Chin Hills of Burma, and this one crowning the Owen Stanley Range at the far eastern end of Papua New Guinea.

MOUNT OXFORD   *14,153ft/4,314m*   *Colorado, USA*
First ascent unknown.
See COLLEGIATE PEAKS.

PAMIRS   *Central Asia*
Highest elevation, 25,325ft/7,719m Kungur Tagh.

If Marco Polo, traveling along the Great Silk Road to China in 1273, had asked the native peoples there the name of the great mountain range surrounding him, they likely would have told him something resembling Bam-i-dunya, "the roof of the world." It's certainly an appropriate name for the 22,000 sq mi/5,690 sq km mountain cluster from whose center some of the world's greatest mountain ranges radiate like the arms of a spiral galaxy—the Himalaya, the Hindu Kush, the Tien Shan, the Karakoram, and the Kun Lun.

Yet it's only one of the ironies of the Pamirs that of the many interpretations suggested for the range's present name, none refers to its extent or height. For example, the mountain writer John Cleare has pointed out that, strictly speaking, the term *pamir* refers not to the mountains but rather to the broad valleys separating the mountains, dividing them into linear groups aligned east to west. This reinforces the prevalent theory that the name comes from the Persian *pai-mir*, meaning "foot of the mountain peaks." But there have been other explanations for the name. One is that it comes from the Sanskrit *upa-Meru*, "under Meru," Meru being the mountain that in Hindu mythology is the center of the world. Or it might come from the Sanskrit *mir*, "lake," of which there are many in the Pamirs. Or it might have evolved from the Persian *pai-mihr*, "at the foot of the sun," or more precisely, "at the foot of Mithras, god of the sun." Or it might

161

have developed from the name by which the range was known to seventh-century Chinese travelers, *po-mi-lo*. Or the name might have had an origin hitherto unknown or unsuspected.

Still, the Persian "foot of the mountain peaks" is a very credible explanation, particularly as the mountains of the Pamirs have had much less historical significance than their valleys. For another irony of the Pamirs is that they were more routinely traveled in ancient and medieval times than they are today. Though the high peaks of the Pamirs form a natural boundary between China and the Soviet Union, their east-west trending valleys have since ancient times been natural trade and invasion routes. Marco Polo may have been the first European to follow the caravans through the mountains, but the peoples of the East—both Near and Far—knew the routes well. Only when sea routes around India were opened up by the Portuguese navigators Vasco da Gama and Ferdinand Magellan in the sixteenth century did the tide of merchants, diplomats, and travelers begin to ebb in the Pamirs. Now, only occasional parties of foreigners desire and are allowed to visit the range. As of 1982, the highest summit of the Pamirs, located in China, remained unclimbed.

PAPSURA   21,165ft/6,451m   *India*
First ascent, 1967, G. Hill and C. Pritchard.

The third highest peak in the Kulu-Lahul-Spiti Divide of the Punjab Himalaya bears an ominous name that means "peak of evil." The origin of the name Papsura, is obscure, and especially so as it is counter to the common Indian practice of giving mountains commendatory names. As the American names scholar George R. Stewart has explained: "Naming a place for a god, with the idea that the god will then be favoring, constitutes one of the commonest manifestations of commendatory naming. The more dominating the religiosity of a culture, the commoner this type of naming. India is an outstanding example, a numerous pantheon making it possible for names of good omen to be placed even upon the smaller natural features."[133] Papsura, however, is hardly a name of good omen.

While names of such dark meaning as Papsura are atypical in the Himalaya, they are found, albeit infrequently, on mountains elsewhere in the world, their meanings subtly different and the circumstances of their naming widely varied. Though Papsura may be unique in embodying the abstract concept "evil," mountain names merely boding ill are more common. In the Lake Hawea-Lake Wanaka region of New Zealand's South Island are Mounts Awful and Dreadful. In the Green Mountains of Vermont is Mount Horrid, while a mountain in the White Mountains of New Hampshire is called the Foolkiller. The Eiger ("ogre") in the Bernese Alps has become famous partly because of the close association between the name and the evil reputation of the mountain. Disgruntled climbers affixed the name Mount Bellicose to a peak in Alaska's Chugach Range, and it's common for climbers to give climbing routes such gallows-humor names as Crack of Doom and In Cold Blood. Names of volcanoes, of course, constitute a special category, for these mountains have unique destructive qualities that make obvious the origins of such names as Pico del Teide ("peak of hell") in the Canary Islands and Sangay ("hell") in Ecuador. Local folklore also contributes many mountain names of ill omen, and especially in places like the Pyrenees, where examples include "the peak of hell" and "the accursed peak"—(see entry)—a name whose meaning is echoed in Mont Maudit, a major summit of the Mont Blanc massif. And local folklore, coupled with religion, is responsible for names such as Agung on the island of Bali; because spirits are believed to haunt the mountains, its name means "mountain of the dead." But as for the origin of the name "peak of evil," Papsura . . . .

MOUNT PARNASSUS 8,061 ft/2,457m Greece
First ascent unknown.

Mount Parnassus, located near Delphi in central Greece, today is a barren massif, but in ancient times its slopes were adorned with laurel, myrtle, olive trees, and conifers—a pleasant, beautiful place. Though we can only conjecture, it's tempting to believe that the mountain's delightful, perhaps even inspirational, ambience had some bearing upon the ancient Greeks' regard for the mountain as sacred to Apollo and the Muses, patrons of poetry and song, and to Dionysus, god of wine. Apollo and Dionysus each were assigned one of the mountain's twin summits, in ancient times called Lycorea and Tithorea. On the summit sacred to Dionysus, priestesses known as the Thyades held orgiastic ceremonies on alternate years, and the mountain's valleys and springs also had mythological significance.

Even the mountain's name was explained by mythology. The name Parnassus was old even in classical times, its true origins lost, and it's not surprising that a folk etymology developed based upon contemporary beliefs regarding the mountain. It was on Parnassus, after all, that the ark of Deucalion, a sort of Greek Noah, came to rest following the flood. The ark's name was Larnax, so the Greeks believed Parnassus had earlier been called Larnassus, after the ark. When the oracle of Delphi was established at the mountain's foot, the name was changed to Parnassus. The ancient writer Peuceris gave another explanation of this, saying it was a corruption of Har Nahas, "hill of divination."

Actually, there might be some slight truth in that explanation. While the ark–mountain connection is sheer myth, the first syllable of the name does mean "hill" or "mountain." The American names scholar George R. Stewart has pointed out that *par-* is found in the names of other Greek mountains— Parnon, Parnes, Parthenios, and even Parthenon, which was the name of the hill before it became the name of the famous temple. As Stewart explains: "By the general principle of repeated generics we can conclude that *par* is especially descriptive of mountains, and most likely means 'mountain' or 'peak'. . . . Even the common noun *parthenon*, 'virgin,' may have been derived from some mountain-dwelling goddess. Since no convincing Indo-European original source exists for *par-*, it may well go back to a pre-Pelasgian [before the Dorian invasion, circa 1200 B.C.] source."[133]

If this is correct, then the names of Greece's two most famous mountains—

163

Olympus and Parnassus—have had remarkably similar evolutions. The name Olympus, like Parnassus, appears to come from an ancient indigenous word of obscure ancestry but likely meaning "mountain," and Olympus, like Parnassus, has acquired such widespread mythological associations that the name has almost become detached from the physical mountain to become part of our civilization's collection of common metaphors. Olympus is the site of lofty divinity, and we climb Parnassus when we aspire to write poetry. Robert Burns used the metaphor in this verse:

> O, were I on Parnassus hill,
> Or had o' Helicon my fill
> That I might catch poetic skill
> To sing how dear I love thee!

MOUNT PELÉE 4,800ft / 1,463m   Martinique
First ascent unknown.

On 8 May 1902, following a month of earthquakes and eruptions, Mount Pelée on the Caribbean island of Martinique exploded, discharging down its slopes a *nuée ardent*—a "fiery cloud" of superheated gasses, rocks, and airborne mud—that overwhelmed the city of St. Pierre and killed all but two of the city's 30,000 inhabitants. Seldom in recorded history had a volcano caused such great loss of life, yet until a schoolteacher noticed some unexpected fumaroles in a valley on the mountain, the people of St. Pierre had no warning that Mount Pelée was anything but benign. Indeed, a lake in the volcano's caldera bore the tranquil name of L'Etang des Palmistes, "lake of the palms," and was a popular picnic site.

The name Pelée means "peeled" or "bare" in French, and the volcano's name sometimes has been translated into English as "bald mountain." Presumably the name was derived from exposed earth or rock near the summit, although Fred Bullard of the University of Texas has pointed out what he suggests is more than a coincidental similarity between the name of the volcano on Martinique and Pele, the Hawaiian goddess of fire whose home is the great volcano Mauna Loa.

The explosion of Mount Pelée on 8 May 1902 followed by only two days the eruption, almost as violent, of La Soufrière (4,500ft / 1,372m), a volcano on the island of St. Vincent approximately 100mi / 160km to the south. There a *nuée ardent* descended on the city of Port Royal and killed 1,600 people. La Soufriére means "sulfur" or "brimstone" in French.

PENDLE HILL 1,813ft / 553m   England
First ascent unknown.

Dominating the landscape of northern Lancashire is a 7mi / 11km ridge whose seemingly unique and specific name actually is a widespread generic name in an elaborate disguise. Pendle Hill honors no person or family named Pendle, nor is

164

the hill associated with a town or river or anything else of that name. Rather, the name Pendle Hill consists of three synonyms for "mountain" brought together by historical accident and welded by the natural processes of language into an onomastic conglomerate.

First came *pen*, a Celtic word for "headland" or "hilltop." With time and with increasing Anglo-Saxon influence, this name lost currency as a generic term and came to refer specifically to the hill, so that local people began calling the ridge Pen Hill, most likely unknowing that *hill* was redundant. This soon coalesced into Penhill, and because Pendle ran more smoothly than Penhill, the ridge became Pendle. But Pendle what? Why, Pendle Hill, of course, so the generic term *hill* again was added. Thus the name Pendle Hill means "hill-hill-hill."

Actually, Pendle Hill is only an exaggerated example of a rather common naming phenomenon, one that most often occurs when different languages meet rather than within a single language. Given how routinely the meanings of words are lost or mutated over time, for names to acquire hidden generics is inevitable, particularly when passed from one language to another. An often-heard example is Mount Fujiyama; *yama* means "mount." Even more common is Mount Ararat; *ara* in Old Persian also means "mount." And occasionally one hears of the Sierra Nevada Range of western North America; *sierra* in Spanish means "range."

Yet curiously, one region where one would most expect explorers to have attached words such as *mount* to names that already convey that meaning is a region whose mountain names actually have very few multiple generics—Central Asia. Perhaps that's because westerners tend to dispense with generic terms altogether when referring to the Himalayan and Karakoram giants; Everest is as common as Mount Everest, and K2, Nanda Devi, Annapurna, Lhotse, and many others are known by their specific names almost exclusively. Whatever the reason for this tendency, it has spared us such grotesqueries as the Gasherbrum Peaks, Mount Dhaulagiri, and Nanga Parbat Mountain, for these already have "mountain" in their names (see entries). Still, names with multiple generics do carry much information about the people who have lived with the names over time, and peeling back a name such as Pendle Hill is somewhat akin to uncovering archaeological stratification.

PENNINE ALPS
Switzerland–Italy

Highest elevation, 15,203ft/4,634m, Monte Rosa.

Today the Celtic peoples are associated with the British Isles and Brittany in France, but names such as that of the Pennine Alps remind us that the Celts once inhabited most of western Europe. Using such evidence as frequency of place-names, scholars have concluded that the ancient homeland of the Celts was in what is now southern Germany. But when the Celts began their great migration in the centuries before Christ they moved south and west. Thus they would have been familiar with the major mountain systems of southern and central Europe, and it is not surprising that some of their names are still found there. Many of these names are derived from the ancient Celtic word *pen*, surviving in modern Welsh as *pen* and in modern Gaelic as *ben* (see Ben Nevis). Strictly speaking, *pen* becomes "head," "top," or "end," but through time it has become a synonym for "mountain" and perhaps is best translated as "peak" or "summit." In this form it appears as Mount Pindus in Greece, in the Apennines of central Italy, and in the name of the range containing the greatest concentration of high mountains in western Europe. The Pennine Alps encompass seven of the nine Alpine peaks exceeding 14,000ft/4,267m: Monte Rosa, 15,203ft/4,634m; Dom, 14,913ft/4,545m; Liskamm, 14,852ft/4,527m; Weisshorn, 14,782ft/4,506m; Matterhorn, 14,690ft/4,478m; Dent Blanche, 14,295ft/4,357m; and Grand Combin, 14,154ft/4,314m. Only Mont Blanc, 15,771ft/4,807m, and the Finsteraarhorn, 14,002ft/4,268m, of the Bernese Alps are missing.

PENNINE CHAIN   *England*
Highest elevation, 2,903ft/885m, Cross Fell.

About all the Pennine Chain of England and the Pennine Alps of Switzerland have in common is their names. Where the Swiss peaks are high and rugged, the English hills are low and rounded. Where there are glaciers in Switzerland, in England there are moors. And even their names, though identical in form and meaning, have had dramatically different histories. The name of the Swiss mountains is a relic of very ancient Celtic habitation (see Pennine Alps), whereas that of the English hills was applied relatively recently. It appears in English records no earlier than the eighteenth century, and it almost certainly was a deliberate invention of one William Bertram (1723–65).

Yet despite their character, certainly humble when compared to the Alps, the Pennines are dear to English rock climbers and hikers, and J.B. Priestly has called the chain "the knobbly backbone of England."[69] For long-distance walkers, the Pennine hills are best known for the Pennine Way, a 250mi/402km footpath from Kinder Scout in Derbyshire to Kirk Yetholm near the Scottish border. And even for less ambitious outdoorsmen, the Pennine hills offer easily accessible respite from the great industrial cities of northern England. Many of the great events of English history took place in the Pennine hills, from Roman times through the Industrial Revolution, and the often bleak but always beautiful landscape there beckons Englishmen still.

PICHINCHA   15,696ft/4,784m   *Ecuador*
First ascent (possibly), 1582, T. Orteguerra; (certainly), 1802, F.H.A. von Humboldt and party.

Looming over Ecuador's capital, Quito, just six miles to the northwest, is the volcano Pichincha. Though it now is dormant, its last eruption in 1881, the volcano's name is a constant reminder of possible volcanic activity in the future; in the local Quechua language *pichincha* means "boiling mountain." Pichincha's

166

proximity to Quito caused it to be well known among early European explorers of the Andes, and its name appeared on a late eighteenth-century list of the world's mountains.

PIKES PEAK   *14,100ft/4,298m*   *Colorado, USA*
First ascent, 1820, E. James and party.

To understand the significance of Pikes Peak for nineteenth-century explorers and pioneers of the American West, one would have to travel as they did, on horseback or in ox-drawn wagons, ploddingly slow, across the seemingly endless grasslands of the Great Plains of what is now eastern Colorado, the horizon on all sides unbroken by any topographical relief. The white tip of a snow-capped peak, tiny in the distance but growing ever larger, would be the welcome signal that soon the grasslands would be left behind and the realm of mountains entered. The peak would be Pikes Peak.

That, doubtless, was how the sight of Pikes Peak affected Lieutenant Zebulon M. Pike when he and his party exploring the Louisiana Territory for the source of the Mississippi in 1806 became the first white men to record seeing the peak. Drawn to the mountain, Pike attempted to climb it, but poor route finding caused him to fail, and he pronounced it unclimbable. He later wrote of how the mountain, which he called Grand Peak, appeared to him from the summit of another mountain: "The summit of Grand Peak, which was entirely bare of vegetation and covered with snow, now appeared at a distance of fifteen or sixteen miles [twenty-four km] from us, and as high again as we had ascended, and would have taken a whole day's march to have arrived at its base, where I believe no human being could have ascended to its pinnacle."[12] Fourteen years later, however, Dr. Edwin James, botanist on Major Stephen Long's expedition, and two other men climbed the mountain without much difficulty, and it has been climbed innumerable times since then. Indeed, the auto road to the summit now is the route of an annual running marathon.

The Indians of the region knew the mountain as "long mountain," for its shape. Though Pike had called it Grand Peak, his maps labeled it simply as the "highest peak" in the wilderness. Alexander von Humboldt's map of New Spain referred to the general mountain uplift around Pikes Peak as the Sierra de Almagre (Spanish, "range of red ochre") but gave no specific name to the peak. Major Long attempted to name the mountain for James, the man who first climbed it, but even by that early time the mountain was more closely associated with the man who discovered it. Colonel Henry Dodge called it Pikes Peak in 1835, and the name was repeated in 1840 by the explorer John C. Fremont, who certainly was echoing a name current among the region's mountain men.

(The name Pikes Peak also appears in Vermont. Although Pike is a local family name there, the "peak" actually is a hill, suggesting that the name was applied as a humorous allusion to the more famous mountain in Colorado.)

Pikes Peak became famous nationally in the 1850s when gold-seekers painted the slogan "Pikes Peak or Bust!" on their wagons. When they found little or nothing, the ebullience turned to bitterness, and they called the venture the

167

"Pikes Peak Fiasco" or the "Pikes Peak Hoax." They were wrong. Thirty years later extremely rich gold deposits were found around the mining camp of Cripple Creek, located at the foot of Pikes Peak.

MOUNT PILATUS   6,994ft/2,132m   Switzerland
First ascent unknown.

Although superstitious fear has inspired many a mountain's name (see Papsura), rare indeed is it for the mountain's name to inspire superstitious fear. Pilatus, a minor but scenic peak overlooking Lake Lucerne in central Switzerland, is perhaps the only example.

The name Mount Pilatus originally came from the Latin Mons Pilatus, "the hooded mountain," derived from the "cap" of clouds the peak wears when the wind is from the west. This characteristic made the mountain a sort of local barometer and inspired the following rhyme:

> If Pilatus wears his cap, serene will be the day.
> If his collar he puts on, then mount the rugged way.
> But if his sword he wields, then keep at home I say.[69]

But perhaps it was inevitable that the close resemblance between the name of the mountain and that of the Roman governor who allowed the crucifixion of Christ would inspire a legend about Pontius Pilate. And so, people living near Mount Pilatus came to believe that Pontius Pilate committed suicide by drowning himself in a tiny lake near the mountain's summit. Moreover, they believed his spirit still haunted the peak, a malevolent, gloomy ghost able to summon bad weather to avenge anyone disturbing the waters of his lake. Thus another local rhyme evolved:

> When the thunderclaps ring out,
> When the storm chorus howls,
> Then rises up from the flood,
> The ghost of a coward.[39]

In 1387 six priests were punished for daring to climb the peak (though it surely had been ascended before then), and centuries later persons climbing the mountain were chaperoned by local officials who ensured that no stone was thrown into the lake. The superstition finally was put to rest in 1855 by the state pastor of Lucerne, who climbed the mountain, tossed rocks into the lake, and challenged Pilate to come forth. He didn't—a coward perhaps, even in legend.

PILOT   North America

During the exploration and settlement of North America, traders, prospectors, explorers, and surveyors often used prominent peaks as landmarks. Because these mountains would "pilot" them in the right direction, Pilot became one of the most common mountain names in North America. In California alone there are at least twenty orographic features named Pilot, and the name also appears in Utah, Nevada, Wyoming, Oregon, Arizona, Washington, North Carolina, and New Hampshire, as well as other states. Usually the names

168

North face of Pilatus. From Francis Gribble, The Early Mountaineers *(London: 1899).*

are old, dating from early exploration of the region. Also characteristic is that the mountains, knobs, and hills bearing the name usually are visible for a great distance.

PISGAH

Widespread

Probably no mountain name better illustrates the type of naming that names scholar George R. Stewart has called "commendatory" than Pisgah. Its appearance in the United States is widespread, and it is found in New York, Pennsylvania, Wyoming, California, North Carolina, Vermont, and other states. But everywhere its origin is the same: the impulse by local Christian settlers to commend to their locality, through the process of naming, the blessings and hope associated with the Mount Pisgah of the Bible. It was from Mount Pisgah in the land of Moab that Moses looked down upon the land that God had promised to the people of Israel at the end of their long journey out of Egypt.

169

Most scholars of the Bible have concluded that Pisgah (the name is mentioned eight times in the Bible) is another name for Mount Nebo. The location of Nebo on the Moab Plateau, commanding a wide view and overlooking the desert, certainly fits the description of Pisgah in Deuteronomy 34:1: "The top of Pisgah, which looketh down upon the desert." Further evidence is the name itself. At least one scholar has derived Pisgah from *pasgah*, which in Hebrew means "to split" or "to cut off," suggesting a mountain whose steep sides appear to have been cut out. That description closely fits Mount Nebo as viewed from the Dead Sea.

POBEDA PEAK   24,406ft/7,439m   China–USSR
First ascent, 1956, V. Abalokov and party.

Pobeda Peak is the highest mountain in the Tien Shan Range and the second highest in the USSR. Thus its first ascent was a prize eagerly desired by Soviet mountaineers. Not until 1932, however, was its existence even suspected, and not until 1946, when A. Letavet's expedition finally topped the Marmornaya Stena—the "marble wall"—and had an unobstructed view to the south, was its location confirmed. The actual ascent of Pobeda required a very strong party, led by Vitali Abalokov, and their success depended, in part, on using snow caves to wait out bad weather. The mountain's name reflects their achievement: *pobeda* in Russian means "victory."

POGRAMNI   6,568ft/2,002m   Alaska, USA
First ascent unknown.

Dominating the southwest end of the Aleutian island of Unimak and rising more than a mile directly from sea level is the volcano Pogramni. The mountain was named by the Russians, who organized and sponsored the earliest explorations of the Bering Strait and the Aleutian Islands and who colonized the region. The name Pogramni often is reported to mean "black, smoldering death." That's not quite accurate, though it is an apt epithet for an active volcano. Rather, the Russian name, as it appeared on an 1847 Russian chart, Sopka Pogramnaya, is best translated as "desolation peak." *Pogramnaya* comes from the same Russian root word meaning "devastation" that appears in Yiddish as *pogrom*, meaning "an organized massacre of helpless people, specifically Jews."

POPOCATAPETL   17,887ft/5,452m   Mexico
First ascent, 1522, Francisco Montaño and Spanish soldiers.

From their great city of Tenochtitlan, the Aztecs of central Mexico could look southeast and see the two volcanoes that are Mexico's second and third highest mountains. One volcano was forever quiet, and they named it Ixtaccihuatl (17,343ft/5,286m), "the white woman," because its profile resembled that of a reclining woman covered with a white sheet. The other volcano, however, slept only fitfully, awakening occasionally to shake the earth and emit clouds of smoke and ash. This volcano they named Popocatapetl, which in Nahuatl, the language of the Aztecs, means "smoking mountain."

Although the Aztec legend linking Ixtaccihuatl and Popocatapetl represents Popocatapetl as a famous warrior (see Ixtaccihuatl), the Aztecs feared the mountain, regarding it as the abode of evil spirits, and they made no attempt to climb it. The first recorded attempt was made in 1519 by Diego de Ordaz and some other soldiers of the Spanish adventurer Hernando Cortez. Though Cortez in a letter to Charles I, King of Spain, says the soldiers were repulsed near the summit by what was likely a minor eruption, the Aztecs regarded the very attempt as further evidence of the awesome and incomprehensible power of the strange white invaders. As the Friar Lopez de Gomara wrote of the venture: "The Indians said, what mean these men? For as yet never mortal man took such a journey in hand."[69] The actual ascent—the first recorded peak ascent in the western hemisphere—was made four years later when Francisco Montaño and some other Spanish soldiers were lured to the top by Cortez's offer of a reward to anyone able to bring down some sulfur needed to make gunpowder. (Sulfur later was mined in the volcano's crater.)

The Aztec civilization collapsed following the conquest of Mexico by Cortez. The capital of the Aztecs eventually became the capital of Mexico, and the lakes that surrounded Tenochtitlan have all but disappeared. But the volcanoes remain as the Aztecs knew them, "Ixty" beautiful in its long sleep and "Popo" still emitting wisps of smoke, dormant only since its last eruption in 1920. And in the villages at the foot of the mountains the Indians still speak the Nahuatl language whose syllables form the mountains' names.

(A mountain in the Coast Range of Oregon also is named Popocatapetl. A government surveyor, aware of the meaning of the Mexican mountain's name, gave the Oregon peak its name because the crew members who climbed it were "smoking hot" when they reached the top.)

PRESIDENTIAL RANGE

New Hampshire, USA

Highest elevation, 6,288ft / 1,917m, Mount Washington

The highest summits in northeastern North America are found in the Presidential Range in the White Mountains of northern New Hampshire. But though many White Mountain peaks now bear the names of United States presidents, the peaks that earned the Presidential Range its name were named when the United States had only five presidents to so honor. On 31 July 1820 a party of seven men, mostly from the northern New Hampshire village of Lancaster, ascended Mount Washington for the stated purpose of naming the high peaks. The party included the map-maker Philip Carrigain and was guided by the famous White Mountain explorer and guide Ethan Allen Crawford.

Mount Washington had already received its name (see entry), so the namers decided to christen the adjacent peaks for the four subsequent presidents—John

Adams, Thomas Jefferson, James Madison, and James Monroe, who was in office at the time. The naming was a momentous event, and the men had brought with them plenty of "O-be-joyful" so that proper toasts could be drunk. Then, running out of presidents, they christened Mount Franklin for Benjamin Franklin, and the next peak to the southwest they called Mount Pleasant (now Mount Eisenhower), a name it facetiously has been suggested was inspired by the O-be-joyful.

Since then, the names of other presidents have been added to the Presidential Range: John Quincy Adams, Franklin Pierce, and most recently, Dwight David Eisenhower. Other presidents having their names on peaks in the White Mountains, though not in the Presidential Range, are Abraham Lincoln, James A. Garfield, Grover Cleveland, and Calvin Coolidge.

Naming mountains for presidents is hardly unique to the White Mountains, however, and presidents' names are found on major and minor mountains throughout the United States. In fact, not long after the New Hampshire peaks were first named a man named Hall J. Kelley campaigned to have the Cascade Range in the Pacific Northwest renamed the Presidential Range, with individual peaks honoring individual presidents (see Mount Adams). The well-intentioned effort failed, allowing the name of the New Hampshire range to remain unique.

MOUNT PRINCETON 14,197ft/4,327m Colorado, USA
First ascent unknown.
See COLLEGIATE PEAKS.

PUMASILLO 19,915ft/6,070m Peru
First ascent, 1957, Cambridge Andean Expedition.

When climbers of the Cambridge Andean Expedition, after long, difficult route-finding and ice-climbing, finally reached what they thought was the summit of Pumasillo, they found that the true summit still was ahead of them, a jagged spire of ice separated from the climbers by a formidable gap. Thus Pumasillo had lived up to the ominous connotations of its name, a Quechua word meaning "puma's claw." The climbers succeeded in crossing the gap and in conquering Pumasillo, but the final assault was only the last of many difficulties that had faced the expedition. Located in a remote, unmapped region of the Cordillera Vilcabamba of Peru, the mountain's existence and position were not recorded until 1956, and a month of difficult and taxing exploration was required before the Cambridge expedition was able even to reach the base of the mountain.

Pumasillo is an especially appropriate name for this mountain, but the Quechua Indians are fond of naming places for animals (see Huayhuash), and Pumasillo is only one of many natural features in Peru named for pumas, just as natural features named for bears are common in North America.

PUMORI   23,442ft/7,145m   *Nepal*
First ascent, 1962, G. Lenser, V. Hurlemann, and H. Rutzer.

Viewed from the Khumbu icefall beneath Everest, Pumori appears as a tower-ing white cone, its steep sides buttressed by formidable ridges. The mountain would have been a familiar sight to the British mountaineer George Leigh Mallory during his 1921 reconnaissance of Everest, and the unnamed peak so impressed him that he named it for his infant daughter, Clare, presumably tak-ing the word *pumori* from the language spoken by his Nepalese guides and porters. The name means "daughter peak."

PYRENEES   *France–Spain*
Highest elevation, 11,168ft/3,404m, Pico Aneto.

The phrase "Europe ends at the Pyrenees" has become a cliché, but that does not diminish its truth. For almost nowhere else do mountains form as clear and effective a boundary as the Pyrenees form to separate the sun-baked Iberian Peninsula, rich with Moorish influence, from the rest of Europe. Actually, the 270mi/434km range is better compared not to a barrier but to a sieve, allowing small elements to pass through but blocking large ones. The Pyrenees have been pierced often—by Hannibal, by Vandals and Visigoths, by the Moors, and by the French and Spanish. Yet the cultures and civilizations flanking the moun-tains, despite strong similarities in origin and development, remain unalterably different.

The origin of the name Pyrenees is uncertain. At least four explanations exist, each plausible. One says Greek colonists and traders transferred to the moun-tains the name of a native town, Pyrene, originally an Iberian word of unknown meaning. If so, this would parallel the origin of the name of the Appalachian Mountains in eastern North America. Another explanation says that the name is derived from the Celtic word *byren*, meaning "ridge." If so, this would parallel the origin of the name of the Apennine Mountains in central Italy. Still another explanation says the name comes from classical mythology, from Pyrene, the nymph whose son Cycnus battled with Hercules and who legend says is buried in the mountains. If so, this would parallel the origin of the name of the Atlas Mountains in northern Africa. And finally, an explanation says the name is derived from a Greek word meaning a "rounded knob," a reference to some Pyrenees foothills. If so, then this would parallel the evolution of the name of the Andes Mountains in South America.

MOUNT RAINIER   14,410ft/4,392m   Washington, USA
First ascent, 1870, H. Stevens and P.B. van Trump.

The naming trait that distinguishes English-speaking peoples from other peoples is the exceptional—some would say excessive—fondness of the English for naming places for people. Everest, McKinley, and Rainier—each mountain was named by an English-speaker for a person who likely never saw the peak named for him. Consequently, each has been embroiled in chronic controversy as to what the proper name for the mountain should be, for in each case the English name has been applied over a native name many people feel would be more appropriate: Everest, McKinley, Rainier—Sagarmatha, Denali, Tacoma.

Yet when the British navigator Captain George Vancouver, exploring the Strait of Juan de Fuca in 1792, named the distant "round, snowy mountain," highest summit in the Cascade Range, for his friend Peter Rainier, he had no inkling or concern that a native name existed, nor would he have suspected that one day people would object to his choice of a name. On the contrary, Vancouver intended the naming to honor both the man and the mountain, for Peter Rainier, in addition to being Vancouver's friend, was a very distinguished British seaman, soon to be a rear admiral, who had won honor in several important campaigns, including the American Revolution. Rainier was the grandson of Huguenot refugees whose name in France had been Regnier. He eventually became an Admiral of the Blue and served in Parliament. To Vancouver he was an important person indeed, a fit eponym for an important mountain.

Unfortunately, many Americans didn't agree, particularly as the mountain did have a prior name, one many people felt was even more appropriate than that of the British seaman. That name was Tacoma (or something close to that), the name the Indians of Puget Sound called the mountain. Yet curiously, and unfortunately for the proponents of Tacoma, the controversy didn't begin until more than half a century after Vancouver's naming, and by then Rainier's name already was firmly established.

No one has questioned that the name Rainier can claim priority among formally bestowed names for the mountain. It was the first name to appear on a map, and it was the name that appeared in the journals of early explorers, who often were casual about its spelling. Lewis and Clark called it both Rainy and Reeaneer. Parker's map of 1833 labeled it Ranier. And on some early maps the name even reverted to its ancestral form, Regnier.

The name Tacoma entered the scene in 1863, when it appeared in Theodore Winthrop's widely read *The Canoe and the Saddle*, where it was used to refer to

Mount Rainier. Actually, transliterations of the original Indian term have varied, the most widespread being *tahoma*, not *tacoma*, and consequently interpretations of the term's meaning also have varied. Common translations are "the mountain," "the gods," "big snow," and others, but the most popular interpretation has been the poetic "the mountain that was God."

Winthrop's use of this name for the mountain coincided with an incipient rivalry in the state of Washington between the burgeoning cities of Seattle and Tacoma, which had taken its name from Winthrop's book. And it was not lost upon the citizens of Tacoma that the prestige of their city would be considerably enhanced if the state's most important mountain bore the same name. Moreover, Indian names were very popular in the latter nineteenth century, when Americans were trying to preserve a rapidly vanishing, already romanticized Indian heritage. The name Tacoma, in addition to being indigenous, also had considerable romantic and patriotic appeal, particularly when it was pointed out that Peter Rainier had been a vigorous foe of the United States during the Revolutionary War. (Rainier partisans countered by saying that Rainier's valor in the cause of his country made him all the more worthy of respect, even in the land of his enemies.)

The controversy smoldered for decades. Among the more substantive issues in the debate was whether the Indian term was, in fact, applied specifically to the mountain or whether it was merely a generic term for any high, snowy mountain. Also undecided was which form of the name should be accepted—Tacoma, Tahoma, Takhoma, Tacobet, or another variant.

The matter finally was resolved—if such issues ever are—in 1924. Following passage in the United States Senate of a joint resolution officially changing the name to Tacoma, the House of Representatives requested a report from the United States Geographic Board—which opposed the change.

But people are stubbornly independent in the names by which they call the familiar natural features around them, and place-name controversies—whether about Everest, McKinley, or Rainier—are like fires in sawdust piles, ready at any time to flare forth anew just when everyone had assumed them dead.

MOUNT ROBSON   12,972ft/3,954m   British Columbia, Canada
First ascent, 1913, A.H. MacCarthy, W.W. Foster, and C. Kain.

To early fur traders of British Columbia, the mountain rising above the junction of the Fraser and Grand Rivers would have been an obvious and compelling landmark. Taller than all others in the Canadian Rockies, the peak is bold and dramatic, its north face rising 10,000ft/3,048m above the lake at its base, the striations of the mountain's sedimentary composition a striking pattern except where erased by near-vertical ice slopes. There, in the shadow of the peak, the traders would rendevous before returning east with their furs, and as early as 1827 the mountain had a name—its present name. It appeared in a diary one George MacDougal kept that year. Describing how the place then known as Tete-jaune Cache got its name—from a fair-haired half-breed who had his fur cache there—MacDougal mentions that it was "near the meeting of the Grand

River—which flows from the base of Mount Robson—and the Fraser River."[12] Fred Beckey, writing about Robson in *Mountains of North America*, quotes an official of the Hudsons Bay Company who gives a plausible explanation for the name: "Years before the Hudsons Bay Company and the Nor'west Company joined [1821], it was the custom for the Nor'west Co. to outfit a party for a two-years trip, hunting and trading. . . . One party (was) under the charge of Peter S. Ogden, some two hundred men, chiefly Iroquoian and French Canadians. When west of the Rockies he [Ogden] scattered his hunters in different parties under the charge of a foreman to hunt for the season. One of his camps, under the charge of a man named Robson, was somewhere in the vicinity of this mountain, and it was the rallying point where all other parties came together for their return east."[12]

The Indians are reported to have called the mountain Yuh-hai-has-kuh, though writers differ as to whether this was the name of the Crees or the Kamloops. This name has been translated as "mountain of the spiral road," the image surely inspired by the striations appearing to encircle the mountain like thread on a spool.

But the respect Mount Robson is accorded among mountaineers is only partly due to the mountain's awesome appearance; by any standards Robson is a formidable mountain to climb. The first ascent of Robson in 1913 culminated six years of attempts and was one of the greatest achievements of Conrad Kain, among the foremost professional guides of his time. High angles, loose rock, malevolent weather, and severe avalanche hazards prohibit safe, easy routes.

ROCKY MOUNTAINS
Western North America

Highest elevation, 14,433ft/4,339m, Mount Elbert.

In a sense, the name Rocky Mountains is a tautology: mountains *are* rocks. But to the French-speaking trappers and explorers who gave the range its name, coming as they were from eastern North America where the rounded, forest-clad mountains only rarely reveal their stone foundations, the jagged, thrusting "rockiness" of the western peaks would have been one of the mountains' most striking characteristics. Thus these French explorers, approaching the Rockies from the Great Lakes, found it easy to translate the Cree Indian word for the mountains into *les montaignes rocheuse*, "the rocky mountains."

Actually, the history of the name is a bit more complex than that. When the Cree Indians told the French explorers of some mountains to the west, they used the Algonquian word for stone, *assin*, or one very much like it, and the French assumed that the Indians were referring to "stone" or "rocky" mountains. But it also is possible the Crees were saying that the mountains were in the land of their friends and allies, the Assiniboine Indians, whose tribal name also comes from *assin*, from their using hot stones to cook (see Mount Assiniboine).

Regardless of what the Crees meant, when the Indian Ochagach in 1730 drew a map for Sieur La Verendrye showing the mountains, the French explorer labeled them the Montaignes de Pierres Brilliantes, or "mountains of bright stones," and for a brief time the mountains were called the Shining Mountains. (The range has had other ephemeral names: Missouri, Mexican, Snowy, and Stony.) But by 1752, the journal of Legardeur St. Pierre referred to the mountains by their present name, Montaignes de Roche, or "rocky mountains."[3]

It's appropriate that the name Rocky Mountains should pass into English from the French, because that parallels the history of the words themselves. *Rock* came into Middle English from the Old Northern French *roque*, which in turn was derived from the Low Latin word *rocca*, which came from a presumed pre-Latin root. That's exactly how the English word *mountain* evolved: into Middle English from Old French, *montaigne*, derived in turn from the Low Latin, *montanea*.

Considering how frequently mountains are named for an obvious and common characteristic, such as their color (Mont Blanc, Green Mountains, Blue Mountains) or their shape (Hogback, Sugarloaf, Aiguilles), it is surprising that the name Rocky Mountains doesn't appear more often, especially as the Rockies have no monopoly on "rockiness." Yet Kelsie Harder's *Dictionary of Place Names: United States and Canada* connects the name Rocky with only five mountains versus eleven rivers and creeks.[61] The name of the Shickshock Mountains of southern Quebec means "rocky mountains" in a local Indian language, and Rocky Mountains once was proposed as a name for the Brooks Range in Alaska. A stony hill in North Carolina bears the name Rocky Mount, and west of Mount Rainier in Washington is a formation called The Rockies. But in North America, in its present form, the name of the continent's greatest range is unique.

THE ROOSTER COMB   10,180ft / 3,103m   *Alaska, USA*

The Rooster Comb is among the peaks comprising the mountain group surrounding Mount McKinley in the Alaska Range. It is separated by a col from Mount Huntington to the west, and climbers attempting Huntington often attempt its neighbor as well. In 1910 Claude Rusk, writing about an expedition of the Mazamas mountain club of Portland, Oregon, described the peak as "a remarkable mountain . . . its tip a succession of corniced spires like a great rooster comb."[100] It was an apt characterization, so much so that in 1957 Bradford Washburn successfully proposed that Rooster Comb be adopted as the mountain's name.

The Rooster Comb is an especially vivid descriptive name, but mountain names based on resemblances to animals' parts are by no means uncommon. For example, one explanation for the names of Crestone Peak and Crestone Needle in the Sangre de Cristo Mountains of southern Colorado is that they come from the Spanish *creston*, "cockscomb." In the Alaska Range with the Rooster Comb there is a peak called the Mooses Tooth. In the Green Mountains of the northeastern United States there is Camels Hump. In the Peruvian Andes there are Pumasillo, "puma's claw," and Jirishanca, "hummingbird's beak." The name of Machapuchare in the Himalaya near Annapurna means

177

"fish's tail." Even the French name for the Matterhorn, Cervin, "deer," is said to have been inspired by the peak's resemblance to a deer's antlers. Similar examples are easily found.

MONTE ROSA   *15,203ft / 4,634m*   *Switzerland–Italy*
First ascent, 1855, J.G. and C. Smyth, E.J. Stephenson, V. Lauener, J. and M. Zumtaugwald.

The name Monte Rosa is descriptive, but despite appearances to the contrary, the name does not mean "red mountain" in Italian but rather "glacier mountain" in Aostan. The name comes from an Aostan patois word *roëse*, meaning "glacier." And from the air Monte Rosa appears almost buried in glaciers, a great, ice-covered dome that has been compared to Mont Blanc, the only mountain in the Alps higher than Monte Rosa. (Monte Rosa, located in the southern Pennine Alps, is the highest mountain in the two countries whose border it forms.)

Monte Rosa is a very complex mountain, with at least eleven summits. By 1854 all but one of these had been climbed, by Italians, Swiss, and others. The summit that remained, the highest, was the Dufourspitz, named for the Swiss surveyor General Dufour, who accurately fixed the position of several summits in the area. The climbing of the Dufourspitz's two rocky horns—the lower in 1854 and the higher in 1855—by Anglo-Swiss parties has been called the dawn of the Golden Age of Mountaineering, a ten-year period that saw all the important peaks of the Pennine Alps climbed by British-inspired parties assisted by local guides.

RUWENZORI RANGE   *Uganda–Zaire*
Highest elevation, 16,763ft / 5,109m, Mount Stanley.

Probably no mountain names better capture the history and character of the mountains they identify than the names borne over the centuries by the Ruwenzori Range on the Uganda–Zaire border. In ancient times the mountains were known as the Mountains of the Moon and were believed to be the source of the Nile. But when the Greek geographer Ptolemy in the second century after Christ included the Montes Lunae on his map, it was only coincidence that he put the mountains approximately where they actually are located. To the ancients, the Mountains of the Moon were more myth than reality; people believed that from the mountains' summits, which no one actually had visited, one could look south to behold a great ocean stretching to the Antipodes.

For centuries persistent rumors and tales of a mysterious mountain range in the heart of Africa continued to excite men's imaginations. Leonardo da Vinci wrote of the Nile: "It is known that it issues from the Mountains of the Moon by several unknown sources. . . . We must conclude those mountains to be of the greatest height upon which clouds, falling in snow, give rise to the Nile."[76]

The Alpine Club at Zermatt, 1864. From Edward Whymper, Scrambles amongst the Alps 1860-1869 (Philadelphia: 1873).

Thus when European and American explorers in the nineteenth century began in earnest to probe Africa's mysteries—and seek the true source of the Nile—the discovery of the fabled Mountains of the Moon was among their most desired prizes.

It was 1876 when the American explorer Henry M. Stanley first appeared in east and central Africa. He, too, had heard rumors of high mountains still deeper in the continent's interior, and he doubtless would have been aware of the name the Arab traders of East Africa had for the fabled mountains; they called them the Mirage Mountains. But it was not until 1888, as he was traveling along the shores of Lake Albert, that he first glimpsed the mountains, appearing, appropriately, almost like a mirage. "I saw a peculiar-shaped cloud of a most beautiful silver color," he wrote, "which assumed the proportions and appearance of a vast mountain covered with snow."[139] Only after watching the apparition for several hours was he convinced that he was looking not at a cloud formation but at distant peaks. Not realizing the significance of his discovery, he named the peaks Mount Gordon Bennett, after the owner of the New York *Herald*, for whom Stanley was working.

To at least some natives of Central Africa, the mountains were called the Mystery Mountains, certainly a fitting title. But when Stanley actually visited the mountains twelve years after discovering them, he chose to adopt for them another native name perhaps even more appropriate: Ruwenzori can be translated to mean "place from whence come the rains," or "rain mountains."

The Ruwenzori are among the wettest mountains on earth. On their upper slopes as much as 150 inches/381 centimeters of rain fall annually—and as often as 350 days a year. Even on the rare days without precipitation, warm, moist air rising from the jungle below is condensed into fog on the mountains' heights. This was why the mountains eluded discovery for so long; even persons in the mountains' immediate vicinity simply could not see them for their perpetual cloak of mist. When the Duke of the Abruzzi in 1906 finally stood on the summit of the range's highest peak, all he could see was an ocean of clouds.

The Duke of the Abruzzi's enormous expedition, equipped and managed like a small army, was a tour de force. Before departing, the party climbed and named all the major summits in the range. In the Ruwenzori six massifs include peaks topping 15,000ft/4,572m: Stanley (16,763ft/5,109m), Speke (16,042ft/4,890m), Baker (15,889ft/4,843m), Emin (15,740ft/4,798m), Gessi (15,470ft/4,715m), and Luigi di Savoia (15,179ft/4,627m). And with consistency rare in mountain naming, each peak is named for a person who figured prominently in the exploration of Africa, including the Duke of the Abruzzi, Luigi di Savoia, himself.

Today the Mystery Mountains have lost much of their mystery, and ascents of the peaks have become common. Yet the dense vegetation and perpetual precipitation that have made the Ruwenzori a mountaineer's nightmare also have made them strange and tantalizing, unlike any other mountains on earth. Normally diminutive plants grow outsize, and above the permanent snowline at 14,250ft/4,343m rime encrustations assume fantastic, unearthly shapes. Thus it's perhaps fitting that the mountains' ancient name survives and that many people still refer to the Ruwenzori as the Mountains of the Moon.

S

MOUNT ST. ELIAS   18,008ft / 5,489m   Alaska, USA
First ascent, 1897, the Duke of the Abruzzi; V. Sella; four Courmayeur guides, including Petigax and Macquinaz; and four others.

The most common explanation for the name of North America's fourth highest mountain is that it was named in 1741 by the Danish navigator Vitus Bering because the day on which he discovered it, July 20, was the day sacred to St. Elias. It's an easy, plausible explanation—the Laurentian Mountains (see entry) and the St. Lawrence River in northeastern North America were named because they were discovered on the feast day of St. Lawrence—but it's only partially correct. The American mountain names scholar Francis P. Farquhar, going to journals and logs kept during Bering's voyage, found that while Bering did sight mountains that most likely included Mount St. Elias, he did so not on the saint's day but three days earlier, on July 17.[42] An entry for that day reads: "We sighted high, snow-covered mountains and among them a high volcano N by W."[42] A name for the mountain is not mentioned. Rather, the name St. Elias apparently was not given originally to the mountain but to a cape. The journal of Sven Waxel, Bering's Swedish lieutenant, chronicled the events: "We sighted land in the direction of N by W and at a distance of about twenty-five German miles [120 nautical miles]. This land consisted of huge, high, snow-covered mountains. We attempted to sail in closer towards land, but as we had only light and shifting winds, it was not until 20th July that we drew near to it. At six o'clock in the evening of that day we let go our anchor in the neighborhood of an island of considerable size, lying at no great distance from the mainland. . . . On our map we called the place Cape Elia, since . . . it was on Elia's day that we had anchored there."[42] The island, too, they named for the saint. For the nearby mountains to assume the name of the island would not have been unusual, and when charts of the area appeared, they showed the name St. Elias on the peak. The irony is that in the meantime the name was disappearing from the island, which now has the name Kayak.

Farquhar has contemplated the meaning of the name St. Elias as applied to this mountain and the range named for it: "Elias is the Greek name of the prophet Elijah. In the Orthodox and Russian churches many of the Old Testament prophets and other worthies are saints. Elias seems particularly appropriate to mountains, witness Hagios Ilias, one of the high peaks of the Greek Olympus, perhaps because 'Elijah went up by a whirlwind into heaven' (2 Kings, 2:11). At all events, the name of the saint has long since left the island . . . and ascended to the mountain."[42]

MOUNT ST. HELENS   8,364ft/2,549m   *Washington, USA*
First ascent, 1853, T. Dryer and party.

Like Mounts Hood and Rainier, Mount St. Helens in southwestern Washington was named in 1792 by the British navigator Captain George Vancouver for an influential figure in British affairs. Vancouver's journal entry for 20 October 1792 records the naming: "The clearness of the atmosphere enabled us to see the high round snowy mountain, noticed when in the southern parts of the Admiralty inlet, to the southward of mount Rainier. . . . Like Rainier [it] seemed covered with perpetual snow, as low down as the intervening country permitted it to be seen. This I have distinguished by the name of Mt. St. Helens, in honor of his Britannic Majesty's ambassador at the court of Madrid."[43]

Vancouver's naming of Mount St. Helens was similar to his other mountain namings. The men Rainier, Hood, and St. Helens now are but footnotes in history and are remembered, when at all, chiefly because of their coincidental association with these important peaks, but in Vancouver's time they were much more well-known than the mountains named for them. Alleyne Fitzherbert, Baron St. Helens, was described in language characteristic of the times as "a man of parts and of infinite zeal and industry."[43] He was ambassador extraordinary to Spain in 1790, and for his role in settling the Nootka Sound dispute he was raised to the Irish peerage as Baron St. Helens. He later joined the British peerage.

Vancouver's naming of Mount St. Helens also paralleled that of Rainier and Hood in that the name was bestowed in ignorance of local Indian traditions regarding the mountain. The best known of these (see Mount Hood) relates Mounts Hood, Adams, and St. Helens. In this legend, two brothers, Wy'east (Mount Hood) and Klickitat, or Pah-to (Mount Adams), sons of the Great Spirit, fought over a beautiful maiden, Loo-wit (Mount St. Helens). In one Indian version of the legend, Loo-wit is called Si Yeet, "woman," while in another she's called Tah-one-lat-clah, "fire mountain."

This last name is a reminder that Mount St. Helens is one of the Cascade Range's great volcanoes—that is, if a reminder is needed after the cataclysmic eruption in 1980 that blew off the mountain's top and devastated the surrounding landscape. As Fred Beckey has pointed out: "St. Helens' recent violence has made people forget that the mountain was once a serene snow cone of classic symmetry, an American counterpart of Japan's Fujiyama."[12] Indeed, Mount St. Helens had been called "the Fujiyama of America." But the two mountains share another similarity: Fuji, like St. Helens, has a history of destructive eruptions.

SANDIA MOUNTAINS   *New Mexico, USA*
Highest elevation, 10,678ft/3,255m, Sandia Peak.
See SANGRE DE CRISTO MOUNTAINS.

SAN FRANCISCO PEAKS   *Arizona, USA*
Highest elevation, 12,633ft/3,851m, Humphreys Peak.

The Hopi Indians of northern Arizona regard as sacred the volcanic cone whose three summits comprise the San Francisco Peaks. Yet the peaks' present name comes not from the religion of the Hopis but from that of their conquerors. And though the name was given by persons living in the Hopi village of Oraibi, those persons were not Indians, but rather were Spanish Franciscan missionaries who by 1629 had named the mountain for the founder of their order, St. Francis of Assisi. It has been suggested that the missionaries gave the name San Francisco to diminish the importance of the peaks in the Hopis' native religion, but though the Franciscans sometimes did give names for this reason, there is no evidence to support that this was a motive for the naming of the San Francisco Peaks.

The early Spanish explorers and settlers have had other names for the peaks. The most common of these has been Sierra Cienega, "mountain of the spring," but it's possible that this is a corruption of an earlier name, Sierra Sinagua, having the opposite meaning, "mountain without water." In 1776 the peaks were referred to as Sierra Napoc, which has been interpreted as referring to the Navajo Indians of the region. Still another name found on old Spanish maps is Sierra de los Cosninos, another reference to a local Indian group. But the name that's survived is the one the missionaries gave, San Francisco.

According to geologists, the "peaks" were once a single mountain, a huge volcano as high as 15,000ft/4,572m, and the occasional use of the name San Francisco Mountain reflects this. But eruptions and erosion have reduced the volcano to its present size and created three distinct summits: Fremont, Agassiz, and Humphreys, the highest point in Arizona.

SANGAY   *17,159ft/5,230m*   *Ecuador*
First ascent, 1929, R. and T. Moore, W. Austin, and L. Thorne.

Sangay, a major summit in Ecuador's eastern chain of volcanoes, has been said to take its name from a Quechua word meaning "hell"; of this, Michael Koerner, who visited the peak, wryly observed: "Getting there is the reason why." (Probably a better translation would include "devil," as "hell" is an alien concept among the local peoples there.) But difficult access is among the lesser obstacles mountaineers face in climbing Sangay, and Sangay's name was inspired not by the mountain being remote, but rather by it being an extremely active volcano, perhaps the world's most active. So frequent and unpredictable are Sangay's eruptions that making the ascent has been likened to running a gauntlet, and in 1976 a British party didn't make it. Overcome by a sudden eruption that buried them in hot rocks and ash, two climbers died, and three others, badly injured, could only be rescued with great difficulty. For them, Sangay's name had become terrifyingly real.

SANGRE DE CRISTO MOUNTAINS

Colorado–New Mexico, USA

Highest elevation, 14,338ft/4,370m, Blanca Peak.

In the late eighteenth century a folk religion began to evolve among the rural Hispanic peoples of northern New Mexico. Its members were called Los Hermanos Penitentes, "the Penitent Brothers." The Penitentes, as the brotherhood's members are more commonly called, did more than conduct pious observances; they also functioned as a mutual aid society and were a powerful force in organizing the isolated communities. Novices and initiates often were called "Brothers of Blood," and though this aspect of the Penitentes has been exaggerated, real blood occasionally was shed by zealots inflicting penance upon themselves.

The naming of the Sangre de Cristo Mountains, in whose villages the Penitentes still are an important part of community life, seems associated with the rise of the sect and what has been called "its accentuated devotion to the Passion and Death of the Savior."[103] Sangre de Cristo in Spanish means "blood of Christ." Penitente Peak (12,249ft/3,733m) is one of the higher summits of the range, and on the summits of other peaks, such as the Truchas Peaks (12,102ft/ 3,689m), shrines have been found. Among the Penitentes, the name Sangre de Cristo gave the mountains great religious significance. Before that name became accepted, the mountains were called the Sierra Madre Mountains, "mother range," but the Penitente name is the one that has survived—as have the Penitentes.

The romantic appeal of the name Sangre de Cristo has inspired other explanations, mostly apocryphal, of its origin. One says that the mountains were named during the Pueblo Revolt of 1680, when the Pueblo Indians of New Mexico rose up to massacre their Spanish oppressors. According to legend, a dying padre named Juan asked for a sign from heaven. When the mountains he beheld turned red at sunset, he exclaimed, "Sangre de Cristo!"

South of the Sangre de Cristo Mountains in New Mexico another mountain range was named because of its reddish hue at sunset. The name of the Sandia Mountains east of Albuquerque means "watermelon" in Spanish, and several explanations for the name have been suggested, such as that it is derived from watermelon-like gourds at a nearby Indian pueblo. The most appealing explanation is that the mountains, composed of a granite base capped by white limestone layers, at sunset strongly resemble a slice of watermelon, its pinkish heart protected by a white rind.

MOUNT SARMIENTO 7,546ft/2,300m Chile
First ascent, 1956, C. Mauri and C. Meffei.

Mountain names honoring specific individuals are relatively rare in South America—certainly compared to North America—but they do occur, particularly outside the Quechua-speaking area of the Andes. Mount Sarmiento, near the southern tip of the continent, is an example.

184

Domingo Faustino Sarmiento (1811–1888) was an Argentine statesman, educator, and gifted journalist who was known as the "teacher president" for his unremitting efforts to foster education in his country. His name on a peak in Chile is not as surprising as it might seem. Like Abraham Lincoln, whom he much admired, Sarmiento was born of humble origins, in western Argentina near the Andes. Also like Lincoln, Sarmiento entered politics after a period of self-education and miscellaneous employment, and his passionate opposition to the cruel dictatorship of Juan Manuel de Rosas led to his exile to Chile. There Sarmiento continued to write pamphlets about education and politics, and there he wrote *Facundo*, the three-part work that has become a classic portrayal of life on the Argentine pampas. When Rosas fell from power in 1852, Sarmiento returned to Argentina, serving as ambassador to the United States, where he met such congenial figures as Horace Mann, Ralph Waldo Emerson, and Henry Wadsworth Longfellow. From 1868 to 1874 Sarmiento served as president of Argentina. Shortly before his death in Paraguay, Sarmiento wrote to a friend: "I must soon start on one last journey. But I am ready. . .for I carry the only acceptable passport, because it is written in every language. It says: Serve mankind."[84]

SCAFELL PIKE   *3,210ft/978m*   *England*
First ascent unknown.

At least two things make Scafell Pike unique among England's mountains: it is the highest point not only in Cumbria but also in all of England, and it is perhaps the only mountain war memorial anywhere, having been given many years ago to England's National Trust to honor the Lake District men who died in World War I. The col of Mickledore separates Scafell Pike from its slightly lower neighbor, Scafell (3,162ft/964m), from which the higher peak most likely takes its name, adding only the Old English mountain generic *pike*, or "peak."

The many names of Norse origin in northern England and Scotland are reminders of the relatively long habitation there of Norse-speaking peoples. The name Scafell combines the two Old Norse words *skali*, "shepherd's hut," and *fjall*, "hill," together meaning "hill on which a small hut is located."

Scafell is not the only Old Norse mountain name in the Lake District. Skiddaw (3,058ft/932m) to the north is believed to take its name from two Old Norse words, *haughr* and *skyti*, interpreted variously to mean "projecting crag" or "ski or snowshoe mountain." Skiddaw is among the least difficult of the higher peaks of the Lake District, and of its ascent a local wag has written:

> Laal brag it is for any man
> To clim opp Skidder side;
> Auld wives and bairns on Jackasses
> To tippy twop ma ride.[111]

SCHIEHALLION   *2,546ft/776m*   *Scotland*
First ascent unknown.
See Introduction.

SENTINEL RANGE
Antarctica

Highest elevation, 16,860ft/5,139m, Vinson Massif.
See VINSON MASSIF.

SGURR ALASDAIR
3,309ft/1,009m
Scotland

First ascent, 1873, A. Nicolson.

It's rare for a mountain to be named for the first person to climb it; even rarer is it for that person to have been born and raised near the mountain. Alexander Nicolson—writer, journalist, and lawyer—was born on the Isle of Skye in northwestern Scotland, and by 1865 he was exploring the mountains of his homeland. He made the first ascent of Sgurr nan Gillean, and in 1873 he climbed the highest point in the Cuillin Hills. The peak was then unnamed, but it afterward was named for him, Sgurr Alasdair being but the Gaelic form of Mount Alexander. (More precisely, *sgurr* means "rocky peaks," but on Skye the word also is used as the generic term *mount*.)

MOUNT SHASTA
14,161ft/4,316m
California, USA

First ascent, 1854, party led by E.D. Pearce.

Under an entry dated 31 January 1814, Alexander Henry and David Thompson, exploring what is now northern California, recorded the names of some Indian tribes they had found there: "They [the Indians] said they were of the Wallawalla, Shatasla, and Halthwypum nations."[56] From the "Shatasla" Indians, Mount Shasta, the northernmost major peak of the Cascade Range in California, takes its name—but the story is more complicated than that.

In 1817 a Spanish expedition led by Luis Argüello into the southern Cascades sighted a very large, snow-covered mountain. The diary of Fray Narcisco, a member of Argüello's party, recorded the mountain's appearance and its naming: "At about ten leagues to the northwest of this place we saw the very high hill called by the soldiers that went near its slopes Jesús María. It is entirely covered by snow."[12] Although scholars have questioned whether or not this mountain was, in fact, Mount Shasta, it's nearly certain that Argüello saw Shasta in 1821 during his second expedition. But like so many names the Spanish planted in the Pacific Northwest, the name Jesús María soon withered, and once again it remained for an English speaker to name the mountain, albeit with an Indian name.

That English-speaking explorer was Peter Skene Ogden, whose journal entries tell of the naming. On 10 February 1827 he wrote: "Here we are among the Sastise." And four days later he wrote: "I have named this river Sastise River. There is a mountain equal in height to Mount Hood or Vancouver, I have named Mount Sastise. I have given these names from the tribes of Indians."[56] Later in his diary Ogden spelled the name Sasty, and the sketchy nature of his entries has caused some persons to doubt whether the river and the mountain he named are the ones bearing those names today. Most people now agree that the river Ogden was referring to is the Rogue River and not the Shasta River, but he is generally credited with naming Mount Shasta.

Five years later the name Shasta appeared on Arrowsmith's "Map of British North America," published in 1832, and by 1841 the name Shasta was firmly affixed to the California mountain, though it took some time for the name's spelling to stabilize. Lieutenant Charles Wilkes, whose overland expedition saw the peak in 1841, wrote of it: "The Shaste Peak is a magnificent sight, its steep sides emerging from the mists which envelop its base. . . . Its cleft summit gave proof of its former active state as a volcano."[12] John C. Fremont, who saw the peak five years later, called it both Shastle and Tsashtl, and other variants have included Shasti, Shasty, and Saste. In 1862 the surveyor William H. Brewer reported hearing an Indian pronounce the name "tschasta," and as the spellings Chasty and Chasta occur on some early maps, it's very possible that these approximate the native pronunciation. For a brief time the mountain was even known as Shasta Butte. But by the latter half of the nineteenth century, the name had settled into its present form. (Shastina, a coined "feminine" or "diminutive" form of Shasta, appears on the mountain's lower summit.)

Although Mount Shasta bears an Indian name, it is not the name by which the Indians themselves knew the mountain. The Sastise, or Shas-ti-ka, Indians living at the mountain's base called the volcano Wai-i-ka, "snowy mountain," the world's most common mountain name. The nearby Wintu Indians also called the peak by a common descriptive name, Bo-lem-poi-yok, "high peak." Fred Beckey reports that the various tribes around Mount Shasta had myths telling of spirits living on the mountain, but as he points out, "The Indians probably knew little about the howling winds and subzero temperatures that can occur on Shasta."[12]

SHAWANGUNK MOUNTAINS New York, USA
First ascent unknown.

The dramatic and difficult cliffs of the Shawangunk Mountains are among the most popular rock-climbing centers in the eastern United States, similar in appeal to the sea cliffs beloved of British rock climbers. Moreover, the cliffs are easily accessible from major population centers, such as New York City only 50 mi/80km to the southeast. Known to climbers simply as "the Gunks," the Shawangunks take their name from three Algonquian words that merely describe the cliffs: *shaw*, "side," *ong*, "hill," and *unk*, "at"—"at the hillside."

Such descriptive names are typical of those that North American Indians—and preliterate peoples generally—gave to natural features. And while their meanings may seem commonplace, even banal, in a contemporary context, these names were very important to these early cultures. For such names served as identifiers in a world without maps; in such a world, a name meaning "at the hillside" would have infinitely greater utility than a name honoring a person, such as George Everest. Consequently, honorific names are virtually unknown among Indians. European peoples, however, have had different needs and tastes, and because early European settlers in New York State valued the sound of the name Shawangunk more than its meaning, the name still survives, untranslated, close to its original form.

SHICKSHOCK MOUNTAINS

Quebec, Canada

Highest elevation, 4,160ft/1,268m, Mount Jacques Cartier.

The great Rocky Mountains spanning western North America and the diminutive Shickshock Mountains on the Gaspe Peninsula in Quebec would seem to have little in common. Yet the names of both passed into English from a French interpretation of Indian names, and the names of both mean the same thing. Shickshock, which appeared on maps in this form as early as 1857, comes from a Micmac Indian term best translated as "rocky mountains." The name also has appeared as Chic Choc, a form the French would pronounce approximately the same as the English would Shickshock. The French explorer Samuel de Champlain labeled these mountains the Notre Dame Mountains on his map of 1632, but now this name is applied to a larger range paralleling the St. Lawrence River, of which the Shickshock Mountains are only a small segment.

SHIPROCK 7,178ft/2,188m

New Mexico, USA

First ascent, 1939, B. Robinson, R. Bedayn, J. Dyer, and D. Brower.

In northwestern New Mexico there is a dramatic rock formation, the eroded core of an ancient volcano, whose spires and buttresses seem to soar, or to sail, above the surrounding high plains. To the region's Navajo Indians, the formation is *tsi bida' hi*, "rock with wings," and to English-speakers it's Shiprock. The huge volcanic plug is sacred to the Navajos—they have often refused permission to climb it—and it figures prominently in three of their myths. One tells of the time the Navajos crossed a narrow sea beyond the setting sun and landed among unfriendly people; to rescue them the Great Spirit sent a stone ship, now Shiprock. Another says that the rescue was effected not by a stone ship but by a great bird, which turned to stone upon alighting safely with the Navajos. The third tells of the Navajos being cast up from the earth at this spot, with the ship of Shiprock the symbol of their voyage. It has been suggested that these myths are of relatively recent origin, because they do not appear in some early ethnological accounts of the Navajos.

There is no easy ascent of Shiprock; the first ascent party not only had to face severe and exposed climbing but also had to solve difficult and deceptive routefinding problems. (The key to the climb was going down, not up, during one pitch.) Though the spires since then have been climbed numerous times by several routes, Shiprock remains a difficult climb, whenever permission to climb it is granted, with many routes still unattempted.

188

SHISHA PANGMA   26,398ft/8,046m   Tibet
First ascent, 1964, Chinese expedition headed by Hsu Ching.

For most of its history, this peak in the Langtang Himal has been known by its Nepalese name, Gosainthan, rather than by its Tibetan name, Shisha Pangma, despite the mountain being entirely within Tibet by a few miles. One reason the Nepalese name is better known is that access to the mountain usually has been through Nepal.

Since the Chinese occupation of Tibet, few westerners have been allowed to visit the mountain. That explains, in part, why Shisha Pangma was the last 8,000m Himalayan peak to be climbed. As the only 8,000m peak entirely within Chinese control, only Chinese parties had been given permission to climb it. The Chinese expedition credited with the first ascent is reported to have included 195 members, and details of their actually reaching the summit are inconclusive because no summit photos have been made available. As Louis C. Baume has explained: "The chronicle of Gosainthan, or Shisha Pangma, is one of endeavors to glimpse the mountain rather than one of attempts to climb it. This most elusive of mountains—geographically, politically, and literally—has been climbed but once, from the north, though whether the actual summit or only the foresummit was attained is still in some slight doubt."[11]

Another reason the name Gosainthan has predominated over Shisha Pangma involves the names themselves. Shisha Pangma is a simple descriptive name meaning in Tibetan "the crest above the grassy plain." Gosainthan, however, can be translated from the Nepalese to mean "place of the saint" or "abode of God." These meanings almost certainly are derived from Gosainthan being near Gosainkund, the largest of many lakes in the area, but more importantly the lake Hindus believe is where sleeps the god Siva, paramount deity of Nepal. Thousands of pilgrims visit the lake and its shrines each year, and the mountain is sacred also. Though most geographers put Shisha Pangma in Tibet, Nepalese maps showing the Nepal–Tibet boundary are drawn to include access to Shisha Pangma's summit.

SHIVLING   21,467ft/6,543m   India
First ascent, 1974, H. Singh, L. Singh, and four Sherpas.
See NANDA DEVI.

SIERRA NEVADA   Spain
Highest elevation, 11,421ft/3,481m, Mulhacen.

The highest mountains in Europe west of the Alps are in Spain, but they are not in the Pyrenees, as many people might suspect, but rather are found in a range in southeastern Spain only 25mi/40km from the Mediterranean. Indeed, the mountains are so high that though the range has no glaciers, winter snow and permanent snowfields make the origin of the name, "snowy range," obvious, almost inevitable, in a region with an otherwise mild climate.

The Sierra Nevada towers over Granada, the Spanish city that more than most has preserved and symbolized the Arab conquest and occupation of Spain. The range's highest summit, Mulhacen, takes its name from Muley Hacén, one of the last Moorish kings. When Muley Hacén's son, Boabdil, in 1492 surrendered Granada to the united Christian kingdoms, the era of Moslem domination of Spain ended. According to legend, Muley Hacén dug his tomb into the peak later named for him.

SIERRA NEVADA
California, USA

Highest elevation, 14,495ft/4,418m, Mount Whitney.

The name Sierra Nevada is merely the Spanish form of the ubiquitous mountain name "snowy range." The name has been applied frequently throughout the Spanish-speaking world, but probably the two best-known applications are the Sierra Nevada of southern Spain (see entry) and the 400mi/644km range in eastern California that includes the highest peak in the United States outside Alaska.

The popularity of the name Sierra Nevada can be seen in the name having been used in California two centuries before it was first applied to the range it now identifies. As early as 1542 the name was given to the mountains south of Carmel now known as the Santa Lucia mountains. In 1556 a Spanish map showed much of California covered by glaciers called "Sierra Neuados." In 1566 another map showed a more well-defined range running east–west in the latitude of Alaska; this, too, was called Sierra Nevada. Other map-makers in the century that followed used the name for other ranges along North America's western coast.

The name was first applied to the present Sierra Nevada in 1776 by the Franciscan missionary Fray Pedro Font, who had come from Mexico to found a colony at San Francisco Bay. After surveying the landscape from a hill near the juncture of the Sacramento and San Joaquin rivers, he wrote: "If we looked to the east we saw on the other side of the plain at a distance of some thirty leagues a great *sierra nevada*, white from the summit to the skirts, and running about from south-southeast to north-northwest."[56] On Font's map of 1776 the name includes not only the present Sierra Nevada but also the Coast Ranges of southern California. Although Font in 1777 published another map depicting with remarkable accuracy the mountain features of the region, his map was not well known, and for a long time there was confusion and ambiguity about the range and its name. The mountains sometimes were mistaken for the Rocky Mountains, and the name Sierra de San Marcos was used by some cartographers for some mountains in the general vicinity of the Sierra Nevada. Further complicating matters, English-speaking trappers and mountain men early in the nineteenth century began calling the mountains the California Range. But by the 1840s the name Sierra Nevada was becoming established, and its use in the widely distributed maps and reports of the explorer John C. Fremont formalized its acceptance.

It's ironic that while the name of the Sierra Nevada dates from very early

Spanish contact with California, the names of the peaks in the range generally are not Spanish and are relatively recent. As Francis P. Farquhar has observed: "Until the coming of the California State Geological Survey [headed by Josiah Dwight Whitney] in the 1860s, none of the high peaks had been named. Consequently, the Whitney men had a clear field. And most of the names they chose were neither Spanish nor descriptive but rather honored specific individuals."[45]

Probably the individual who was most closely associated with the Sierra Nevada was the naturalist John Muir (1838–1914), who found in the range an almost mystical communion with nature. (The Whitney group of mountains, which includes six 14,000ft/4,267m peaks, is often called the Muir Crest.) Muir suggested that the mountains be called the Range of Light. Though map-makers and geographers have never recognized the name, it doubtless will survive among mountain travelers who are reminded of it as they find in the Sierra Nevada some of the beauty and clarity found there, before them, by Muir.

MOUNT SINAI   8,652ft/2,637m   Egypt
First ascent unknown.

Without doubt, the most momentous mountain ascent in all human history was that of Moses up Mount Sinai: "Moses was in the mount . . . with the Lord forty days and forty nights . . . he did neither eat bread nor drink water. And he wrote upon the tables the words of the covenant, the Ten Commandments."[99] These events, and the laws Moses brought down from the mountain, have become central to the beliefs of three of the world's major religions: Judaism, Christianity, and Islam. And because most scholars have accepted the Exodus as having roots in an actual historical event, it becomes legitimate to ask: which mountain was the Sinai Moses ascended?

Scholars and explorers for centuries have attempted to answer that question, and the evidence they've gathered is very strong, though not conclusive, for accepting the traditional site, the prominent massif at the southern tip of the Sinai Peninsula. For one thing, the mountain there is consistent with Biblical accounts of the Exodus. The people of Israel could have reached the mountain in the time mentioned in the Bible, and water sources near the mountain could have supported their encampment there for more than a year. Moreover, the ancient Hebrews, like other early peoples, regarded high mountains as mysterious and sacred, and as Josephus, the historian of the Jews, wrote in the first century after Christ, Sinai is "the highest of all the mountains that are in that country, and is not only very difficult to be ascended by men, on account of its vast altitude, but because of the sharpness of its precipices . . . and besides this it was terrible and inaccessible on account of the rumor that passed about that God dwelt there."[99] Nearly two thousand years later, the nineteenth-century traveler and scholar Dr. Durbin climbed the mountain and wrote: "No one who has not seen them can conceive the ruggedness of these vast piles of granite rock, rent into chasms, rounded into smooth summits, or splintered into countless peaks, all in wildest confusion. . . . Here and here only could the wondrous displays of

Sinai have been visible to the assembled host of Israel. . . ."⁹⁹

Even in Josephus's time, Sinai was accepted to be part of the great granitic block called el Tur (*el tur* is an Arabic term applying to any lofty mountain). The highest peak in this block—and in the Sinai massif—is Jebel Katarin (8,652ft/2,637m), Arabic for "Mount Catherine," so named because the bones of the saint are said to have miraculously appeared on the summit, where they still repose in a chapel. To the northwest, lower but more conspicuous, is Jebel Musa (7,497ft/2,285m), the "mountain of Moses," where for centuries 3,000 steps cut into stone have taken pilgrims by tens of thousands to the summit. Jebel Musa, topped by a long, jagged ridge, actually has two summits. The one to the southeast is crowned by a chapel; the other, separated from the chapel by three precipitous crags, is called in Arabic Ras-es-Safsafeh, or "the willow top."

While scholarship and tradition both have settled upon the Sinai massif as the historical Sinai, uncertainty has remained regarding the name. Sinai is mentioned thirty-five times in the Bible, but sometimes the word refers to the mountain and sometimes to the nearby desert. The word Sinai is thought to come from a Hebrew root meaning "to shine." (The Babylonian word *sinu*, "the moon," comes from the same root.) Given this meaning, Sinai could plausibly apply to the desert of Sin, perhaps named for the glare of its white sands, but it also could apply to the mountain, especially when the Book of Exodus says "the glory of Jehova was like devouring fire on the top of the mount in the eyes of the children of Israel."⁹⁹

A further complication comes from the fact that the names Sinai and Horeb (from a Hebrew word meaning "waste") are often used interchangeably in the Bible to refer to both the mountain and the desert. Scholars now are convinced that Sinai and Horeb both refer to the same mountain, or at least to the same locality, but as to their meanings and applications at the time of the Exodus there is only conjecture.

SKIDDAW   3,058ft/932m   England
First ascent unknown.
See SCAFELL PIKE.

SNOW MOUNTAINS   Irian Jaya
Highest elevation, 16,500ft/5,029m, Sukarno Peak.

The name complex "white-snowy mountain" is without doubt the most common in the world, appearing in some form almost everywhere there are mountains. But the name is perhaps nowhere more appropriately applied than here, on a mountain range only four degrees from the equator on an island synonymous with jungle. In more temperate regions the name often lacks meaning, the mountains it supposedly identifies actually no more white than others. On these mountains in the western portion of Irian Jaya, however, the name points out the mountains' most distinguishing characteristics: their unexpected snowfields and the elevations that permit them at this latitude.

Mount Sinai, Egypt. From William H.D. Adams, Mountains and Mountain Climbing (London: 1883).

The snowline in the Snow Mountains is at 14,500ft/4,420m, yet several peaks in the range exceed 16,000ft/4,877m, and glaciers stretch for several miles through the main massif, which includes Sukarno Peak and several other summits. The nomenclature of the region is very uncertain, having undergone several changes since Indonesian acquisition of western New Guinea, including a change of the range's highest mountain's name from Ngapalu to Sukarno Peak. Uncertainty about elevations also has caused confusion. The names Mount Carstencz and Carstencz Top are still used, but without unanimity as to which mountains they identify.

The early history of the name Snow Mountains is unknown, but it likely was first applied by the Dutch, who colonized the island, and some English maps still label the range with the Dutch form of the name, Sneeuw Gebergte.

SNOWDON   *3,560ft/1,085m*   *Wales*
First ascent unknown.

In any mountain region the likelihood is high that the dominant mountain will bear a name that can be translated as "white, or snowy, mountain." One example is the highest mountain in the British Isles, Ben Nevis in Scotland (see entry), and another is the highest peak in Britain south of Scotland, Snowdon in Wales.

Like most "white mountain" names throughout the world, Snowdon is relatively old. It's a combination of two Anglo-Saxon words: *snaw*, "snow," and *dun*, "hill." It appeared as Snawdune in 1095 and as Snoudon in 1283, but differences in orthography mean little, and for nearly a thousand years the name has remained close to its original form.

Persons sensitive to the meanings of names will refrain from attaching *mount* to Snowdon—*dun* means "hill" in Celtic—but no great harm is done if it is added. Such multilingual redundancies are among the things that make British mountain names so interesting, and Snowdon, despite its prosaic meaning, is a particularly interesting name. For instance, it suggests that when English adventurers entered Wales sometime in the eleventh century, it must have been in early winter or late spring, when snow would have lingered longer on Snowdon than on nearby peaks. Also, Snowdon is one of only a few English names that have survived being planted in the alien soil of Wales. In some counties one can hardly find a name that is not Welsh, and in Caernarvonshire the only one is Snowdon. This name, however, must share the mountain with the Welsh name Yr Wyddfa (pronounced "with-fa"), and as the English names scholar C.M. Matthews has pointed out, "Wherever one finds an English name in Wales one may be sure that the native one exists beside it."[87]

In form Snowdon has been compared to a starfish, the mountain's five ridges radiating armlike from the central summit of Yr Wyddfa. This name can be translated from the Welsh as "cairn place" or "tumulus," but "lookout" also has been offered as a meaning; each is an apt description of the mountain.

Snowdon has given its name to Snowdonia National Park, which encompasses many other important Welsh mountains: the Glyders, Tryfan, Cader

Idris, Carnedd Llewelyn, and others. The region often is known by its Welsh name Eryri, sometimes translated as "place of the eagles" (*eryr* is "eagle" in Welsh), but also as "highlands." It's a region whose wild and beautiful landscape easily evokes its romantic history and folklore, and the mountains figure prominently in Welsh mythology. The summit of Snowdon, for example, is said to be the tomb of Rhita Gawr, greatest of the giants, who wove his robe from the beards of vanquished kings. Legends live long in Eryri; King Arthur, Merlin, and the ancient warriors are still remembered. Indeed, if Sir Thomas Malory is believed, King Arthur made the first recorded ascent in Wales: "King Arthur yoed up to the creste of the cragge, and than he comforted himself with the cold winde."[111]

Especially beautiful in Eryri are many of its place names. As Amory Lovins has written: "I cannot imagine a Welshman who could call a place by a plain ugly name when he can think of names as beautiful as these: Lake of Longing, Valley of Sound, Cliff of the Wine, Mare, Citadel of Light, Silent Moor, Torrents of Clouds, Hill of the Hawk, River Running, Stream that Lies in the Eye of the Sun."[80] And a passage by the English writer and mountaineer, Hamish Brown, describing one of his journeys in Snowdonia, also conveys some of the magic the mountains' Welsh names impart to the already magical landscape: "We turned southeast . . ., down to Craig yr Ysfa, 'crag of craving,' an array of historic climbing crags above lonely Cwm Eigiau, beyond which we found a surprisingly narrow sweep of ridge overlooking Lynnon Llugwy. . . . It led to Penyr-helgi, 'hill of the black hound.' Tryfan looked like Suilven: cloud-creating and bold. Onwards, to the east, were the 'pass of the three knights' and 'the slippery hill of the witch.'"[18]

For rock climbers, Snowdon has special significance. One of the most popular and certainly among the most respected climbing faces in Britain is the formidable 600ft/183m cliff on Snowdon's shoulder known as Clogwyn du'r Arddu, "Cloggy" to its many climbing devotees. The name is Welsh and can be translated as "the black cliff of the black height." This difficult, forbidding name conveys something of the character of the cliff itself. As Alan Rubin has written: "Its name hints of the feeling of intimidation felt by most who visit the cliff. This intimidating atmosphere, coupled with the very real difficulties of the climbing problems presented by the crag, limited exploration to a few minor lines on the fringes until the 1920s."[125] All that changed after World War II, with routes of the highest standards being developed, and now Cloggy occupies roughly the same position among British rock climbers that El Capitan does among climbers in North America.

STORE SKAGASTØLSTIND   7,887ft/2,404m   Norway
First ascent, 1876, W.C. Slingsby.

Store Skagastølstind is Norway's third highest peak, but Wilfred Noyce has called it the finest in southwestern Norway's Jotunheimen Mountains, the range that includes the only peaks higher—Galdhøpiggen (8,097ft/2,468m) and Glittertinden (8,045ft/2,452m). Noyce also called Store Skagastølstind "a magnificent peak,"[95] and his praise was deserved. Store Skagastølstind is a stark, dramatic, chisel-shaped, difficult peak, and W.C. Slingsby's solo first ascent was the apex of his long career of mountain exploration in Norway. Norwegian mountaineers, who know the peak well, call it Storen, "the big one."

But as with Galdhøpiggen and Glittertinden, the name by which Store Skagastølstind was known to earlier residents of the region had a less imposing meaning. Each of Norway's three highest peaks has a name that merely identifies the mountain with reference to some other feature. With Store Skagastølstind, the other feature is a shieling, or small summer farm. Tom Schmidt of the Institute of Name Research at the University of Oslo explains the history and meaning of the name thus: "Composed with the common peak-name element *tind*, this name describes the peak's situation above Skagastølen, the *støl* belonging to the farm Skagen in the parish of Luster in the county of Sogn og Fjordane. A well-known mountaineer's cabin, Skagastølsbu, also has its name from this shieling. Locally, the shieling is also known as Skardsstølen, describing its position in a *skard*, 'mountain pass,' and the mountains as Skardsstøltindan. These names may well be older than Skaga-, but the latter name is now the only one used on maps and other printed matters."[127]

SUGARLOAF   *Widespread*

Why is it that those of us who have never seen a "loaf" of sugar nonetheless know in advance the general shape of a mountain named Sugarloaf? In fact, people who never even knew sugar ever came in loaves nonetheless are aware that hills and mountains with a symmetrical conical shape are likely to have that name. The reason is that the noun *sugarloaf*, its original referent gone, has acquired another, and now the term refers not to a loaf of sugar but instead to a kind of mountain. Sugarloaf no longer is a confectioner's term but a geographer's.

The term's history began sometime after the advent of the sugar trade in the seventeenth century. Then, sugar commonly was marketed not in its familiar granulated form but in cones, or "loaves," created when hot, liquid sugar was poured into molds. A favorite size was about five and a half inches in diameter at the bottom, three inches at the top, and thirteen inches high. Grocers would break off pieces from the sugarloaves and sell them by the pound. The shape of these sugarloaves was as familiar and recognizable to people in the eighteenth and nineteenth centuries as the shape of an ice cream cone is to us today, and nothing could have been more natural than for mountains shaped like sugarloaves to be named for them. As George R. Stewart has observed: "Apparently the world lacked not only a sweetener but also a word for a conical or conoidal form."[132]

By the hundreds, mountains received this name, and in many languages: *pan de azucar* in Spanish, *Zuckerhut* in German, *pain de sucre* in French, *zucchero in pani* in Italian, and many more. In the mountains of Papua is a peak called the Sugarloaf. The great rock hulk overlooking the bay of Rio de Janiero in Brazil is the Sugarloaf. Diminutive Vermont has four Sugarloaf Mountains. In the

American Southwest, the name appears not only in its English form but also in its American-Spanish form, *peloncillo*, and Arizona and New Mexico both have Peloncillo mountains. (Arizona's Peloncillo Range was named not for all its peaks looking like sugarloaves but rather for one of them.) The student of California place-names, Erwin G. Gudde, has estimated that in California there are some hundred orographic features named Sugarloaf or some variant. He has observed that when used as a descriptive generic term the name usually is broken into two words but when used with another term, such as peak or mountain, it is one word, Sugarloaf.[56]

Again, Stewart: "Worldwide, the most famous metaphorical name is Sugarloaf.... As a metaphorical descriptive for an upstanding hill, mountain, or rock it came to dot, in appropriate languages, all the newly explored parts of the world, and even to make incursions into regions already named. A Sugarloaf Hill appears in Kent. The sugarloaf itself eventually became obsolete, but by that time the use of the word in topography had become established."[132]

Surely, few persons in the eighteenth century could have guessed that one day almost no one would be familiar with a loaf of sugar but that virtually everyone would recognize a mountain named for one. In Alaska there is a peak named Ice Cream Cone Mountain. Will our descendents one day wonder what curious thing could have inspired so common a mountain name?

TABLE MOUNTAIN   *3,567ft / 1,087m*   *South Africa*
First ascent, 1503, Antonio de Soldhana.

Anyone approaching the tip of South Africa from the sea could hardly help noticing what the Portuguese navigator Antonio de Soldhana saw in 1503: a huge mountain whose top is so extensive and flat that a comparison with a table is almost inevitable. Reinforcing the comparison is a distinctive white cloud, formed by moisture-laden southeast winds, that occasionally is draped over the mountain like a tablecloth and that has acquired that name. The first European to sight the mountain was another Portuguese navigator, Bartholomew Diaz, who saw it when he discovered the Cape of Good Hope prior to 1500, but the mountain was first climbed by de Soldhana, who went up it to see whether he had rounded the cape, an ascent repeated often by subsequent navigators. De Soldhana gave the mountain its name, calling it in his language Mesa, and the Dutch and English who followed the Portuguese to South Africa merely translated his name, calling the mountain Taafel and Table.

While the name Table Mountain is particularly appropriate for this mountain in South Africa, the name is not unique. Indeed, the Spanish word for "table," *mesa*, has become a generic term for any mountain or hill characterized by steep sides and a flat top. The name Table Mountain itself has similarly become a generic term for the flat-topped landforms resulting from old basalt flows. In County Wicklow in Ireland there is another Table Mountain (1,760ft/536m), very likely named for the better-known mountain in Africa.

TACONIC MOUNTAINS

New York–Massachusetts–Vermont, USA
Highest elevation, 3,816ft/1,163m, Mount Equinox.

The Taconic Mountains are scenic, forest-covered summits closely related geographically to the nearby Green Mountains of Vermont. The name Taconic is reported to come from an Indian word meaning "wilderness." Perhaps, but some skepticism is warranted because wilderness was an alien concept among early Indians, who knew nothing else and had no basis for comparison or definition. Moreover, using a name meaning "wilderness" to identify a large and rather poorly defined area not necessarily more wild than any other would have been atypical indeed of Indian naming, which tended to focus on distinctive, easily observable characteristics. More likely, the name Taconic is like many in the eastern United States, possibly having an Indian origin, but adopted and applied by English-speaking peoples with an imperfect knowledge of the sounds and meanings of the words they were borrowing.

Two explanations exist for the intriguing name of the Taconic's highest summit, Mount Equinox. The more likely is the one that gives credit for the name to a Colonel Partridge, who in 1823 surveyed the mountain; he is said to have named it for the time of year he was there, the autumnal equinox. Attempts also have been made to find an Indian origin for the name, but John C. Huden, an authority on the place-names of the eastern Indians, has been skeptical of the results.[67] Still, it's possible that the name evolved from an Abenaki word for "place of fog," a fitting and plausible descriptive name.

TAI SHAN   5,056ft/1,541m   China
First ascent unknown.

Of China's five sacred mountains—north, south, east, west, and central—the most sacred is that of the east, Tai Shan. Located south of Beijing in Shandong Province, Tai Shan was venerated even before Confucius climbed it sometime prior to 500 B.C. Confucius wrote about the impressive view from Tai Shan's summit. His works, quoted by generations of Chinese, have perpetuated the name by which the mountain was known to him, making Tai Shan among the world's oldest mountain names in continuous use.

Semantically, the character representing Tai Shan has many meanings, but according to Lin Ziyu, who has specialized in Chinese place-names, the most likely is "safe" or "peaceful."[158] This is because the ancient Chinese emperors climbed this most sacred of mountains hoping to appease the powers governing the unruly Yellow River 35mi/56km to the north. Since then, the mountain has been adopted by Daoists, Buddhists, and Confucians, all of whom have decorated its niches with temples and carved its granite boulders with laudatory inscriptions. On a single day as many as 10,000 pilgrims have climbed the 6,700 stone steps leading to the summit and the Temple of the Jade Emperor.

As a result, Tai Shan has become a symbol of great importance, loftiness, and grandeur. Zhu Bin, another Chinese place-names scholar, reports that the character *tai* thus also means "highest and greatest." He points out that two Chinese provinces, Shandong and Shanxi, were named for this mountain. *Shan* in Chinese means simply "mountain," but it is Tai Shan, first among China's sacred five, to which the names refer.[14]

In addition to Tai Shan, China's five sacred mountains include Heng Shan, Hunan Province, of the south; Hua Shan, Shanxi Province, of the west; Heng Shan, Hebei Province, of the north; and Song Shan, Henan Province, of the center. According to Ziyu, the five sacred mountains are known generally as Wu Yue; *wu* means "five," and *yue* means "sacred, lofty, splendid, and magnificent mountain." Legend has it that these *yue* were the residences of different gods. As a result, emperors and kings of different dynasties held sacrificial rites on these mountains. Ziyu has found two explanations for the origin of the Wu Yue: "One says that the Wu Yue system existed as early as the ancient period of Shun (2179–2140 B.C.). However, it was later proved that such an assertion is a wrong conclusion drawn by scholars of Confucian classics. According to contemporary research, the Wu Yue system started during the regime of Emperor Wu Di (140–87 B.C.) of the Han Dynasty." While the sacred mountains of the east and west, Tai Shan and Hua Shan, have remained fixed throughout history, the names for the southern and northern sacred mountains have shifted from mountain to mountain according to the decrees of various emperors.

TAKHT-E-SULEIMAN GROUP   Iran
Highest elevation, 15,817ft/4,821m, Alam Kuh.

Wilfred Noyce has called the Takht-e-Suleiman massif west of Demavend "the most interesting mountain group of the Elburz."[95] Like many place names in the Islamic world, Takht-e-Suleiman has its origins in religious lore: *takht* in Persian means "seat of a ruler" ("throne" probably is the nearest English equivalent), and Suleiman is the Solomon of the Old Testament. Thus Takht-e-Suleiman is similar to peaks such as Adams Peak in Sri Lanka and Croagh Patrick in Ireland whose names identify them with a religious personage.

MOUNT TASMAN   11,475ft/3,498m   New Zealand
First ascent, 1895, E.A. Fitzgerald, M. Zurbriggen, and J. Clarke.

The two highest summits of New Zealand's Southern Alps both bear the names of European explorers who came to the isolated islands, stayed only briefly, and then departed, never to return. Mount Cook (see entry) was named for the English captain, James Cook, while Mount Tasman, second highest mountain in the range, was named for the Dutch navigator Abel Janszoon Tasman (1603–1659), who discovered and named New Zealand. Tasman's visit was even briefer than Cook's. Sailing into a New Zealand bay in 1642, Tasman's party was attacked by Maori warriors defending their homeland. Tasman saw little advantage in further exploration, and he sailed away, but not before he had marked the site of the attack on his map as Mordenaars Baai, "murderers bay." This name has found little favor among New Zealanders, whose sympathies have been with the Maoris, but they have respected Tasman, whose name appears not only on this peak but also on the great glacier in Mount Cook National Park, where its 19mi/30km length makes it one of the longest in the world outside of Asia and the polar regions.

Ever since the Maoris repulsed Tasman, New Zealanders have maintained a tradition of protecting their territory against what they have seen as conquest by outsiders. When news reached New Zealand in 1894 that the famous European mountaineers E.A. Fitzgerald and Matthias Zurbriggen were coming to make the first ascent of Mount Cook, which had resisted all previous attempts, three young and relatively inexperienced New Zealand climbers made a desperate Christmas Day attempt to beat them. They succeeded. Disappointed, Fitzgerald and Zurbriggen had to settle for first ascents of Tasman and other mountains, joined by seventeen-year-old Jack Clarke, one of the three who had succeeded on Mount Cook.

TEEWINOT   12,317ft/3,754m
First ascent, 1929, F. Fryxell and P. Smith.

Wyoming, USA

Although it is only the sixth tallest summit in the Teton Range, Teewinot is among the most impressive, and according to Orrin Bonney, "Many tourists who view this graceful Teton peak dominating the view from Jenny Lake go home believing it is the Grand Teton."[15] The Indians had names for all the major summits of the Tetons, but Teewinot is the only one that has survived in general use; the current spelling approximates a Shoshonean word meaning "many pinnacles," describing the peak's distinctive appearance.

PICO DEL TEIDE   12,128ft/3,697m
First ascent, 1582, R.E. Scory.

Canary Islands

The highest mountain in the Atlantic Ocean is the volcanic Pico del Teide, which dominates the island of Tenerife in the Canary group. The huge formation rises from the caldera of an earlier volcano, and Pico del Teide's 12,128ft/3,697m summit is made all the more impressive by its being only ten miles from the sea on the north side. The mountain's name is Spanish. Like the names of many volcanoes (see Sangay and Tungurahua) it reflects a history of destructive eruptions; it means "peak of hell."

TETON RANGE
Wyoming, USA

Highest elevation, 13,766ft/4,196m, Grand Teton.

So striking and common is the resemblance between mountain shapes and the shapes of certain other objects that the naming of mountains for them is inevitable. Examples include needles, castles, towers, sugarloaves, teeth, and, of course, women's breasts. The Teton Range of Wyoming is the best known of the "breast mountains," but the name Teton is only one of a large and varied subset of mountain names. In French they occur not only as *teton*, "breast," but also as *mamelle*, with the same meaning. In Missouri there is a rock formation called Les Mamells (sic), a name given by French traders and explorers for the obvious reasons.

But breast names appear to be much more common in English, and especially in the New World, where a spirit of ribald irreverence characterized much of the naming by frontiersmen and pioneers. In California there is a formation called the Two Teats. Tit Butte occurs throughout the American West, and the name Wildhorse Tit in Colorado probably was intended to distinguish one teatlike eminence from another and not to indicate part of a wild horse's anatomy. (Very infrequently, *tit* appears in place-names not because of any association with breasts but rather as a colloquial contraction of the French *petite*, "small," as in Tit Chateau and Tit Blis, both in Louisiana.) In Arizona there is a hill commonly called the Nipple; however, this name usually appears in print as Maidens Breast (said to be a translation of a Havasupai Indian name) because the formation is in a national park. Elsewhere, local sensibilities have been less delicate. In Wyoming cowboys named a mountain Maggies Nipples for a certain Maggie Baggs, not otherwise identified, while California has formations named Nellies Nipples and the even more specific Clara Birds Nipples, this name having been given by the girl's father. Other forms of the name include *pap*—Alaska has a

"The key to the ascent." From Edward Whymper, Scrambles Amongst the Alps
1860-1869 (Cleveland: 1899)

formation called the Paps, and Idaho has a Paps Mountain—and *bosom*, appearing as the Left Bosom and the Right Bosom in the Gannett Peak region of Wyoming.

To the Shoshone Indians of Wyoming, the mountains now called the Tetons were known as the "hoary headed fathers," a name many people have felt is more descriptive of the craggy, almost martial mountains than a word meaning "breasts." These people are correct; the name Tetons originally was applied to another, more breastlike group of mountains. Early travelers to northwestern Wyoming called the present Teton peaks the Pilot Knobs. For example, that was how the exploring party affiliated with John Jacob Astor and led by Wilson Price Hunt and Robert Stuart, referred to them when they passed through the region in 1811–1812. Following his visit in 1824 Alexander Ross wrote: "The great backbone of America are three elevated insular mountains or peaks. They are seen at a distance of one hundred and fifty miles, and the hunters very aptly designate them the Pilot Knobs."[15] Of the name Tetons, Ross applied it to the breast-shaped cratered buttes now known as Twin Buttes and Big Southern Butte near the Craters of the Moon National Monument in Idaho. But when Peter Skene Ogden and his trappers passed through the region in 1825, they transferred the name from the buttes to the more prominent mountains. In his journal entry for 10 June 1825 Ogden wrote: "We had a sight of the Trois Tettons [note spelling] bearing due East, they appear not very distant, but as they are very high the distance must be great."[15]

THABANA NTLENYANA   11,425ft / 3,482m   *Lesotho, Africa*
First ascent, 1951, D. Watkins, B. Anderson, and R. Goodwin.

The relatively late date for the first ascent of this mountain was not due to any technical difficulties. On the contrary, Thabana Ntlenyana appears so unassuming and insignificant that not until 1951 did people realize that it is the highest point in Africa south of Kilimanjaro and thus worthy of an ascent; one was promptly and easily undertaken. The mountain's name comes from two native words that reflect Thabana Ntlenyana's modest character despite its impressive elevation; they mean "little black mountain." (The mountain also sometimes goes by the native names Thabantshonyana and Thadentsonyane.)

TIEN SHAN   *China–USSR*
Highest elevation, 24,406ft / 7,439m, Pobeda Peak.

When the British explorer Sir Francis Younghusband traveled through Central Asia in 1887, he followed for much of his journey the old silk caravan route known as the Tien Shan Nan Lu. For 700mi / 1,126km, the ancient track led him between the Tarim Basin and the Takla Makan Desert to the south and a great arc of mountains to the north, a range as remote and vast as Central Asia itself. Younghusband later wrote that seeing the gleaming summits of the Tien

Shan against the Central Asian sky helped him to understand how early camel drivers had come to know the mountains as the "mountains of heaven"[76]—and that's what the two Chinese words *tien* ("sky" or "heaven") and *shan* ("mountain") together mean. Despite being adjacent to the Takla Makan Desert, the Tien Shan are less arid than the Pamirs to the west, and Colonel Reginald Schomberg, who for several years lived in the region, wrote: "Entrancingly lovely is the Tien Shan with its dancing vistas, its dazzling peaks, and its glorious flowers."[76]

The first scientific exploration of the Tien Shan came in 1857 when the region was penetrated by the Russian geographer P.P. Semenov, who subsequently was known as Semenov Tyan-Shansky. Semenov made the first sighting of Khan Tengri (22,949ft/6,995m), and for seventy-five years that mountain was believed to be the highest in the range. In 1932 the presence of a higher mountain was suspected, but it was not until 1946, when the Marmornaya Stena, the "marble wall," was topped, that the location of the higher peak, Pobeda Peak (24,406ft/7,439m), was confirmed.

MOUNT TIMPANOGOS   *11,750ft/3,581m*   *Utah, USA*
First ascent unknown.

Rising 7,000ft/2,134m above the flat floor of Utah's Jordan River Valley southeast of Salt Lake City and commanding views of the entire Utah Lake drainage, Mount Timpanogos is probably Utah's best known and most popular mountain. Its name preserves the memory of the Indian people who lived on the shore of Utah Lake beneath the Wasatch Mountains. They were known as the *timpanogos*, or "rock river," branch of the Utes for their association with a local river known to the Indians by that name. The river eventually acquired another name, but the name Timpanogos by that time had been transferred to the mountain.

The American explorer John C. Fremont passed through the region during his 1844 expedition, and his report mentioned both the mountains and the river: "It [Utah Lake] is almost entirely surrounded by mountains, walled on the north and east by a high and snowy range, which supplies to it a fan of tributary streams. Among these, the principal river is the Timpan-ogo—signifying Rock River—a name which the rocky grandeur of its scenery, remarkable even in this country of rugged mountains, has obtained for it from the Indians."[12]

TONGARIRO   *6,517ft/1,986m*   *New Zealand*
First ascent unknown.

The English place-names scholar C.M. Matthews has written, "I know of no other people who have such fanciful names as the Polynesians."[87] A good example is that of Tongariro, the dormant volcano that is the central peak and third highest summit in the thermal region of New Zealand's North Island. The name joins *tonga*, "south wind," and *riro*, "carried." When the Polynesian people that were to become the Maoris undertook their great ocean migration that culminated in their arrival at New Zealand, they took with them a rich tradition of myths. Tongariro has become part of a myth telling of a hero who came from Hawaiiki, their homeland. The hero climbed this mountain, and being nearly dead from cold, he called out for help. The south wind heard him and carried his words to his home, from whence his sisters sent a magical fire (a volcanic eruption?) to burst from the mountain and warm him. Thus the name, "south wind carried."

TRANGO TOWERS   *20,600ft/6,279m*   *China–Pakistan*
First ascent, 1977, D. Hennek, J. Morrisey, J. Roskelly, G. Rowell, and K. Schmitz.

According to the mountaineer and linguist H. Adams Carter, the alliterative name of this group of spires in the Baltoro region comes from a campsite of the same name. Carter points out that Ardito Desio's map identifies the mountains as "Tramgo," which could indicate a connection with the Balti *tramga*, meaning "sheepfold."

The use of the term *towers* to identify these dramatic peaks is echoed in the *torres* of Patagonia, whose thrusting verticality is reminiscent of the Baltoro towers. And curiously, both the Patagonian and the Baltoro mountains include a "no-name" mountain (see Innominate). In Patagonia there is Torre Innominata, while in the Trango Towers the peak said to be the "most elegant" is called the Nameless Tower (20,500ft/6,248m).

TRISUL   *23,360ft/7,120m*   *India*
First ascent, 1907, T. Longstaff, the brothers Brocherel, and K. Burathoki.

One of the mountains ringing the "Sanctuary" of Nanda Devi, Trisul, at the time of its first ascent in 1907, was the first 7,000m mountain ever to be climbed. Like Nanda Devi, whose access it guards, Trisul has been sanctified by Hindu lore, and the name Trisul often is translated as "the trident of Siva," whose consort is here manifested as the goddess Nanda. (There are many other manifestations.) But H. Adams Carter, a linguist and mountaineer, recently has had reason to question whether the trident is, in fact, Siva's. As he explains: "Ever since my first visit to the region forty years ago, I had associated the mountain Trisul [Trident] with Siva's deadly weapon. This year on two or three occasions my suggestion to the porters that the peak represented Siva's trident brought speedy denials. 'No, sahib. Not Siva's but Nanda's trident. When she needs to protect someone and becomes angry, she gets eight arms, each holding a weapon. But the most important is the trident, and it is that which she uses to kill the demons.'"[23]

Snow travel at 20,000 feet. From Edward Whymper, Travels amongst the Great Andes of the Equator (London: 1883).

TRONADOR   11,253ft / 3,430m   *Chile*
First ascent, 1934, G. Clausen.

One of the more scenic and challenging peaks in the Lakes District of Chile is Tronador, which in the 1930s was the object of much nationalistic "do-or-die" mountaineering of the sort then focused on such Alpine challenges as the Eiger-wand and the Grandes Jorasses. Tronador's evil reputation was enhanced by its name, which is Spanish and means "thunderer," from frequent avalanches on the mountain.

TRUCHAS PEAKS   *New Mexico, USA*
Highest elevation, 13,102ft / 3,993m, South Truchas.
See Introduction.

TRYFAN   3,010ft / 917m   *Wales*
First ascent unknown.

The English mountaineer and writer Hamish Brown has called Tryfan, one of the best-known summits in Snowdonia National Park in northern Wales, "that prince of Welsh peaks, which from all angles is grand and unmistakable."[18] Author Amory Lovins has described it as "a thin, triangular knife-blade of volcanic rock, set on edge on a slanted sea of grass and boulders." Especially conspicuous when Tryfan is viewed from certain perspectives, as from the Glyders to the southeast, is its tripartite summit.

The name Tryfan is Welsh and means simply "three-headed mountain," and for generations people have compared the mountain to a cocked hat. On Tryfan's highest point are two monoliths known as Adam and Eve, often mistaken for people by observers below. Tryfan is connected with nearby Glyder Fach by the appropriately named Bristly Ridge.

As one surveys Welsh mountains, it sometimes seems almost obligatory that each have some connection with Welsh mythology, and Tryfan is no exception. Just as nearby Snowdon is identified with King Arthur, so Tryfan is identified with Bedivere, last of King Arthur's knights. Legend says that Bedivere's grave is somewhere on the mountain, and that the sword Excalibur was cast into Lyn Ogwen, the lake at Tryfan's base.

TUNGURAHUA   16,457ft / 5,016m   *Ecuador*
First ascent, 1873, W. Reiss and A. Stubel.

An American writer and climber has remembered Tungurahua as "a perfect little volcano right next to Banos—elegant, exotic, and exquisitely beautiful."[74] The people of Banos, however, have reason to remember another Tungurahua, one more in keeping with the mountain's Quechua name, which has been

206

translated variously as "black giant" and "little hell." Both names fit. Tungurahua is a volcano characterized by violent eruptions followed by long periods of quiescence. After sleeping a hundred years, Tungurahua in 1886 awakened suddenly; Banos was devastated.

THE TWELVE BENS
Ireland
Highest elevation, 2,395ft / 730m, Benbaun.

It's characteristic of Irish mountain naming that even a seemingly straightforward name like the Twelve Bens has somewhere in its history a figure from Irish mythology. The "bens" are a group of mountains in southwestern Connemara radiating like spokes from the central cone of Benbaun. *Ben*, meaning "summit" in Gaelic, also is found in Scotland and comes from the same ancient Celtic root as *pen* (see Pennine Alps), which survives in modern Welsh and is found on hill and mountain names throughout England. Mariners called the Twelve Bens "the twelve stakes," because the hills were the first land they sighted returning from the sea. But the original Gaelic name for the group was Beanna Beola, "Beola's mountains." Beola was a mythological figure who tradition says was buried by the sea in Connemara at Toombeola, "Beola's burial mound." The name of Benbaun, highest of the Bens, is simply descriptive; it comes from the Gaelic *beann ban*, "the white mountain," appropriate for a quartzite peak, even though the name most likely was inspired by snow on the mountain.

MOUNT TYNDALL   *14,018ft / 4,273m*
California, USA
First ascent unknown.

John Tyndall (1820–1893) was a prominent British scientist and mountaineer whose works and reputation were well known to Clarence King of the California Geological Survey. In July 1864 King and another surveyor, Richard Cotter, made the first recorded ascent of this peak near Mount Whitney in Sequoia National Park, and in his classic book *Mountaineering in the Sierra Nevada* King told of the peak's naming: "I rang my hammer upon the topmost rock; we grasped hands, and I reverently named the grand peak Mount Tyndall."[45] King and Cotter did not make the first ascent, however; when the two reached the summit, they found an Indian arrow there.

Tyndall had published his influential and controversial *Glaciers of the Alps* in 1860, only four years before King and Cotter made their climb. That same year he made an attempt on the Matterhorn, reaching the Great Tower on the Italian ridge, then the highest point reached. In 1861 he made the first ascent of the Weisshorn. Then in 1862 he made another attempt on the Matterhorn, reaching the Shoulder, whose subsequent name, Pic Tyndall, echoes that of the mountain in California.

Some of the esteem King had for Tyndall is mirrored in the writings of William H. Brewer, who was King's supervisor when King and Cotter made their ascent: "Science will advance, new generations will need new books, and his, which now so delight us, will then have almost lost their individuality in the great mass of scientific literature. But the man will not be forgotten. Science will not lose sight of his works, and a grand monument of Nature's building will link him with the future and keep his memory green."[45]

MOUNT TYREE   16,290ft/4,965m   *Antarctica*
First ascent, 1967, ten members of American Alpine Club expedition.
See VINSON MASSIF.

UINTA MOUNTAINS   *Utah, USA*
Highest elevation, 13,528ft/4,123m, Kings Peak.

The Uinta Mountains east of Salt Lake City include the highest peak in Utah, as well as five other summits topping 13,000ft/3,962m, but probably the most distinctive feature of the Uinta Mountains is that they are one of very few east–west trending major ranges in the western hemisphere. The naming of the mountains was not unusual, however; like many other North American mountains, the Uintas take their name from that of a tribe of Indians living in the area, here the Uintat branch of the Utes. The surveyor and geologist Henry Gannett interpreted the name to mean originally "pine land," an accurate, if not very specific, description of the Indians' former territory.

The list is long of North American peaks and ranges named for associated Indian tribes, the namers almost invariably non-Indians. For example, a Ute tribal name appears not only on the Uinta Mountains but also on Mount Timpanogos east of Utah Lake. A small sample of similar North American mountain names includes Mount Shasta in California, Mount Assiniboine in Alberta–British Columbia, the Adirondacks in New York State, the Absaroka Range in Wyoming, Blackfoot Mountain in Montana, the Jicarilla Mountains in New Mexico, Mount Klickitat in Oregon, the Wenatchee Mountains in Washington, and the Chugach Mountains in Alaska.

ULUGH MUZTAGH   25,340ft / 7,724m   *China*
No first ascent.

Like many of the world's highest mountains, the highest peak in the Kun Lun Range of Central Asia bears a name that means simply "ice mountain." *Muztagh* is an Altaic word applied throughout the region not only to individual peaks but also to any high, snowy group of mountains; *ulugh* means "ice." Before this name was accepted, however, the mountain was identified merely by the surveyor's designation E61, just like K2 in the Karakoram. The remoteness of the Kun Lun Range, coupled with political obstacles imposed by the Peoples Republic of China, has made the mountains virtually inaccessible to western mountaineers, and though the Englishman Sir Aurel Stein has described the approaches to Ulugh Muztagh, the mountain has not yet been climbed.

URAL MOUNTAINS   *USSR*
Highest elevation, 6,214ft / 1,894m, Gora Norodnaya.

Of the many Eurasian mountain ranges, the Urals are among the lowest, and only infrequently along their 1,200mi / 1,931km length do rocky summits rise above the enveloping forest. Yet the range's significance transcends its elevation, for its mountains form one of the earth's few true boundary ranges, separating peninsular Europe from the truly continental landmass of Asia. The name Ural reflects this: it is a Turkish (Altaic) word meaning "belt" or "girdle."

The Urals, a remarkably straight-trending mountain system, were formed during the so-called "Hercynian movement" when other Eurasian mountain ranges were being formed, such as the Harz of Europe and the Altai and Tien Shan of Asia. Like the Rocky Mountains of North America, the Urals form a climatic as well as a topographic barrier, and deciduous trees on their western slopes indicate a moister, milder climate than on the conifer-covered eastern slopes. Only a few ranges constitute boundaries as do the Urals. Other examples include the Pyrenees between France and Spain, the Caucasus between Europe and Asia Minor, and the Himalaya separating the Indian subcontinent from Central Asia.

MOUNT VANCOUVER 15,825ft/4,823m

*First ascent, 1949, A. Bruce-Robertson,
W. Hainsworth, R. McCarter, and N. Odell.*

*Alaska, USA-
Yukon, Canada*

This mountain, one of the major peaks of the St. Elias Range, was named for Captain George Vancouver, the British navigator who from 1791 to 1795 conducted extensive explorations of the northwest coast of North America and himself named many of the region's features. The name Vancouver was given to the mountain in 1874 by W.H. Dall and Marcus Baker of the United States Coast Survey, and they named nearby Mount Cook at the same time. Some writers have suggested that because the two surveyors mistakenly put Mount Cook's elevation on Mount Vancouver and vice versa, the names that now appear on the mountains are not what the surveyors intended; rather, argue these writers, the surveyors would have preferred that the higher mountain— Vancouver—honor Captain James Cook, as he was the better known of the two navigators. Be that as it may, the elevations were switched and not the names, and Mount Vancouver now tops nearby Mount Cook.

Although Vancouver often is listed as one of the boundary peaks of the St. Elias Range, it actually has multiple summits, the highest of which clearly is in Canada. The summit that truly straddles the Alaska–Yukon border now is called Good Neighbor Peak (15,700ft/4,785m). This summit was named by the party that in 1967 first climbed it, a binational expedition made up of representatives of the American Alpine Club and the Alpine Club of Canada, with Montague Ewart Alford and Vincent Hoeman as co-leaders.

MOUNT VESUVIUS 3,891ft/1,186m

First ascent unknown.

Italy

Twice in the history of the ancient Mediterranean civilizations, volcanoes erupted with such destructive force that whole societies were disrupted. The first was the eruption of Mount Thera on Crete that destroyed the Minoan civilization there and likely gave rise to the legend of Atlantis. The other, less cataclysmic but far better known, was the eruption in A.D. 79 of Mount Vesuvius that destroyed the Roman cities of Pompeii, Herculaneum, and Stabiae. The story of the latter eruption has become famous, largely through the writings of the

Eruption of Vesuvius, Italy. From William H.D. Adams, Mountains and Mountain Climbing *(London: 1883).*

Roman philosopher Pliny the Younger, who was at Pompeii when Vesuvius exploded. He described vividly the holocaust that killed thousands of Romans, including his uncle, Pliny the Elder. Since then, Vesuvius and the ruined cities beneath it have been meccas for the curious seeking relics of the mountain's long eruptive history. But one of the most enduring of such relics is the volcano's name. It comes from the language of the Oscans, an Indo-European people who inhabited Campania before the Romans and who gave to the volcano a name meaning "the emitter of smoke and sparks."

The Greek geographer Strabo (63 B.C.?–?A.D. 24) was ahead of his time in his observations and theories regarding volcanoes, and though Vesuvius—then called Mons Vesbius—was covered with dense vegetation when he examined it, he correctly deduced its volcanic nature from burnt rocks in the area. Other evidence is the mountain's characteristic volcanic shape; Monte Somma, the mountain partially surrounding the cone of Vesuvius, is the remains of an ancient caldera.

The eruptions of Vesuvius, the only active volcano on the European mainland, have been so well-known and well-documented that they have contributed to the lexicon of vulcanology, inspiring names for two classes of eruptions: Vesuvian, denoting normal eruptive behavior, and Plinian, a much more violent type of the sort that killed Pliny the Elder.

The name Vesuvius was consciously transferred to a mountain near Los Angeles in California, and though the namers there probably were not aware of the original meaning of the name—"emitter of fire and sparks"—the borrowing was particularly appropriate. The California mountain was named because beginning in 1893 fireworks were displayed every Saturday night on the summit, ending with an effusion of fire and sparks intended to be a representation in miniature of the Italian volcano.

MOUNT VICTORIA   13,363ft/4,073m   Papua New Guinea
First ascent, 1889, party led by W. MacGregor.
See OWEN STANLEY RANGE.

VIGNEMALE   10,800ft/3,292m   France
First ascent, 1837, H. Cazeaux and B. Guillembet.
See MALADETA MASSIF.

VINSON MASSIF   16,860ft/5,139m   Antarctica
First ascent, 1966, N. Clinch and party.

On 23 December 1935, an airplane piloted by H. Hollick Kenyon and having as passenger the polar explorer Lincoln Ellsworth took off from Dundee Island in the Antarctic Panhandle to begin a flight over the unexplored regions of western Antarctica. The plane made three landings on the ice during its journey, and when it arrived at its destination Ellsworth had a major announcement to make. He had found, rising from the featureless white plain, a huge mountain chain whose peaks stood like sentinels overlooking the Ronne Ice Shelf to the east and the vast polar plateau to the west. Ellsworth named the chain the Sentinel Range.

For decades thereafter the remote and forbidding Sentinel Range was the focus of considerable speculation by Antarctic researchers and explorers. Because its peaks lie between Marie Byrd Land, the Antarctic Panhandle, and the Transantarctic Mountains, the Sentinel Range was considered crucial to understanding the geological history of the continent. The mountains were not easy to study, however. The nearby Heritage Range is easily accessible by motor toboggan, but surface travel in the higher Sentinel Range is difficult and dangerous. Moreover, the Sentinel Range, like most Antarctic mountains, is guarded from approach by a huge moat of crevassed ice.

Nonetheless, the mountains beckoned explorers. In 1957 a twenty-nine-year-old glaciologist named Charles R. Bentley wrote in his diary: "What a range it is, full of extremely steep faces and jagged edges."[60] Some persons in Bentley's party climbed some of the outlying mountains, but they made no attempt on the higher peaks. Yet in that year it was recognized that the high peaks of the Sentinel Range sooner or later would have to be reckoned with, because in 1957 two peaks in the range were discovered to be the highest in Antarctica: the 16,860ft/5,139m Vinson Massif and 16,290ft/4,965m Mount Tyree.

Peaks of such significance clearly needed names, and by the early 1960s names had been assigned. Mount Tyree was named for Rear Admiral David M. Tyree, commander of the United States Naval Support Force in Antarctica from 1959 to 1962. He was a popular figure, especially in New Zealand, and his men and ships played an important role in United States Antarctic research and exploration.

The Vinson Massif was named for a man whose connection with Antarctica was less direct but whose support also was critical to United States Antarctic exploration—Congressman Carl Vinson of Georgia. Representative Vinson first went to Washington in 1914 at the age of thirty-one; when he retired in 1964 at the age of eighty-one, he was the first congressman to have served in the House for fifty years. He was chairman of the House Armed Services Committee, where he was largely responsible for the United States government's support of Antarctic research and exploration from 1935 to 1961.

With the recognition that the Vinson Massif was the continent's highest mountain came the challenge to climb it; Antarctica was the last continent whose highest peak had never been successfully assaulted. In the fall of 1966 two rival parties embarked for the cold continent, each hoping to be the first to make the historic ascent. But the race for the summit was decided early when delays—an unaffordable luxury in Antarctica—forced the smaller, four-man party to abandon its attempt.

The second party stood a better chance. Sponsored by the National Geographic Society and the American Alpine Club and coordinated by the National Science Foundation, the party consisted of three Antarctic scientists and seven experienced mountaineers. An airplane landed them twenty miles west of the mountains on a flat snow plain. From there, they transported their equipment and supplies on sleds to the extremely steep western escarpment of the mountains.

On 20 December 1966 all ten climbers stood on top of the bulky Vinson Massif. They planted on the summit the flags of the twelve nations that had signed the Antarctic Treaty of 1959. The party was led by Nicholas Clinch, a thirty-six-year-old lawyer from Los Angeles. Soon thereafter, in January, they climbed Mount Tyree, actually a more difficult mountain than the Vinson Massif because its slopes are steeper.

With the success of this party in making these ascents, a long and important era in mountaineering ended. Other high peaks remain to be climbed in Antarctica, but not the highest—not there nor on any other continent.

VIRUNGA MOUNTAINS
Eastern Central Africa

Highest elevation, 14,782ft/4,506m, Karisimbi.

Eight great volcanoes make up the Virunga Mountains shared by Zaire, Ruanda, and Uganda. The Virungas were born of the same tectonic instability along the Great Rift Valley of East and Central Africa that created the region's well-known lakes, and the volcanoes are located in the Rift's western branch between Lake Edward and Lake Kivu. Although only two of the eight volcanoes have showed any life in recent history, evidence of past vulcanism is everywhere, and the Virungas rise above an expanse of lava covering 1,200 sq mi/ 3,108 sq km. The name Virunga is the plural form of a Swahili word, *kirunga*, that means "cone mountain" or "volcano," as does Mfumbiro, another local name for the mountains.

As with the Ruwenzori, the other great volcanic mountains of Central Africa, the ecology and human history of the Virungas have tended to the bizarre. The dense forests surrounding the mountains are the habitat of the rare mountain gorilla, while on the slopes above are giant senecios and lobelias. One of the worst tragedies in mountaineering history occurred in the Virungas. In 1907 an expedition including lowland Africans and the geologist Kirschstein were caught in an unexpected snow and hail storm on Karisimbi. The Africans, believing God intended them to die, sat down; twenty perished despite Kirschstein's efforts to move them. Less tragic but also extraordinary was the achievement of one Earl Denman, who became the first man to climb all eight volcanoes —wearing no shoes and accompanied only by African guides. (Denman later attempted to climb Everest alone.)

MONTE VISO
12,602ft/3,841m
France–Italy

First ascent, 1861, W. Mathews and W. Jacomb with M. and J. Croz.

Though the Romans for centuries explored and conquered in the region that includes the Alps, the names of only a very few Alpine peaks are mentioned in all the surviving Roman records—and Monte Viso is one of them. Like most ancient peoples, the Romans saw mountains only as nettlesome obstacles, to be avoided wherever possible—but two things made the Romans notice Monte Viso more than other mountains. First, its position as the highest summit of the Cottian Alps, located at the source of the Po River on the French–Italian border, put it in the way of much of the commerce and conquest that flowed

214

between the Italian peninsula and the rest of western Europe.

Second, Monte Viso stands isolated from the other Cottian peaks and is visible over a wide area. Indeed, the name Monte Viso can be translated from the Latin as "sight mountain" or even "watchtower." But much as Monte Viso would have captured the attention of the Romans, its first ascent, though not technically difficult, waited until 1861, during the Golden Age of Mountaineering in the Alps. As James Ramsay Ullman has written: "The Romans were conquerors and explorers, but they were not mountaineers." [140]

VULCANO   1,637ft/499m   Italy
First ascent unknown.

On Italy's Lipari Islands, west of the Strait of Messina, there is a volcano that has shared its name with all the other volcanoes of the world. The name since ancient times has been Vulcano, and the Romans believed the fiery mountain to be the mythical site of the forge of Vulcan, god of fire and metalworking. Linguists, however, believe the god's name can be traced to a still earlier Etruscan word, which in turn was derived phonetically from the Cretan *welkhanos.* According to the etymologist Eric Partridge, the Etruscans brought the Cretan term to Italy and there gave it its meaning, "the god of destructive fire," a meaning the name has carried ever since. [102]

W

MOUNT WASHINGTON   6,288ft/1,917m   New Hampshire, USA
First ascent, 1642, D. Field.

Mount Washington in the White Mountains of New Hampshire is the highest peak in northeastern North America. Although its summit is reached by both an auto road and a cog railway, the mountain still commands respect, especially in winter when the weather approximates arctic conditions. The world's highest wind velocity—231 miles per hour—was recorded on the summit of Mount Washington on 12 April 1934.

The earliest names for the mountain were simply descriptive. To the Abenaki-speaking peoples of the region the peak was known as Kodaak Wadjo, "summit of the highest mountain." It wasn't merely another peak to them, however, for they believed that a *maji neowaska,* or "bad spirit," dwelt there. The Indians also called the mountain Agiochook, which has been interpreted to mean "the place

215

of the Great Spirit." To some tribes, the peak and its neighbors were called Waumbekket-methna, "snowy mountains." And the Algonquian Indians called the peak Waumbik, meaning "white rocks."

A 1628 narrative refers to the mountain as the "Christall Hill," and John Winthrop, governor of the Massachusetts Bay Colony, writing in his journal of 1642 about Darby Field's ascent that year of the mountain, called the peak both "the White Hill" and "the Sugarloaf." In 1784 a scientific party consisting of Dr. Manasseh Cutler, Dr. Jeremy Belknap, and several others climbed Mount Washington as part of their explorations. Also in 1784, General George Washington retired from the Army to Mount Vernon, an event believed to have inspired the name Mount Washington.

The naming of the highest peak in the White Mountains for the nation's first president prompted subsequent namers to name other peaks for other early United States presidents, and today the Presidential Range of the White Mountains includes Mounts Washington, Jefferson, John Adams, John Quincy Adams, Madison, Monroe, Pierce, and Eisenhower. Other presidents having their names on peaks in the White Mountains, though not in the Presidential Range, are Lincoln, Garfield, Cleveland, and Coolidge. (Mount Jackson in the White Mountains was named to honor not President Jackson but Dr. Charles T. Jackson, New Hampshire state geologist.)

MOUNT WASHINGTON   7,794ft/2,376m   Oregon, USA
First ascent, 1923, six local youths.

It's not surprising that several United States mountains were named for George Washington, hero of the Revolutionary War, the nation's first president, and "father of his country." The best known of these mountains is the one in New Hampshire (see entry), but they also include this rocky spire between Mount Jefferson and the Three Sisters in the Oregon Cascades. The peak doubtless received its name because of its proximity to Mount Jefferson, but who applied the name and when is not known; it was not mentioned by any early explorers nor shown on any early maps.

Mount Washington is the eroded core of a pre-Pleistocene volcano, and despite its relatively low elevation, its unusual appearance and technical difficulties make it an important mountain, especially among rock climbers. It defied all attempts at a first ascent until 1923 when six boys from Bend, Oregon, reached the summit.

WEISSHORN   14,782ft/4,506m   Switzerland
First ascent, 1861, J. Tyndall and J. Bennen.

The well-known nineteenth-century Alpine mountaineer and traveler John Ball once described the Weisshorn in the southern Pennine Alps as "perhaps the most beautifully sharp and symmetrical of the pyramidal peaks of the Alps." [69]

Thus it's perhaps unfortunate that such a distinctive peak doesn't have a more distinctive name instead of one shared by literally scores of other mountains world-wide. Weisshorn is German and means simply "white mountain."

The first ascent of the Weisshorn was one of the great events in the Golden Age of Mountaineering (1855–1865). Leslie Stephen attempted the mountain in 1859, and C.E. Mathews and Melchior Anderegg the following year also sought a route to the top. But it remained for Professor John Tyndall and his Swiss guides, particularly Johann-Joseph Bennen, to solve the problem Tyndall called the "snow catenary" barring the way to the summit.

The fame of the Weisshorn in Switzerland has caused the name to be transferred to other mountains. Near Mount Hubbard in the Yukon there is an 11,620ft/3,542m peak named the Weisshorn, doubtless after the Alpine mountain.

WHEELER PEAK   *13,160ft/4,011m*   *New Mexico, USA*
First ascent unknown.

The highest summits in five states in the western United States were named for geologists and surveyors involved in the mapping and exploration of the American West: Mount Whitney in California, Gannett Peak in Wyoming, Humphreys Peak in Arizona, Kings Peak in Utah, and Wheeler Peak in New Mexico. Major George M. Wheeler of the United States Army was in charge of surveys west of the one-hundredth meridian between 1871 and 1878, and New Mexico's highest peak, located in the southern Sangre de Cristo Range behind Taos, now bears his name.

The name Wheeler Peak also appears on Nevada's second highest and perhaps most noteworthy mountain (13,063ft/3,982m), with its north face nearly vertical for 1,800ft/549m. And in California there are four orographic features named Wheeler, including a Wheeler Peak in the Sierra Nevada, and these too were named for the Army surveyor.

Men such as Wheeler, Josiah Whitney, Henry Gannett, Andrew Humphreys, and Clarence King played major roles in the scientific exploration of the West. And while Whitney urged his subordinates not to name new discoveries for him—they easily found a way around that edict—many of these early explorers saw nothing wrong when their fellows named natural features for them, even while they were living, a practice now officially discouraged. Given the close association between these men and the mountains, they may have been right.

WHITE MOUNTAINS   *New Hampshire–Maine, USA*
Highest elevation, 6,288ft/1,917m, Mount Washington.

"White mountain" is the most common of all mountain names, appearing virtually wherever mountains are found. (Antarctica, for obvious reasons, is a possible exception.) In the United States the best known example is the White Mountains of northern New Hampshire and western Maine, a loosely defined mountain complex that includes the highest summits of northeastern North America. Like most "white mountain" names, this one is old, very likely predating European settlement of the region. Some Indian tribes are reported to have called the highest summit of the range, now named Mount Washington, Waumbekket-methna, meaning "white mountain," or "snowy mountain." And some writers have said that the high peaks also were known as *kan-ran-vugarty*, a phrase referring to their supposed resemblance to the whiteness of a gull.

The English mariner Christopher Levett is believed to have been the first white man to have given the mountains a name. Writing in 1628 in his *A Voyage into New England*, Levett called one of the peaks "the Christall Hill," a name later writers attributed to quartz crystals being found on the peaks.[65] Darby Field found some of these crystals—he thought they were diamonds—in 1642 when he made the first ascent of Mount Washington. The name Crystal Hills was short-lived, however; less than fifty years later the name White Mountains appeared in print. In 1672 John Josselyn in his *New England Rarities Discovered* wrote of the Indians: "Ask them whither they go when they die, they will tell you, pointing with their finger, to heaven beyond the White Mountains."[65]

Josselyn also wrote in his account: "The original of all the great rivers in the country, the snow lies on the mountains the whole year excepting the month of August; the black flies are so numerous that a man cannot draw his breath but he will suck some of them in. Some suppose that the White Mountains were first raised by earthquakes, but they are hollow, as may be guessed by the resounding of the rain upon the level on the top."[65]

MOUNT WHITNEY   14,495ft/4,418m   *California, USA*
First ascent, 1873, A.H. Johnson, C.D. Begole, and J. Lucas.

In July 1864 two men stood on top of what is now known as Mount Brewer in the southern Sierra Nevada of California. They were William H. Brewer and Charles F. Hoffman, assistants of Josiah Dwight Whitney (1819–1896), chief of the California Geological Survey, and from the mountain's summit they beheld what they correctly assumed to be the highest peak of the range. Whitney previously had forbidden his subordinates to name the mountain that is now Mount Hamilton after him, but on this occasion his two assistants stood upon their rights as discoverers and named the high peak, now recognized as the highest United States mountain outside Alaska, Mount Whitney. (Brewer's and Hoffman's names appear on other mountains in the Sierra Nevada.)

In 1871 another of Whitney's surveyors, Clarence King, attempted a first ascent of Mount Whitney, but by mistake he instead climbed the nearby mountain now known as Mount Langley. His error was discovered two years later, and he hastened to the mountain to make another attempt, but before he arrived three local men from Inyo County made the ascent. The three were fishermen camped in Kern Canyon, and upon hearing of King's mistake they hastened to the summit themselves. Soon, a brief but intense controversy flared in the weekly newspaper *The Inyo Independent* as to who had actually made the

218

ascent, the three fishermen or two other local men. Local feeling also ran high as to what the peak should be called. When the three fishermen on 20 September 1873 repeated their ascent to validate their claim, they also proposed that the peak be named Fisherman's Peak in defiance of the name Whitney, proposed by the surveyors in 1864. (Local people called Whitney, the geology professor, "the old earthquake sharp.") As *The Inyo Independent* editorialized: "Some people are trying to take the credit of their [the fishermen] being the first away from them, but they won't succeed. Prof. Whitney's agent has just returned from the mountain and finds fault with the people here for their lack of romance in calling it 'Fisherman's Peak.' Ain't it as romantic as 'Whitney'? The fishermen who found it looked mighty romantic on their return to Soda Springs. Wonder who the old earthquake sharp thinks is running this country anyhow?"[45]

The naming controversy didn't subside with the gradual acceptance of the fishermen's first ascent. As the mountain names expert Francis P. Farquhar tells the story: "For a long time a determined effort was made by the people of Inyo County to keep the name of the 'old earthquake sharp' from being established on their mountain. When they couldn't make 'Fisherman's Peak' stick they tried 'Dome of Inyo.' That, too, failed, so they went back to 'Fisherman's'; in 1881 a bill was introduced in the Legislature by an Inyo County assemblyman providing that 'The peak shall be known as Fisherman's Peak, and the same is hereby declared to be the official name of said peak, and the only name to be regarded as legal.' The bill passed in the Assembly, but it reached the Senate on April Fool's Day and the jolly senators amended it to read 'Fowler's Peak' in honor of one of their colleagues. Neither Fish nor Fowl prevailed, however; the Governor vetoed the bill, the storm subsided, and Whitney, like McKinley and Rainier, has become less a personal memorial than an integral part of the mountain."[45]

Actually, Whitney's name does considerable honor to the mountain, the early residents of Inyo County notwithstanding. Whitney's reputation as a geologist was widespread and deserved; his survey of California was a very important and very formidable undertaking, and as Farquhar has written: "Whitney demonstrated his greatness by coming much nearer to fulfilling it than any other man of his time could have done. . . . He should also be given credit for the appointment of such a remarkable group of men as his assistants."[45] Less well-known has been Whitney's work as a place-names scholar. His little book *Names and Places*, published in 1888, was the first book-length work on American names. It was a book he was eminently qualified to write, for few persons have given so many names or have had their own name applied to such a notable feature as Mount Whitney.

WIND RIVER RANGE
Wyoming, USA

Highest elevation, 13,785ft/4,202m, Gannett Peak.

For mountains to take the names of rivers is not unusual. Rivers historically have been more important than mountains and have usually been named before them. A convenient way of identifying a mountain, therefore, has often been to name it after a nearby river. Examples of mountains with river names include Mount Cameroon in West Africa, the Finsteraarhorn in Switzerland, and this range in the Rocky Mountains of Wyoming. The name Wind River is a translation of an Indian name, and Orrin Bonney, long familiar with the region, explains its origin thus: "The constant gusts that rushed down the valley, shaking man and pony, peppering faces with flying sand and filling eyes with dust, gave the river its name."[15]

The Wind River Range is becoming increasingly popular among mountaineers, despite its remoteness and difficult access. The range includes Wyoming's highest summit, Gannett Peak (see entry), as well as numerous smaller but still important summits. But the range's reputation among mountaineers is due mainly to the high quality and standards of the climbing, along with opportunities for new routes and ascents. These qualities are best exemplified in the now famous Cirque of the Towers, a ridge of some seventeen summits, most approximately 12,000ft/3,658m, with names such as Watchtower, Sharks Nose, Overhanging Tower, and Wolfs Head.

At the southern end of the range stands Wind River Peak (13,225ft/4,031m), formerly known as Snow Peak. Bonney suggests that its present name arose spontaneously from the fact that it is the highest peak in the range visible from the South Pass region. It also was the highest peak visible from the Oregon Trail as pioneers approached the Continental Divide from the east, and thus it was easily identified with the name of the entire range.

WRANGELL MOUNTAINS
Alaska, USA

Highest elevation, 16,390ft/4,996m, Mount Blackburn.

That the Wrangell (with two l's) Mountains in southeastern Alaska bear the name of Ferdinand Petrovich von Wrangel (1794–1870) is both appropriate and ironic. Wrangel was an admiral in the Imperial Russian Navy, and from 1829 he was closely identified with the Russian territories in North America, serving as governor there for several years. He achieved prominence as an explorer of Alaska, and he was the first European to see the range later to bear his name. But Wrangel, as a Russian, bitterly opposed the sale of Russian Alaska to the United States, and while he certainly would have been honored by his name appearing so frequently in the land to which he contributed so much, he also would have resented the names being in "foreign" territory.

Actually, it's only through chance that this range is called the Wrangell Mountains and not the Tillman Mountains. In 1885 a Lieutenant Allen of the United States Army sighted a tall mountain that he named Mount Wrangell

(14,163ft/4,317m). But apparently the same lieutenant also named the same peak Mount Tillman, for Samuel Escue Tillman, a professor at the United States Military Academy at West Point. Eventually the name Wrangell was accepted and the name Tillman dropped, and in 1901 F.C. Schrader of the United States Geological Survey called the range the Wrangell Mountains, presumably for Mount Wrangell, which at the time was thought to be the highest peak in the range. Since then, the peaks of the Wrangell Mountains have been called "the jewels of Alaska." A dozen summits exceed 12,000ft/3,658m, including the ice-capped volcanoes Mounts Sandford and Wrangell.

THE WREKIN   *1,335ft/407m*   *England*
First ascent unknown.

The Wrekin is an isolated summit that stands along the Welsh border and has served as a beacon for centuries. On its summit, as on other western summits, fires in 1588 flared forth signalling the arrival of the Spanish armada off the coast. The hill's name has nothing to do with "beacon," however, despite the rhyming resemblance. Rather, the name Wrekin is of unknown meaning and very old, possibly dating back to when an Iron Age fort stood on the hill's summit. The name first appeared as the Wrokene in a charter of 975, but it is far older than that because the Roman town of Viroconium, now Wroxeter, built on the hill's lower slopes, clearly took its name from a preexisting name for the hill. As the English names scholar C.M. Matthews has written of the Wrekin: "The abandonment of bleak hilltops in favor of more comfortable positions lower down was one of the regular processes of civilization, and in hill country many villages bear names that belonged earlier to the heights above them. No meaning is known for Wrekin, and many other hill names that emerge from the same pre-English obscurity have unknown origins." [87]

A border legend tells of the Wrekin's creation. The Devil once set out with a spadeful of earth to make mischief by damming the Severn River and flooding Shrewsbury, but by the time he had reached Wellington he already was tired and discouraged. He asked a shoemaker he met how much farther was Shrewsbury, and the shoemaker, pointing to a bag of old shoes he carried, replied, "Just look how many pairs of shoes I have worn out on the way." Thereupon the Devil, in disgust, threw down the spadeful of earth, forming the Wrekin.

 **Y**

MOUNT YALE 14,196ft/4,327m Colorado, USA
First ascent, 1869, members of Whitney surveying expedition.
See COLLEGIATE PEAKS.

YERUPAJA 21,759ft/6,632m Peru
First ascent, 1950, D. Harrah and J. Maxwell.

Yerupaja, the second highest separate peak in Peru and the highest summit in the Cordillera Huayhuash north of Lima, has two names, one Quechua, the other Spanish, both obscure in origin. According to César Morales Arnao, Peruvian mountaineer and fluent speaker of Quechua, the most likely interpretation of the Quechua name Yerupaja is that it comes from *yuri*, "to be born," and *huacan*, "weeping." Says Arnao: "It seems that the mountain is giving birth as avalanches sweep its precipitous slopes while the winds howl and weep." Arnao says that the name also could come from *keru*, "wood," and *huaje*, "to put to pasture," adding: "In this inhospitable region the animals graze even on wood."[2] But given the mythological nature of many Quechua mountain names, literal interpretations are to be viewed with skepticism, and it's very possible that there's more to this name than has yet been revealed.

Locally, Yerupaja also is commonly known by its Spanish name, El Carnicero, "the butcher." The mountain is indeed a difficult and dangerous one, known for its treacherous cornices. But Yerupaja's mountaineering hazards surely are not the inspiration for the name El Carnicero, whose true origins remain obscure.

 **Z**

ZINAL ROTHORN 13,848ft/4,221m Switzerland
First ascent, 1864, L. Stephen and F. Grove with M. and J. Anderegg.

The name of the Zinal Rothorn, one of the major peaks of the Pennine Alps, means "red peak of Zinal" in German. Zinal is a village that also has given its name to the Zinal Glacier, fed by such mountains as the Obergabelhorn and the

Dent Blanche. The reference in the name to the mountain's redness is reported to come not from the hue of its rocks but rather from the pinkish alpenglow on the peak at sunset, a phenomenon also believed responsible for the names of the Sangre de Cristo Mountains in Colorado and New Mexico in the western United States and the Sandia Mountains in New Mexico (see Sangre de Cristo).

Reference List

1   Alvarez, Grace de Jesus C. *Toponimos en Apellidos Hispanos*. Estudios de Hispanofila No. 7. Garden City, New York: Adelphi University. 1968.

2   Arnao, César Morales. "Quechua Names in the Northern Peruvian Andes and Their Meanings," translated by H. Adams Carter. *American Alpine Journal*. 1966: 63–74.

3   Arps, Louisa Ward, and Kingery, Elinor Eppich. *High Country Names: Rocky Mountain National Park*. Denver: Colorado Mountain Club. 1966.

4   Armstrong, G.H. *The Origin and Meaning of Place Names in Canada*. Toronto: Macmillan. 1930.

5   Ataee, Mohammed. 1982. Personal communication.

6   Azimov, Isaac. *Words on the Map*. Boston: Houghton Mifflin. 1962.

7   Aurousseau, M. *The Rendering of Geographical Names*. Westport, Connecticut: Greenwood. 1975.

8   Baedecker, Karl. *Switzerland Together with Chamonix and the Italian Lakes: Handbook for Travelers*. Twenty-sixth edition. New York: Scribners. 1922.

9   Barbezat, Alain. "The Hoggar and Its Mountains," *The Mountain World*. 1955: 196–211.

10 Barnes, Will C. *Arizona Place Names*, revised and enlarged by Byrd H. Granger. Tucson: University of Arizona Press. 1973.

11 Baume, Louis C. *Sivalaya: Explorations of the 8000-metre Peaks of the Himalaya*. Seattle: The Mountaineers. 1979.

12 Beckey, Fred. *Mountains of North America*. San Francisco: Sierra Club. 1982.

13 Belloc, Hillaire. *The Pyrenees*. New York: Alfred A. Knopf. 1923.

14 Bin, Zhu. 1983. Personal communication.

15 Bonney, Orrin H., and Bonney, Lorraine. *Guide to the Wyoming Mountains and Wilderness Areas*, second revised edition. Denver: Sage Books. 1965.

16 *Brewers Dictionary of Phrase and Fable*. New York: Harpers. (No date.)

17 Brniak, Marek. *American Alpine Journal*. 1980:619.

18 Brown, Hamish. *Hamish's Groat's End Walk: One Man and his Dog on a Hill Route through England and Ireland*. North Pomfret, Vermont: David and Charles. 1981.

19 Buck, Carl Darling. *A Dictionary of Selected Synonyms in the Principal Indo-European Languages*. Chicago: University of Chicago Press. 1949.

20 Bueler, William. *Mountains of the World: a Handbook for Climbers and Hikers*. Seattle: The Mountaineers. 1977.

21 Busk, Douglas. "The Mountains of Ethiopia," *The Mountain World*. 1955: 213–222.

22 Carter, H. Adams. "Balti Place Names in the Karakoram," *American Alpine Journal*. 1975: 52–60.

23 Carter, H. Adams. "The Goddess Nanda and Place Names of the Nanda Devi Region," *American Alpine Journal*. 1975: 24–29.

24 Cheney, Roberta Carkeek. *Names on the Face of Montana*. Missoula: University of Montana Press. 1971.

25 Clark, Ronald W. *Men, Myths, and Mountains*. New York: Thomas Y. Crowell. 1976.

26 Clark, Ronald W., and Pyatt, Edward C. *Mountaineering in Britain*. London: Phoenix House. 1957.

27   Cleare, John. *The World Guide to Mountains and Mountaineering*. Exeter, England: Mayflower Books. 1979.

28   Connor, H.E., ed. *Mount Cook National Park*. Christchurch, New Zealand: Mount Cook National Park Board. 1966.

29   Coolidge, W. A.B. *The Alps in Nature and History*. New York: E.P. Dutton. 1908.

30   Coolidge, W. A.B. *Swiss Travel and Swiss Guide Books*. London: Longmans, Green. 1889.

31   Copley, G.J. *English Place-names and Their Origins*. Newton Abbot, Devon: David and Charles. 1968.

32   Delpar, Helen, ed. *The Discoverers: An Encyclopedia of Explorers and Exploration*. New York. 1980.

33   Douglas, William O. *Beyond the High Himalayas*. New York. 1952.

34   Eberhart, Perry, and Schmuck, Philip. *The Fourteeners: Colorado's Great Mountains*. Chicago: Swallow Press. 1970.

35   Echevarria, Evelio. "Survey of Andean Ascents," *American Alpine Journal*. 1973.

36   Eichler, George R. *Colorado Place Names*. Boulder, Colorado: Johnson Publishing. 1977.

37   Embick, Andrew. "Kichatna Spires," *American Alpine Journal*. 1982:15.

38   *Enciclopedia de Mexico*. Mexico City: Instituto de la Enciclopedia de Mexico. 1966.

39   Engeln, O.D. von, and Urquhart, Jane McKelway. *The Story Key to Geographic Names*. Port Washington, New York: Kennikat Press. 1924.

40   Engle, Claire Elaine. *A history of mountaineering in the Alps*. London. 1950.

41   Evans, E. Estyn. *Mourne Country: Landscape and Life in South Down*. Dundalk, Ireland: Dundalgan Press. 1967.

42   Farquhar, Francis P. "Naming Alaska's Mountains," *American Alpine Journal*. 1959: 211–232.

43   Farquhar, Francis P. "Naming America's Mountains—the Cascades," *American Alpine Journal*. 1960: 49–65.

44   Farquhar, Francis P. "Naming America's Mountains—the Colorado Rockies," *American Alpine Journal*. 1961: 319–346.

45   Farquhar, Francis P. "Naming America's Mountains—the Sierra Nevada of California," *American Alpine Journal*. 1962: 131–158.

46   Farquhar, Francis P. *Place Names of the High Sierra*. San Francisco: Sierra Club. 1926.

47   Farrington, Oliver Cummings. "Observations on Popocatapetl and Ixtaccihuatl, with a review of the geographic and geological features of the mountains," *Geological Series*, v. 1, no. 2: Field Columbian Museum, pub. 18. Chicago. 1897.

48   Fear, Ronald. "Dhaulagiri II," *American Alpine Journal*. 1972: 21–25.

49   Field, John. *Place Names of Great Britain and Ireland*. London: David and Charles. 1980.

50   Frome, Michael. *Strangers in High Places*. New York: Doubleday. 1960.

51   Frost, Tom. "Ama Dablam's South Ridge," *American Alpine Journal*. 1980.

52   Galarza, Max Espinoza. *Toponimos Quechuas del Peru*. Lima, Peru. (No date.)

53   Gannett, Henry. *American Names: a Guide to the Origin of Place Names*. Washington, D.C.: Public Affairs Press. 1947.

54   Goody, Richard. "Tayapampa in the Alpamayo Valley," *American Alpine Journal*. 1967: 316–321.

55   Green, Vivian H. *The Swiss Alps*. London: P.T. Batsford. 1961.

56   Gudde, Erwin G. *California Place Names: a Geographical Dictionary*. Berkeley: University of California Press. 1949.

57   Hagen, Toni, et al. *Mount Everest*. New York. 1963.

58 Hamilton, William B. *The Macmillan Book of Canadian Place Names*. Toronto: Macmillan. 1978.

59 Hann, Phil Townsend, compiler. *The Dictionary of California Land Names*. Los Angeles: Automobile Club of Southern California. 1946.

60 Harder, Kelsie, ed. *Illustrated Dictionary of Place Names: United States and Canada*. New York: Van Nostrand. 1976.

61 Hatherton, Trevor, ed. *Antarctica*. New York. 1965.

62 Hedrick, Basil C., and Hedrick, Anne K. *Historical and Cultural Dictionary of Nepal*. Metuchen, New Jersey: Scarecrow Press. 1972.

63 Heim, Arnold. "The Virungas (Volcanoes)," *The Mountain World*. 1956–57: 82–101.

64 Hewitt, Rodney, and Davidson, Mavis. *The Mountains of New Zealand*. Wellington. 1954.

65 Hixson, Robert and Mary. *The Place Names of the White Mountains*. Camden, Maine: Down East. 1980.

66 Hohle, Per. *The Mountain World of Norway*. Oslo: Dreyers Forlag. (No date.)

67 Huden, John C. *Indian Place Names of New England*. New York. 1962.

68 Hughes, John. "Popo and Ixta: Mountains, Myth, and Symbol," *Century: a Southwest Journal of Observation and Opinion*. 6 July 1983: 23–26.

69 Huxley, Anthony, ed. *Standard Encyclopedia of the World's Mountains*. New York: G.P. Putnam's. 1962.

70 Irving, R.L.G. *Ten Great Mountains*. London: Travel Book Club. 1940.

71 Irwin, William Robert, ed. *Challenge: an Anthology of the Literature of Mountaineering*. New York. 1950.

72 Jerome, John. *On Mountains*. New York: Harcourt, Brace, Jovanovich. 1978.

73 Klier, Heinrich. "Cordillera Huayhuash: Andes Expedition of the Austrian Alpine Club, 1954," *The Mountain World*. 1955.

74 Koerner, Michael. *The Fool's Climbing Guide to Ecuador and Peru: a Work of Fiction and Plagiarism*. Birmingham, Michigan: Buzzard Mountaineering. 1976.

75 Kurz, Marcel. "Himalayan Chronicle," *The Mountain World*. 1955: 111–128.

76 Lane, Ferdinand C. *The Story of Mountains*. New York: Doubleday. 1950.

77 Leigh, Rufus Wood. *Five Hundred Utah Place Names: Their Origin and Significance*. Salt Lake City: Deseret News Press. 1961.

78 Lenser, Gerhard. "Pumori—the Daughter Mountain," *The Mountain World*. 1962–63: 127–132.

79 Lewis, Richard S. *A Continent for Science: the Antarctic Adventure*. New York. 1965.

80 Lovins, Amory, and Evans, Philip. *Eyri, the Mountains of Longing*. San Francisco: Friends of the Earth. 1971.

81 Lunn, Sir Arnold. *The Swiss and Their Mountains: a Study of the Influence of Mountains on Man*. London: George Allen and Unwin. 1963.

82 McArthur, Lewis A. *Oregon Geographic Names*. Portland: Binford and Mort for the Oregon Historical Society. 1952.

83 *McGraw-Hill Dictionary of World Biography*. New York: McGraw-Hill. 1973.

84 McLintock, A.H., ed. *An Encyclopedia of New Zealand*. Wellington: R.E. Owen, Government Printer. 1966.

85 McPhee, A. Marshall. *Kenya*. New York: Frederick A. Praeger. 1968.

86 *Maori Place Names and Their Meanings*. Wellington. 1950.

87 Matthews, C.M. *Place Names of the English-speaking World*. New York: Charles Scribners. 1972.

88 Mitre, Bartholome, *Historia de San Martin y de la Emancipacion Sudamerica*. Argentina, 1952:332.

89 Molony, Eileen. *Portraits of Mountains*. London. (No date.)

90   Mould, D.D.C. Pochlin. *The Mountains of Ireland.* New York: Robert M. McBride. 1955.
91   Murray, James A.H. *A New English Dictionary on Historical Principles.* Oxford: Clarendon Press. 1888.
92   Neate, W.R. *Mountaineering and its Literature.* Seattle: The Mountaineers. 1980.
93   Nievergelt, Bernhard. "Simien: Ethiopia's Threatened Mountain Area," *The Mountain World.* 1968-69: 132-17.
94   Noyce, Wilfred, and Lukan, Karl. *The Alps.* New York: Putnam's. 1963.
95   Noyce, Wilfred, and McMorrin, Ian, eds. *World Atlas of Mountaineering.* London: Thomas Nelson and Sons. 1969.
96   Oakley, Amy. *Hill-towns of the Pyrenees.* New York: Century. 1923.
97   O'Brien, Bart. "Climbing Half Dome—Twenty Years After," *American Alpine Journal.* 1978: 466-470.
98   Olson, Jack. *The Climb up to Hell.* New York: Harper and Row. 1962.
99   Orr, James, ed. *The International Standard Bible Encyclopedia.* Chicago: Howard-Severance. 1930.
100 Orth, Donald J. *Dictionary of Alaska Place Names.* Washington, D.C.: Government Printing Office. 1967.
101 Papinot, E. *Historical and Geographical Dictionary of Japan.* Ann Arbor, Michigan: Overlook. 1948.
102 Partridge, Eric. *Origins: a short etymological dictionary of English,* second edition. New York: Macmillan. 1956.
103 Pearce, Thomas Matthew, ed. *New Mexico Place Names: a Geographical Dictionary.* Albuquerque: University of New Mexico Press. 1975.
104 Peattie, Roderick, ed. *The Cascades.* New York: Vanguard. 1949.
105 Peattie, Roderick, ed. *The Pacific Coast Ranges.* New York: Vanguard. 1946.
106 Perkins, Henry A. "The Mountains of Iceland," *American Alpine Journal.* 1946: 1-13.
107 Phillips, James W. *Alaska-Yukon Place Names.* Seattle: University of Washington Press. 1973.
108 Phillips, James W. *Washington State Place Names.* Seattle: University of Washington Press. 1971.
109 Pukui, Mary Kawena; Elbert, Samuel H.; and Mookini, Esther T. *Place Names of Hawaii.* Honolulu: University Press of Hawaii. 1974.
110 Pyatt, Edward C. *The Guiness Book of Mountains and Mountaineering Facts and Feats.* London: Guiness Superlatives. 1980.
111 Pyatt, Edward C. *Mountains of Britain.* London: P.T. Batsford. 1966.
112 Reader, John. "The Beckoning Snow of Kilimanjaro, Africa's 'mountain of greatness'" *Smithsonian.* August 1982: 39-51.
113 Reaney, P.H. *The Origin of English Place-names.* London: Routledge and Kegan Paul. 1960.
114 Rebuffat, Gaston. *The Mont Blanc Massif: the 100 Finest Routes,* trans. Jane and Colin Taylor. New York: Oxford University Press. 1974.
115 Ricker, John F. "Cordillera Vilcanota—1969," *American Alpine Journal.* 1970: 42-47.
116 Ricker, John F. *Yuraq Janka: Guide to the Peruvian Andes Part I: Cordillera Blanca and Rosko.* New York: American Alpine Club. 1977.
117 Ridgeway, Rick. "Park at the Top of the World," *National Geographic.* June 1982: 704-725.
118 Ritchie, David. *The Ring of Fire: Volcanoes, Earthquakes, and the Violent Shore.* New York: Atheneum. 1981.
119 Rittman, A. and L. *Volcanoes.* New York: Putnam's. 1976.

120   Robbins, Royal. "Tis-sa-ack," *American Alpine Journal.* 1970:7.
121   Roberts, David S., and Millikan, Richard G.C. "Kichatna Spire," *American Alpine Journal.* 1967: 272–278.
122   Room, Adrian. *Place-names of the World.* Plymouth, England: David and Charles. 1974.
123   Rostaing, Charles. *Les Noms de Lieux.* Paris: Presses Universitaires de France. 1965.
124   Rowell, Galen A. "On or Around Anyemaqen," *American Alpine Journal.* 1982.
125   Rubin, Alan. Review of *Clogwynn du'r Arddu: the Black Cliff* by Peter Crew, Jack Soper, and Ken Wilson. *American Alpine Journal.* 1973:534.
126   Russell, Franklin. *The Mountains of America: From Alaska to the Smokies.* New York: Harry N. Abrams. 1975.
127   Schmidt, Tom, Institute for Names Research, Oslo, Norway. 1983. Personal communication.
128   Sealock, Richard B. *Bibliography of Place-name Literature—U.S. and Canada.* Chicago: American Library Association. 1967.
129   Shaw, A.G.L., and Clark, C.M.H., eds. *Australian Dictionary of Biography:1788–1850.* New York: Cambridge University Press. 1966.
130   Simpson, W. Douglas. *Portrait of the Highlands.* London: Robert Hale. 1979.
131   Stahl, Kathleen M. *History of the Chagga People of Kilimanjaro.* London. 1964.
132   Stewart, George R. *American Place-names: a Concise and Selective Dictionary for the Continental United States of America.* New York: Oxford University Press. 1970.
133   Stewart, George R. *Names on the Globe.* New York: Oxford University Press. 1975.
134   Stewart, George R. *Names on the Land.* Boston: Houghton Mifflin. 1958.
135   Swift, Esther Munroe. *Vermont Place-names: Footprints of History.* Brattleboro, Vermont: Stephen Greene Press. 1977.
136   Taylor, Isaac. *Words and Places: Illustrations of History, Ethnology, and Geography.* New York: E.P. Dutton. 1911.
137   Thomas, Lowell. *Lowell Thomas' Book of the High Mountains.* New York: Messner. 1964.
138   Thorarinsson, Sigurdur. *The Eruption of Hekla: 1947–1948.* Reykjavik: H.F. Leiftur. 1967.
139   Ullman, James Ramsay. *The Age of Mountaineering.* New York: J.B. Lippincott. 1954.
140   Ullman, James Ramsay. *High Conquest: the Story of Mountaineering.* New York: J.B. Lippincott. 1941.
141   Ullman, James Ramsay. *Kingdom of Adventure.* New York: William Sloan. 1947.
142   *United Nations Conference on the Standardization of Geographic Names, v. 1, Report of the Conference.* Geneva, Switzerland. 1967.
143   Unsoeld, Willi. "Nanda Devi from the North," *American Alpine Journal.* 1977.
144   Unsworth, Walt. *Encyclopedia of Mountaineering.* New York: St. Martin's Press. 1975.
145   U.S. Board on Geographic Names. *Geographic Names of the Antarctic.* Washington, D.C.: National Science Foundation. 1980.
146   U.S. Board on Geographic Names. *Guidelines: Proposing Names for Unnamed Domestic Features.* 1977.
147   Waddell, L.A. *Among the Himalayas.* Westminster: Archibald Constable. 1899.
148   Walton, W.H. Murray. "Ontake, the Sacred Peak," *American Alpine Journal.* 1977: 566–569.
149   Ward, Michael, ed. *The Mountaineers Companion.* London: Eyre and Spottiswoode. 1966.
150   Way, Ruth. *A Geography of Spain and Portugal.* London: Dutton. 1962.
151   Weber, Klaus. 1983. Personal communication.

152 Wells, Matthew. "West Ridge of Nevado Santa Cruz," *American Alpine Journal.* 1981.
153 White, Stuart. 1983. Personal communication.
154 Whymper, Edward. *Scrambles Amongst the Alps in the Years 1860–69.* 7th ed. London: Murray. 1965.
155 Wickwire, James. "The Northwest Ridge of K2," *American Alpine Journal.* 1976: 359–367.
156 Yeats, William Butler. *Collected Poems.* New York: Macmillan. 1956.
157 Younghusband, Sir Francis. *Everest: the Challenge.* New York: T. Nelson and Sons. 1936.
158 Ziyu, Lin. 1983. Personal communication.

Selective Index:

The following list includes mountains whose names are explained or translated in the text but for which there is not a separate alphabetical entry. It does not include mountains' names mentioned in the text whose meanings or origins are apparent from the name itself, such as Round Mountain. It also does not include mountains with the same name as a mountain for which there is an alphabetical entry; e.g. a mountain such as the Matterhorn of California would be discussed under the entry for the Matterhorn in Switzerland.

Stargazer (New Zealand)   47

Taranaki (New Zealand)   83
Mount Terror (Antarctica)   87
Thlauhatke Hills (Florida, USA)   8
Mount Thor (Baffin Island, Canada)
   46
Torre Innominata (Chile)   116
Mont Tremblant (Quebec, Canada)
   131
El Tronador (Chile)   9
Trossachs (Scotland)   5
Tullujuto (Peru)   12
El Tur (Egypt)   192
TV Mountain (Montana, USA)   12
Mount Tyee (Oregon, USA)   17

Mount Ulmer (Antarctica)   90
Ulrichshorn (Switzerland)   22
Unaka Mountains (Tennessee, USA)   7

Mount Verdi (California, USA)   18
Mount Victoria (Burma)   161
Mount Victoria (British Columbia,
   Canada)   161
Mount Victoria (Papua New Guinea)
   161
Nevado Viscacha (Peru)   11

Wagontire Mountain (Oregon, USA)
   11
Wallowa Mountains (Oregon, USA)
   25
Nevada Wamanripa (Peru)   11
Mount Waumbek (New Hampshire,
   USA)   7
Weissmies (Switzerland)   6
Mount Wister (Wyoming, USA)   18

Yuraqraju (Peru)   6

About the author:

The combination of the outdoors and geographical names has long held a fascination for Robert Hixson Julyan. Born in Boulder, Colorado, he grew up roaming the Rockies. He has since hiked and climbed in the Atlas Mountains of Morocco and the Swiss Alps, as well as Vermont's Green Mountains, New Hampshire's White Mountains, the Mexican volcanic peaks, and numerous ranges in New Mexico, where he is a member of the New Mexico Mountain Club.

Julyan receive a bachelor's degree in English from the University of Colorado and a master's degree in natural resources from Cornell University. He is now a publications editor at the University of New Mexico, Albuquerque.

His published writings include *Place Names of the White Mountains* (Down East Books, 1980), *Lawrie Tatum Indian Agent* (Pendle Hill Publications, 1981), and "New Mexico Place Names," in *New Mexico in Maps*, University of New Mexico Press, 1985. Julyan is a member of the American Name Society.